# WALLACE STEVENS

*Harmonium* (1923, 1931, 1937)

*The Man With the Blue Guitar* INCLUDING *Ideas of Order*
(1936, 1937; IN ONE VOLUME, 1952)

*Parts of a World* (1942, 1951)

*Transport to Summer* (1947)

*The Auroras of Autumn* (1950)

*The Collected Poems of Wallace Stevens* (1954)
(INCLUDES ALL TITLES LISTED ABOVE)

Opus Posthumous: Poems, Plays, Prose (1957; 1989)
(REVISED, ENLARGED, AND CORRECTED EDITION EDITED BY MILTON J. BATES)

*The Palm at the End of the Mind: Selected Poems and a Play* (1971)
(EDITED BY HOLLY STEVENS)

*The Necessary Angel: Essays on Reality and the Imagination* (1951)

*Letters of Wallace Stevens* (1966)
(SELECTED AND EDITED BY HOLLY STEVENS)

*Souvenirs and Prophecies: The Young Wallace Stevens* (1977)
(BY HOLLY STEVENS)

# OPUS

# POSTHUMOUS

# OPUS

# POSTHUMOUS

### BY

# WALLACE STEVENS

*Revised, Enlarged, and Corrected Edition*

*Edited by Milton J. Bates*

ALFRED A. KNOPF  NEW YORK 1989

THIS IS A BORZOI BOOK,
PUBLISHED BY ALFRED A. KNOPF, INC.

Some of the material included in this work was originally published in the following publications:

Atlanta Journal, Eastern Underwriter, Harvard Advocate, New Verse, Others, Partisan Review, Poetry, Semi-Colon, The Trend, Twentieth Century Verse, View, and Yale Literary Magazine.

"A Note on Poetry" by Wallace Stevens was originally published in The Oxford Anthology of American Literature, edited by Benét and Pearson, Oxford University Press.

The original edition thanked the editors of magazines and books in which material originally appeared, as follows: Accent, Alcestis, The Atlantic Monthly, Briarcliff Quarterly, The Chapbook, Contact, Contempo, Direction, The Hudson Review, Imagi, Life and Letters Today, The Little Review, The Measure, The Modern School, New World Writing, Perspective, Poetry Quarterly, Quarterly Review of Literature, The Rocking Horse, Saturday Review, Seven Arts, Sewanee Review, Shenandoah, Smoke, Soil, Times Literary Supplement, Vogue, Wake, Westminster Magazine, Yale Review, and Zero; Pierre Beres, Inc., Louis Carré et Cie, College English Association, Creative Age Press, Cummington Press, Galleon Press, Harcourt, Brace & Company, The Macmillan Company, Objectivist Press, Prairie Press, the Saint Nicholas Society of New York and the Bollingen Foundation, for the "Two Prefaces" to Paul Valéry's Dialogues (Volume Four of The Collected Works of Paul Valéry), copyright 1956 by Bollingen Foundation, Inc.

Grateful acknowledgment is made to the following for permission to reprint previously published material:

Dobson Books Limited: "Responses to Modern American Poetry Questionnaire" from Modern American Poetry, edited by Rajan et al. Reprinted by permission of Dobson Books Limited, Durham, England.

The Hartford Fire Insurance Company: "Insurance and Social Change" by Wallace Stevens, published in The Hartford Agent (October, 1937, No. 29). Copyright 1937 by Hartford Fire Insurance Company. All rights reserved. Reprinted by permission.

Heldref Publications: "Poetry and Meaning" by Wallace Stevens, from The Explicator (November, 1948, No. 7), published by Heldref Publications, 4000 Albemarle St., NW, Washington, DC 20016. Copyright 1948. Reprinted by permission of the Helen Dwight Reid Educational Foundation.

Alfred A. Knopf, Inc.: "Poetry and War" from Parts of a World by Wallace Stevens. Copyright 1942 by Wallace Stevens. Copyright renewed 1970 by Holly Stevens. Reprinted by permission of Alfred A. Knopf, Inc.

Princeton University Press: "I have lived so long with the rhetoricians . . ." by Wallace Stevens from Wallace Stevens: The Making of Harmonium by Robert Buttel. Copyright © 1967 by Princeton University Press. Reprinted by permission of Princeton University Press.

Library of Congress Cataloging-in-Publication Data

Stevens, Wallace, 1879–1955.
Opus posthumous.

Includes index.
I. Bates, Milton J.  II. Title.
PS3537.T4753A6  1989      811'.52      88–46045
ISBN 0-394-57792-2

Manufactured in the United States of America
First Published August 19, 1957
Reprinted Seven Times
First Revised, Enlarged, and Corrected Edition

# Preface

WHEN SAMUEL FRENCH MORSE was preparing the first edition of *Opus Posthumous*, he was determined that the book should contain only the best of Wallace Stevens' uncollected and unpublished writings, omitting material he considered "merely fugitive." The resulting volume has served us admirably for over thirty years, passing through eight printings in hardcover before being issued as a Vintage paperback. Besides giving the reader more of the kind of pleasure to be found in Stevens' *Collected Poems* and *The Necessary Angel: Essays on Reality and the Imagination*, it hinted at riches yet to be divulged, in the form of manuscripts and notebooks. Since most of this material has now been edited, published, and in some cases analyzed exhaustively, Morse's Introduction to the first edition is no longer the indispensable guide it was in 1957. It has been replaced in this edition with notes providing textual information on some of the selections.

This edition also includes more of Stevens' poetry and prose than the first; in fact, it contains virtually all of the uncollected pieces he wrote for publication after his Harvard years, plus more than three dozen items still in manuscript at his death. Several of the new additions, notably the poem "From the Journal of Crispin" (an early version of "The Comedian as the Letter C"), came to light after the first edition appeared. Others—and these constitute the bulk of the new material—would once have seemed too slight or ephemeral to share the same pages with "The Course of a Particular" and the *Adagia*. In keeping with the formalist orthodoxy of its day, the

1957 *Opus Posthumous* preserved, with significant exceptions like *Owl's Clover*, the timeless Wallace Stevens of aesthetics, epistemology, and questions of belief. To this rather Olympian figure the current edition adds, without apology, the timely and even time-bound poet who engages today's biographers and literary historians.

Among the new additions, "Carnet de Voyage" stands out as an early sequence in which the apprentice poet began to sound his mature themes. The early war poems "Phases" and "Lettres d'un Soldat," here reprinted in as full a form as the extant manuscripts allow, find him struggling with a profound dislocation between idiom and event. Also reprinted complete are the two *Adagia* notebooks, portals to the poetry inscribed with nearly three hundred fitful tracings. Essays like "Cattle *Kings* of Florida," "Insurance and Social Change," and "Surety and Fidelity Claims" all grew out of Stevens' working life and serve to bridge the apparent chasm between that realm and the one he created in his poetry. His responses to the questionnaires sent out by the *Partisan Review* and other publications address, as intelligently as the questions permit, the contemporary state of poetry and its relation to American politics and culture.

The selections in this volume are arranged chronologically within each category. In the case of items published during Stevens' lifetime or shortly thereafter, the year of publication appears parenthetically in roman type following the title in the table of contents. For items that were still in manuscript at his death, the year of composition appears in italics—either with a question mark when conjectural or without a question mark when the date can be established.

Although the conditions of publication precluded a full scholarly or critical edition, this *Opus Posthumous* is based on an examination of most versions of each selection, whether in manuscript or in print. Two selections are reprinted directly from the first edition because no other printed or manuscript source could be located: "Stanzas for 'Examination of the Hero in a Time of War'" (two of three stanzas) and "Notes on Jean Labasque." Generally speaking, the text of a published work follows the printed version over which Stevens is likely to have exercised the most control. The notes specify cases where versions in manuscript have been favored over those in print. For complete citations of the published works—except for "Surety and Fidelity Claims," which is cited in the notes—the reader may consult J. M. Edelstein's *Wallace Stevens: A Descriptive Bibliography* (Pittsburgh: University of Pittsburgh Press, 1973). For works surviving only in manuscript, the text represents what appears to be the latest stage of composition or revision; thus a typescript is usually preferred to a holograph manuscript.

Misspellings have been silently corrected, as have errors in the accenting and capitalization of foreign words. Periods have been added where necessary for terminal punctuation or to regularize Stevens' ellipses.

This edition would have been impossible without the cooperation of the libraries that house Stevens manuscripts consulted in its preparation: the Henry E. Huntington Library, San Marino, California; the Department of Special Collections, University of Chicago Library; the Collection of American Literature, Beinecke Rare Book and Manuscript Library, Yale University; the Poetry/Rare Books Collection, University Libraries, SUNY at Buffalo; the Houghton Library, Harvard University; the Van Pelt Library, University of Pennsylvania; and the Princeton University Library, *Story Magazine* archive, Box 6. That indebtedness extends likewise to the editors and publishers in whose magazines and books (listed on the copyright page) many items first saw the light of day. To all of these and to Holly Stevens I am grateful for permission to publish or reprint the selections in this volume.

Much of the credit for launching a new edition of *Opus Posthumous* belongs to Holly Stevens and A. Walton Litz, who did all they could to help this volume measure up to the lofty standard they set in their own editions of Wallace Stevens' writings. I am further indebted to Robert J. Bertholf, Brigitte Coste, Philip N. Cronenwett, Vicki Denby, J. M. Edelstein, Margarethe V. Fitzell, Harry Ford, Sara S. Hodson, George S. Lensing, James Longenbach, Glen MacLeod, Lori Misura, and Nancy M. Shawcross for their helpful responses to my queries. This, finally, must be said in appreciation of Julie Gores and her persistent staff in the Interlibrary Loan Department, Marquette University Library: they always got their book.

MILTON J. BATES

# Contents

## PLAYS

## APHORISMS

## ESSAYS, SPEECHES, NOTES

## QUESTIONNAIRE RESPONSES

# POEMS

## CHIAROSCURO

The house-fronts flare
In the blown rain.
The ghostly street-lamps
Have a pallid glare.

A wanderer beats,
With bitter droop,
Along the waste
Of vacant streets.

Suppose some glimmer
Recalled for him
An odorous room,
A fan's fleet shimmer

Of silvery spangle,
Two startled eyes,
A still-trembling hand
And its only bangle.

## COLORS

### I

Pale orange, green and crimson, and
white, and gold and brown.

Lapis-lazuli and orange, and opaque green,
faun-color, black and gold.

## TESTAMENTUM

Plant the tea-plant on my grave,
And bury with me funerary cups,
Of which let one be such
That young Persephone will not resist.

## DOLLS

The thought of Eve, within me, is a doll
That does what I desire, as, to perplex,
With apple-buds, the husband in her sire.

There's a pious caliph, now, who prays and sees
A vermeil cheek. He is half-conscious of
The quaint seduction of a scented veil.

Playing with dolls? A solid game, greybeards.
Think of the cherubim and seraphim,
And of Another, whom I must not name.

## INFERNALE

(A boor of night in middle earth cries out,)
Hola! Hola! What steps are those that break

This crust of air? . . . (*He pauses.*) Can breath shake
The solid wax from which the warmth dies out? . . .

I saw a waxen woman in a smock
Fly from the black toward the purple air.
(*He shouts.*) Hola! Of that strange light, beware!
(*A woman's voice is heard, replying.*) Mock

The bondage of the Stygian concubine,
Hallooing haggler; for the wax is blown,
And downward, from this purple region, thrown;
And I fly forth, the naked Proserpine.

(*Her pale smock sparkles in a light begun
To be diffused, and, as she disappears,
The silent watcher, far below her, hears:*)
Soaring Olympus glitters in the sun.

◇◇◇◇◇◇◇◇◇◇◇◇◇◇◇◇◇◇◇◇◇◇◇◇◇◇◇◇◇◇◇◇◇◇◇◇◇◇◇◇◇◇◇◇◇◇◇◇◇◇◇◇◇◇◇

## CARNET DE VOYAGE

### I

An odor from a star
Comes to my fancy, slight,
Tenderly spiced and gay,
As if a seraph's hand
Unloosed the fragrant silks
Of some sultana, bright
In her soft sky. And pure
It is, and excellent,
As if a seraph's blue
Fell, as a shadow falls,
And his warm body shed
Sweet exhalations, void
Of our despised decay.

5

The green goes from the corn,
The blue from all the lakes,
And the shadows of the mountains mingle in the sky.

Far off, the still bamboo
Grows green; the desert pool
Turns gaudy turquoise for the chanting caravan.

The changing green and blue
Flow round the changing earth;
And all the rest is empty wondering and sleep.

III

Here the grass grows,
And the wind blows.
And in the stream,
Small fishes gleam,
Blood-red and hue
Of shadowy blue,
And amber sheen,
And water-green,
And yellow flash,
And diamond ash.
And the grass grows,
And the wind blows.

IV

She that winked her sandal fan
Long ago in gray Japan—

She that heard the bell intone
Rendezvous by rolling Rhone—

How wide the spectacle of sleep,
Hands folded, eyes too still to weep!

6

I am weary of the plum and of the cherry,
And that buff moon in evening's aquarelle,
I have no heart within to make me merry.
I nod above the books of Heaven or Hell.

All things are old. The new-born swallows fare
Through the Spring twilight on dead September's wing.
The dust of Babylon is in the air,
And settles on my lips the while I sing.

Man from the waste evolved
The Cytherean glade,
Imposed on battering seas
His keel's dividing blade,
And sailed there, unafraid.

The isle revealed his worth.
It was a place to sing in
And honor noble Life,
For white doves to wing in,
And roses to spring in.

VII   *Chinese Rocket*

There, a rocket in the Wain
Brings primeval night again.
All the startled heavens flare
From the Shepherd to the Bear—

When the old-time dark returns,
Lo, the steadfast Lady burns
Her curious lantern to disclose
How calmly the White River flows!

It was a simple thing
For her to sit and sing,
   "Hey nonino!"

This year and that befell,
(Time saw and Time can tell),
   With a hey and a ho—

Under the peach-tree, play
Such mockery away,
   Hey nonino!

## FROM A JUNK

A great fish plunges in the dark,
Its fins of rutted silver; sides,
Belabored with a foamy light;
And back, brilliant with scaly salt.
It glistens in the flapping wind,
Burns there and glistens, wide and wide,
Under the five-horned stars of night,
In wind and wave . . . It is the moon.

## HOME AGAIN

Back within the valley,
Down from the divide,
No more flaming clouds about,
O! the soft hillside,
And my cottage light,
And the starry night.

8

{{IMG_p0_0}} ❁◇❁◇❁◇❁◇❁◇❁◇❁◇❁◇❁◇❁◇❁◇❁◇❁◇❁◇❁◇❁◇❁◇❁◇❁◇❁◇❁◇❁◇❁◇

# PHASES

*"La justice sans force est contredite, parce qu'il y a toujours des méchants; la force sans la justice est accusée."* PASCAL

I

There was heaven,
Full of Raphael's costumes;
And earth,
A thing of shadows,
Stiff as stone,
Where Time, in fitful turns,
Resumes
His own . . .

A dead hand tapped the drum,
An old voice cried out, "Come!"
We were obedient and dumb.

II

There's a little square in Paris,
Waiting until we pass.
They sit idly there,
They sip the glass.

There's a cab-horse at the corner,
There's rain. The season grieves.
It was silver once,
And green with leaves.

There's a parrot in a window,
Will see us on parade,
Hear the loud drums roll—
And serenade.

9

This was the salty taste of glory,
That it was not
Like Agamemnon's story.
Only, an eyeball in the mud,
And Hopkins,
Flat and pale and gory!

But the bugles, in the night,
Were wings that bore
To where our comfort was;

Arabesques of candle beams,
Winding
Through our heavy dreams;

Winds that blew
Where the bending iris grew;

Birds of intermitted bliss,
Singing in the night's abyss;

Vines with yellow fruit,
That fell
Along the walls
That bordered Hell.

Death's nobility again
Beautified the simplest men.
Fallen Winkle felt the pride
Of Agamemnon
When he died.

What could London's
Work and waste
Give him—
To that salty, sacrificial taste?

What could London's
Sorrow bring—
To that short, triumphant sting?


VI

*[first part missing]*

The crisp, sonorous epics
Mongered after every scene.
Sluggards must be quickened! Screen,

No more, the shape of false Confusion.
Bare his breast and draw the flood
Of all his Babylonian blood.


VII

The vaguest line of smoke, (a year ago),
Wavered in evening air, above the roof,
As if some Old Man of the Chimney, sick
Of summer and that unused hearth below,

Stretched out a shadowy arm to feel the night.
The children heard him in their chilly beds,
Mumbling and musing of the silent farm.
They heard his mumble in the morning light.

Now, soldiers, hear me: mark this very breeze,
That blows about in such a hopeless way,
Mumbling and musing like the most forlorn.
It is that Old Man, lost among the trees.

## VIII

What shall we say to the lovers of freedom,
Forming their states for new eras to come?
Say that the fighter is master of men.

Shall we, then, say to the lovers of freedom
That force, and not freedom, must always prevail?
Say that the fighter is master of men.

Or shall we say to the lovers of freedom
That freedom will conquer and always prevail?
Say that the fighter is master of men.

Say, too, that freedom is master of masters,
Forming their states for new eras to come.
Say that the fighter is master of men.


IX

Life, the hangman, never came,
Near our mysteries of flame.

When we marched across his towns,
He cozened us with leafy crowns.

When we marched along his roads,
He kissed his hand to ease our loads.

Life, the hangman, kept away,
From the field where soldiers pay.


X

Peace means long, delicious valleys,
In the mode of Claude Lorraine;
Rivers of jade,
In serpentines,

About the heavy grain;
Leaning trees,
Where the pilgrim hums
Of the dear
And distant door.
Peace means these,
And all things, as before.

## XI

War has no haunt except the heart,
Which envy haunts, and hate, and fear,
And malice, and ambition, near
The haunt of love. Who shall impart,

To that strange commune, strength enough
To drive the laggard phantoms out?
Who shall dispel for it the doubt
Of its own strength? Let Heaven snuff

The tapers round her futile throne.
Close tight the prophets' coffin-clamp.
Peer inward, with the spirit's lamp,
Look deep, and let the truth be known.

⸻

## "ALL THINGS IMAGINED
## ARE OF EARTH COMPACT . . ."

All things imagined are of earth compact,
Strange beast and bird, strange creatures all;
Strange minds of men, unwilling slaves to fact:

Struggling with desperate clouds, they still proclaim
The rushing pearl, the whirling black,
Clearly, in well-remembered word and name.

Even the dead, when they return, return
Not as those dead, concealed away;
But their old persons move again, and burn.

❀◈❀◈❀◈❀◈❀◈❀◈❀◈❀◈❀◈❀◈❀◈❀◈❀◈❀◈❀◈❀◈❀◈❀◈❀◈❀◈❀◈❀◈❀◈❀◈❀◈❀◈❀◈❀◈◈

## L'ESSOR SACCADÉ

Swallows in the elderberry,
Fly to the steeple.
Then from one apple-tree
Fly to another.

Fly over the stones of the brook,
Along the stony water.
Fly over the widow's house
And around it.

Never mind the white dog
That barks in the bushes.
Fly over the pigeons
On the chimney.

◈◈◈◈◈◈◈◈◈◈◈◈◈◈◈◈◈◈◈◈◈◈◈◈◈◈◈◈◈◈◈◈◈◈◈◈◈◈◈◈◈◈◈◈◈◈◈◈◈◈◈◈◈◈◈

## AN EXERCISE FOR PROFESSOR X

I see a camel in my mind.
I do not say to myself, in English,
"There is a camel."
I do not talk to myself.
On the contrary, I watch
And a camel passes in my mind.
This might happen to a Persian.
My mind and a Persian's
Are as much alike, then,
As moonlight on the Atlantic
Is like moonlight on the Pacific.

## HEADACHE

The letters of the alphabet
Are representations of parts of the head.
Ears are $q$ s
$L$ s are the edges of the teeth
$M$ s are the wrinkled skin between the eyes
In frowns.
The nostrils and the bridge of the nose
Are $p$ s or $b$ s.
The mouth is $o$.
There are letters in the hair.
Worms frown, are full of mouths,
Bite, twitch their ears . . .
The maker of the alphabet
Had a headache.


## "I HAVE LIVED SO LONG
## WITH THE RHETORICIANS . . ."

I have lived so long with the rhetoricians
That when I see a pine tree
Broken by lightning
Or hear a crapulous crow
In dead boughs,
In April
These are too ready
To despise me
It is for this the good lord
Gave the rooster his lustre
And made sprats pink
Who can doubt that Confucius
Thought well of streets
In the spring-time

15

It is for this the rhetoricians
Wear long black equali
When they are abroad.

❀◇❀◇❀◇❀◇❀◇❀◇❀◇❀◇❀◇❀◇❀◇❀◇❀◇❀◇❀◇❀◇❀◇❀◇❀◇❀◇❀◇❀◇❀◇❀◇❀◇❀◇❀◇

## "THE NIGHT-WIND OF AUGUST . . ."

The night-wind of August
Is like an old mother to me.
It comforts me.
I rest in it,
As one would rest,
If one could,
Once again—
It moves about, quietly
And attentively.
Its old hands touch me.
Its breath touches me.
But sometimes its breath is a little cold,
Just a little,
And I know
That it is only the night-wind.

◇◇◇◇◇◇◇◇◇◇◇◇◇◇◇◇◇◇◇◇◇◇◇◇◇◇◇◇◇◇◇◇◇◇◇◇◇◇◇◇◇◇◇◇◇◇◇◇◇◇◇◇◇◇◇◇◇◇

## TO MADAME ALDA, SINGING A SONG,
## IN A WHITE GOWN

So much sorrow comes to me out of your singing.
A few large, round leaves of wan pink
Float in a small space of air,
Luminously.
A white heron rises.
From its long legs, drifting, close together,
Drops of water slide
And glisten.
It drifts from sight.

16

## THE SILVER PLOUGH-BOY

A black figure dances in a black field.
It seizes a sheet, from the ground, from a bush, as if spread there
      by some wash-woman for the night.
It wraps the sheet around its body, until the black figure is
      silver.
It dances down a furrow, in the early light, back of a crazy
      plough, the green blades following.
How soon the silver fades in the dust! How soon the black
      figure slips from the wrinkled sheet! How softly the sheet
      falls to the ground!

## BLANCHE McCARTHY

Look in the terrible mirror of the sky
And not in this dead glass, which can reflect
Only the surfaces—the bending arm,
The leaning shoulder and the searching eye.

Look in the terrible mirror of the sky.
Oh, bend against the invisible; and lean
To symbols of descending night; and search
The glare of revelations going by!

Look in the terrible mirror of the sky.
See how the absent moon waits in a glade
Of your dark self, and how the wings of stars,
Upward, from unimagined coverts, fly.

17

# FOR AN OLD WOMAN IN A WIG

### I

                    . . . There is a moment's flitter
Of silvers and of blacks across the streaking.
                         . . . a swarming chitter

Of crows that flap away beyond the creaking
Of wooden wagons in the mountain gutters.
. . .

The young dogs bark . . .
. . .
                    . . . It is the skeleton Virgil utters

The fates of men. Dogs bay their ghosts. The traces
Of morning grow large and all the cocks are crowing
And . . .        the sun . . .      paces

The tops of hell . . . Death, . . . knowing,
Grieves . . . our spirits with too poignant grieving,
                         . . . keeps on showing

To our still envious memory, still believing,
The things we knew. For him the cocks awaken.
He spreads the thought of morning past deceiving

And yet deceives. There comes a mood that's taken
From water-deeps reflecting opening roses
And rounding, watery leaves, forever shaken,

And floating colors, which the mind supposes
In an imagination cut by sorrow.
Hell is not desolate Italy. It closes

                    . . . above a morrow
Of common yesterdays: a wagon's rumble,
Loud cocks and barking dogs. It does not borrow,

18

Except from dark forgetfulness, the mumble
Of sounds returning, or the phantom leaven
Of leaves so shaken in a water's tumble.


II

Is death in hell more death than death in heaven?
And is there never in that noon a turning—
One step descending one of all the seven

Implacable buttresses of sunlight, burning
In the great air? There must be spirits riven
From out contentment by too conscious yearning.

There must be spirits willing to be driven
To that immeasurable blackness, or . . .
To those old landscapes, endlessly regiven,

Whence hell, and heaven itself, were both begotten.
There must be spirits wandering in the valleys,
And on the green-planed hills, that find forgotten

Beggars of earth intent
On maids with aprons lifted up to carry
Red-purples home—beggars that cry out sallies

Of half-remembered songs . . . sing, "Tarry,
Tarry, are you gone?" . . . Such spirits are the fellows,
In heaven, of those whom hell's illusions harry.


III

When summer ends and changing autumn mellows
The nights . . .                    and moons glance
Over the dreamers . . . and bring the yellows

Of autumn days and nights into resemblance,
The dreamers wake and watch the moonlight streaming.
They shall have much to suffer in remembrance.

19

They shall have much to suffer when the beaming
Of these clear moons, long afterward, returning,
Shines on them, elsewhere, in a deeper dreaming.

...   Suns, too, shall follow them with burning
Hallucinations in their turbid sleeping ...
...

*O pitiful lovers of Earth, why are you keeping*
*Such count of beauty in the ways you wander?*
*Why are you so insistent on the sweeping*

*Poetry of sky and sea? Are you, then, fonder*
*Of the circumference of earth's impounding,*
*Than of some sphere on which the mind might blunder,*

*If you, with irrepressible will, abounding*
*In ...                wish for revelation,*
*Sought out the unknown new in your surrounding?*

◇◇◇◇◇◇◇◇◇◇◇◇◇◇◇◇◇◇◇◇◇◇◇◇◇◇◇◇◇◇◇◇◇◇◇◇◇◇◇◇◇◇◇◇◇◇◇◇

## THE FLORIST WEARS KNEE-BREECHES

My flowers are reflected
In your mind
As you are reflected in your glass.
When you look at them,
There is nothing in your mind
Except the reflections
Of my flowers.
But when I look at them
I see only the reflections
In your mind,
And not my flowers.
It is my desire
To bring roses,
And place them before you
In a white dish.

20

# SONG

There are great things doing
In the world,
Little rabbit.
There is a damsel,
Sweeter than the sound of the willow,
Dearer than shallow water
Flowing over pebbles.
Of a Sunday,
She wears a long coat,
With twelve buttons on it.
Tell that to your mother.

# EIGHT SIGNIFICANT LANDSCAPES

## I

An old man sits
In the shadow of a pine tree
In China.
He sees larkspur,
Blue and white,
At the edge of the shadow,
Move in the wind.
His beard moves in the wind.
The pine tree moves in the wind.
Thus water flows
Over weeds.

The night is of the color
Of a woman's arm:
Night, the female,
Obscure,
Fragrant and supple,
Conceals herself.
A pool shines,
Like a bracelet
Shaken in a dance.

III

I measure myself
Against a tall tree.
I find that I am much taller,
For I reach right up to the sun,
With my eye;
And I reach to the shore of the sea
With my ear.
Nevertheless, I dislike
The way the ants crawl
In and out of my shadow.

IV

When my dream was near the moon,
The white folds of its gown
Filled with yellow light.
The soles of its feet
Grew red.
Its hair filled
With certain blue crystallizations
From stars,
Not far off.

Wrestle with morning-glories,
O, muscles!
It is useless to contend
With falling mountains.

Not all the knives of the lamp-posts,
Nor the chisels of the long streets,
Nor the mallets of the domes
And high towers,
Can carve
What one star can carve,
Shining through the grape-leaves.

Crenellations of mountains
Cut like strummed zithers;
But dead trees do not resemble
Beaten drums.

Rationalists, wearing square hats,
Think, in square rooms,
Looking at the floor,
Looking at the ceiling.
They confine themselves
To right-angled triangles.
If they tried rhomboids,
Cones, waving lines, ellipses—
As, for example, the ellipse of the half-moon—
Rationalists would wear sombreros.

## INSCRIPTION FOR A MONUMENT

To the imagined lives
Evoked by music,
Creatures of horns, flutes, drums,
Violins, bassoons, cymbals—
Nude porters that glistened in Burma
Defiling from sight;
Island philosophers spent
By long thought beside fountains;
Big-bellied ogres curled up in the sunlight,
Stuttering dreams . . .

## BOWL

For what emperor
Was this bowl of Earth designed?
Here are more things
Than on any bowl of the Sungs,
Even the rarest—
Vines that take
The various obscurities of the moon,
Approaching rain
And leaves that would be loose upon the wind,
Pears on pointed trees,
The dresses of women,
Oxen . . .
I never tire
To think of this.

❀◇❀◇❀◇❀◇❀◇❀◇❀◇❀◇❀◇❀◇❀◇❀◇❀◇❀◇❀◇❀◇❀◇❀◇❀◇❀◇❀◇❀◇❀◇❀◇❀◇❀◇❀◇❀◇❀◇❀◇

# PRIMORDIA

## *In the Northwest*

### 1

All over Minnesota,
Cerise sopranos,
Walking in the snow,
Answer, humming,
The male voice of the wind in the dry leaves
Of the lake-hollows.
For one,
The syllables of the gulls and of the crows
And of the blue-bird
Meet in the name
Of Jalmar Lillygreen.
There is his motion
In the flowing of black water.

### 2

The child's hair is of the color of the hay in the haystack,
    around which the four black horses stand.
There is the same color in the bellies of frogs, in clays,
    withered reeds, skins, wood, sunlight.

### 3

The blunt ice flows down the Mississippi,
At night.
In the morning, the clear river
Is full of reflections,
Beautiful alliterations of shadows and of
    things shadowed.

25

## 4

The horses gnaw the bark from the trees.
The horses are hollow,
The trunks of the trees are hollow.
Why do the horses have eyes and ears?
The trees do not.
Why can the horses move about on the ground?
The trees cannot.
The horses weary themselves hunting for green grass.
The trees stand still,
The trees drink.
The water runs away from the horses.
La, la, la, la, la, la, la, la,
Dee, dum, diddle, dee, dee, diddle, dee, da.


5


The birch trees draw up whiteness from the ground.
In the swamps, bushes draw up dark red,
Or yellow.
O, boatman,
What are you drawing from the rain-pointed water?
O, boatman,
What are you drawing from the rain-pointed water?
Are you two boatmen
Different from each other?


*In the South*


6


Unctuous furrows,
The ploughman portrays in you
The spring about him:
Compilation of the effects
Of magenta blooming in the Judas-tree
And of purple blooming in the eucalyptus—

Map of yesterday's earth
And of tomorrow's heaven.


                          7


The lilacs wither in the Carolinas.
Already the butterflies flutter above the cabins.
Already the new-born children interpret love
In the voices of mothers.
Timeless mother,
How is it that your aspic nipples
For once vent honey?

*The pine-tree sweetens my body*
*The white iris beautifies me.*


                          8


    The black mother of eleven children
    Hangs her quilt under the pine-trees.
    There is a connection between the colors,
    The shapes of the patches,
    And the eleven children . . .
    Frail princes of distant Monaco,
    That paragon of a parasol
    Discloses
    At least one baby in you.


                          9


The trade-wind jingles the rings in the nets around the racks
        by the docks on Indian River.
It is the same jingle of the water among the roots under the
        banks of the palmettoes,
It is the same jingle of the red-bird breasting the orange-trees
        out of the cedars.

Yet there is no spring in Florida, neither in boskage perdu, nor
on the nunnery beaches.

*To the Roaring Wind*

What syllable are you seeking,
Vocalissimus,
In the distances of sleep?
Speak it.

◇◇◇◇◇◇◇◇◇◇◇◇◇◇◇◇◇◇◇◇◇◇◇◇◇◇◇◇◇◇◇◇◇◇◇◇◇◇◇◇◇◇◇◇◇◇◇◇◇◇

## MEDITATION

How long have I meditated, O Prince,
On sky and earth?
It comes to this,
That even the moon
Has exhausted its emotions.
What is it that I think of, truly?
The lines of blackberry bushes,
The design of leaves—
Neither sky nor earth
Express themselves before me . . .
Bossuet did not preach at the funerals
Of puppets.

❀◇❀◇❀◇❀◇❀◇❀◇❀◇❀◇❀◇❀◇❀◇❀◇❀◇❀◇❀◇❀◇❀◇❀◇❀◇❀◇❀◇❀◇❀◇❀◇❀◇❀◇❀◇❀◇❀◇❀◇❀◇❀◇❀◇❀◇

## GRAY ROOM

Although you sit in a room that is gray,
Except for the silver
Of the straw-paper,
And pick

At your pale white gown;
Or lift one of the green beads
Of your necklace,
To let it fall;
Or gaze at your green fan
Printed with the red branches of a red willow;
Or, with one finger,
Move the leaf in the bowl—
The leaf that has fallen from the branches of the
    forsythia
Beside you . . .
What is all this?
I know how furiously your heart is beating.

◇◇◇◇◇◇◇◇◇◇◇◇◇◇◇◇◇◇◇◇◇◇◇◇◇◇◇◇◇◇◇◇◇◇◇◇◇◇◇◇◇◇◇◇◇◇◇◇◇◇◇◇

# LETTRES D'UN SOLDAT
## (1914–1915)

> Combattre avec ses frères, à sa place, à son
> rang, avec des yeux dessillés, sans espoir de
> gloire et de profit, et simplement parce que
> telle est la loi, voilà le commandement que
> donne le dieu au guerrier Arjuna, quand
> celui-ci doute s'il doit se détourner de l'ab-
> solu pour le cauchemar humain de la bataille.
> . . . Simplement, qu'Arjuna bande son arc
> avec les autres Kshettryas!
>
> PRÉFACE D'ANDRÉ CHEVRILLON

I

> 7 septembre
> . . . Nous sommes embarqués dans l'aventure, sans aucune
> sensation dominante, sauf peut-être une acceptation assez
> belle de la fatalité. . . .

COMMON SOLDIER

No introspective chaos . . . I accept:
War, too, although I do not understand.
And that, then, is my final aphorism.

I have been pupil under bishops' rods
And got my learning from the orthodox.
I mark the virtue of the common-place.

I take all things as stated—so and so
Of men and earth: I quote the line and page,
I quote the very phrase my masters used.

If I should fall, as soldier, I know well
The final pulse of blood from this good heart
Would taste, precisely, as they said it would.


## II

*27 septembre*
*Jamais la majesté de la nuit ne m'apporta autant de con-*
*solation qu'en cette accumulation d'épreuves. Vénus, étince-*
*lante, m'est une amie.*

### IN AN ANCIENT, SOLEMN MANNER

The spirit wakes in the night wind—is naked.
What is it that hides in the night wind
Near by it?

Is it, once more, the mysterious beauté,
Like a woman inhibiting passion
In solace—

The multiform beauty, sinking in night wind,
Quick to be gone, yet never
Quite going?

She will leap back from the swift constellations,
As they enter the place of their western
Seclusion.

*22 octobre*
*Ce qu'il faut, c'est reconnaître l'amour et la beauté triom-*
*phante de toute violence.*

ANECDOTAL REVERY

The streets contain a crowd
Of blind men tapping their way
By inches—
This man to complain to the grocer
Of yesterday's cheese,
This man to visit a woman,
This man to take the air.
Am I to pick my way
Through these crickets?—
I, that have a head
In the bag
Slung over my shoulder?
I have secrets
That prick
Like a heart full of pins.
Permit me, gentlemen,
I have killed the mayor,
And am escaping from you.
Get out of the way!
(*The blind men strike him down with their sticks.*)

IV

*31 octobre*
*Jusqu'à présent j'ai possédé une sagesse de renoncement,*
*mais maintenant je veux une Sagesse qui accepte tout, en*
*s'orientant vers l'action future.*

MORALE

And so France feels. A menace that impends,
Too long, is like a bayonet that bends.

*7 novembre*
*Si tu voyais la sécurité des petits animaux des bois, souris,*
*mulots! L'autre jour, dans notre abri de feuillage, je suivais*
*les évolutions de ces petites bêtes. Elles étaient jolies comme*
*une estampe japonaise, avec l'intérieur de leurs oreilles rose*
*comme un coquillage.*

### COMME DIEU DISPENSE DE GRACES

Here I keep thinking of the Primitives—
The sensitive and conscientious schemes
Of mountain pallors ebbing into air;

And I remember sharp Japonica—
The driving rain, the willows in the rain,
The birds that wait out rain in willow leaves.

Although life seems a goblin mummery,
These images return and are increased,
As for a child in an oblivion:

Even by mice—these scamper and are still;
They cock small ears, more glistening and pale
Than fragile volutes in a rose sea-shell.

VI

*26 novembre*
*J'ai la ferme espérance, mais surtout j'ai confiance en la*
*justice éternelle, quelque surprise qu'elle cause à l'humaine*
*idée que nous en avons.*

### THE SURPRISES OF THE SUPERHUMAN

The palais de justice of chambermaids
Tops the horizon with its colonnades.

If it were lost in Übermenschlichkeit,
Perhaps our wretched state would soon come right.

For somehow the brave dicta of its kings
Make more awry our faulty human things.

*29 novembre au matin, en cantonnement*
*Telle fut la beauté d'hier. Te parlerai-je des soirées précé-*
*dentes, alors que sur la route, la lune me dessinait la broderie*
*des arbres, le pathétique des calvaires, l'attendrissement de*
*ces maisons que l'on sait des ruines, mais que la nuit fait*
*surgir comme une évocation de la paix.*

### LUNAR PARAPHRASE

The moon is the mother of pathos and pity.

When, at the wearier end of November,
Her old light moves along the branches,
Feebly, slowly, depending upon them;
When the body of Jesus hangs in a pallor,
Humanly near, and the figure of Mary,
Touched on by hoar-frost, shrinks in a shelter
Made by the leaves, that have rotted and fallen;
When over the houses, a golden illusion
Brings back an earlier season of quiet
And quieting dreams in the sleepers in darkness—

The moon is the mother of pathos and pity.

*7 décembre*
*Bien chère Mère aimée. . . . Pour ce qui est de ton coeur, j'ai*
*tellement confiance en ton courage, qu'à l'heure actuelle*
*cette certitude est mon grand réconfort. Je sais que ma mère*
*a atteint à cette liberté d'âme qui permet de contempler le*
*spectacle universel.*

There is another mother whom I love,
O chère maman, another, who, in turn,

33

Is mother to the two of us, and more,
In whose hard service both of us endure
Our petty portion in the sacrifice.
Not France! France, also, serves the invincible eye,
That, from her helmet, terrible and bright,
Commands the armies; the relentless arm,
Devising proud, majestic issuance.
Wait now; have no rememberings of hope,
Poor penury. There will be voluble hymns
Come swelling, when, regardless of my end,
The mightier mother raises up her cry;
And little will or wish, that day, for tears.


IX


*15 janvier*
*La seule sanction pour moi est ma conscience. Il faut nous*
*confier à une justice impersonnelle, indépendante de tout*
*facteur humain, et à une destinée utile et harmonieuse mal-*
*gré toute horreur de forme.*

NEGATION

Hi! The creator too is blind,
Struggling toward his harmonious whole,
Rejecting intermediate parts,
Horrors and falsities and wrongs;
Incapable master of all force,
Too vague idealist, overwhelmed
By an afflatus that persists.
For this, then, we endure brief lives,
The evanescent symmetries
From that meticulous potter's thumb.


X


*4 février*
*Hier soir, rentrant dans ma grange, ivresse, rixes, cris, chants*
*et hurlements. Voilà la vie!*

34

John Smith and his son, John Smith,
    And his son's son John, and-a-one
    And-a-two and-a-three
And-a-rum-tum-tum, and-a
Lean John, and his son, lean John,
    And his lean son's John, and-a-one
    And-a-two and-a-three
And-a-drum-rum-rum, and-a
Rich John, and his son, rich John,
    And his rich son's John, and-a-one
    And-a-two and-a-three
And-a-pom-pom-pom, and-a
Wise John, and his son, wise John,
    And his wise son's John, and-a-one
    And-a-two and-a-three
And-a-fee and-a-fee and-a-fee
    And-a-fee-fo-fum—
Voilà la vie, la vie, la vie,
    And-a-rummy-tummy-tum
    And-a-rummy-tummy-tum.

## XI

*5 mars*

*La mort du soldat est près des choses naturelles.*

Life contracts and death is expected,
As in a season of autumn.
The soldier falls.

He does not become a three-days personage,
Imposing his separation,
Calling for pomp.

Death is absolute and without memorial,
As in a season of autumn,
When the wind stops,

When the wind stops and, over the heavens,
The clouds go, nevertheless,
In their direction.


## XII

*17 mars*
*J'ai oublié de te dire que, l'autre fois, pendant la tempête,
j'ai vu dans le soir les grues revenir. Une accalmie permet-
tait d'entendre leur cri.*

In a theatre, full of tragedy,
The stage becomes an atmosphere
Of seeping rose—banal machine
In an appointed repertoire . . .


## XIII

*26 mars*
*Rien de nouveau sur notre hauteur que l'on continue d'or-
ganiser. . . . De temps à autre la pioche rencontre un pauvre
mort que la guerre tourmente jusque dans la terre.*

Death was a reaper with sickle and stone,
Or swipling flail, sun-black in the sun,
A laborer.

Or Death was a rider beating his horse,
Gesturing grandiose things in the air,
Seen by a muse. . . .

Symbols of sentiment . . . Take this phrase,
Men of the line, take this new phrase
Of the truth of Death—

Death, that will never be satisfied,
Digs up the earth when want returns . . .
You know the phrase.

# ARCHITECTURE

### I

What manner of building shall we build?
Let us design a chastel de chasteté.
De pensée. . . .
Never cease to deploy the structure.
Keep the laborers shouldering plinths.
Pass the whole of life earing the clink of the
Chisels of the stone-cutters cutting the stones.

### II

In this house, what manner of utterance shall there be?
What heavenly dithyramb
And cantilene?
What niggling forms of gargoyle patter?
Of what shall the speech be,
In that splay of marble
And of obedient pillars?

### III

And how shall those come vested that come there?
In their ugly reminders?
Or gaudy as tulips?
As they climb the stairs
To the group of Flora Coddling Hecuba?
As they climb the flights
To the closes
Overlooking whole seasons?

## IV

Let us build the building of light.
Push up the towers
To the cock-tops.
These are the pointings of our edifice,
Which, like a gorgeous palm,
Shall tuft the commonplace.
These are the window-sill
On which the quiet moonlight lies.

## V

How shall we hew the sun,
Split it and make blocks,
To build a ruddy palace?
How carve the violet moon
To set in nicks?
Let us fix portals, east and west,
Abhorring green-blue north and blue-green south.
Our chiefest dome a demoiselle of gold.
Pierce the interior with pouring shafts,
In diverse chambers.
Pierce, too, with buttresses of coral air
And purple timbers,
Various argentines,
Embossings of the sky.

## VI

And, finally, set guardians in the grounds,
Gray, gruesome grumblers.
For no one proud, nor stiff,
No solemn one, nor pale,
No chafferer, may come
To sully the begonias, nor vex
With holy or sublime ado
The kremlin of kermess.

## VII

Only the lusty and the plenteous
Shall walk
The bronze-filled plazas
And the nut-shell esplanades.

◇◇◇◇◇◇◇◇◇◇◇◇◇◇◇◇◇◇◇◇◇◇◇◇◇◇◇◇◇◇◇◇◇◇◇◇◇◇◇◇◇◇◇◇◇◇◇◇

## STANZAS FOR "LE MONOCLE DE MON ONCLE"

I peopled the dark park with gowns
In which were yellow, rancid skeletons.
Oh! How suave a purple passed me by!
But twiddling mon idée, as old men will,
And knowing the monotony of thought,
I said, "She thumbs the memories of dress."
Can I take fire from so benign an ash?
It is enough she comes upon the eye.
A maid of forty is no feathery girl.
Green bosoms and black legs, beguile
These ample lustres from the new-come moon.

## VIII

Poets of pimpernel, unlucky pimps
Of pomp, in love and good ensample, see
How I exhort her, huckstering my woe.
*"Oh, hideous, horrible, horrendous hocks!"*
Is there one word of sunshine in this plaint?
Do I commend myself to leafy things
Or melancholy crows as shadowing clouds?
I grieve the pinch of her long-stiffening bones.
*"Oh, lissomeness turned lagging ligaments!"*
Eheu! Eheu! With what a weedy face
Black fact emerges from her swishing dreams.

39

## AN EARLY VERSION OF "ANECDOTE OF THE PRINCE OF PEACOCKS"

In the land of the peacocks, the prince thereof,
Grown weary of romantics, walked alone,
In the first of evening, pondering.

"The deuce!" he cried.

And by him, in the bushes, he espied
A white philosopher.
The white one sighed—

He seemed to seek replies,
From nothingness, to all his sighs.

"My sighs are pulses in a dreamer's death!"
Exclaimed the white one, smothering his lips.

The prince's *frisson* reached his fingers' tips.

## PETER PARASOL

*Aux taureaux Dieu cornes donne*
*Et sabots durs aux chevaux . . . .*

Why are not women fair,
All, as Andromache—
Having, each one, most praisable
Ears, eyes, soul, skin, hair?

Good God! That all beasts should have
The tusks of the elephant,

Or be beautiful
As large, ferocious tigers are.

It is not so with women.
I wish they were all fair,
And walked in fine clothes,
With parasols, in the afternoon air.

❀◈❀◈❀◈❀◈❀◈❀◈❀◈❀◈❀◈❀◈❀◈❀◈❀◈❀◈❀◈❀◈❀◈❀◈❀◈❀◈❀◈❀◈❀◈❀◈❀◈❀◈❀◈❀◈❀◈❀

## EXPOSITION OF THE CONTENTS OF A CAB

Victoria Clementina, negress,
Took seven white dogs
To ride in a cab.

Bells of the dogs chinked.
Harness of the horses shuffled
Like brazen shells.

Oh-hé-hé! Fragrant puppets
By the green lake-pallors,
She too is flesh,

And a breech-cloth might wear,
Netted of topaz and ruby
And savage blooms;

Thridding the squawkiest jungle
In a golden sedan,
White dogs at bay.

What breech-cloth might you wear,
Except linen, embroidered
By elderly women?

## PIANO PRACTICE AT THE ACADEMY
## OF THE HOLY ANGELS

The time will come for these children, seated before their long
    black instruments, to strike the themes of love—
All of them, darkened by time, moved by they know not what,
    amending the airs they play to fulfill themselves;
Seated before these shining forms, like the duskiest glass, re-
    flecting the piebald of roses or what you will.
Blanche, the blonde, whose eyes are not wholly straight, in a
    room of lustres, shed by turquoise falling,
Whose heart will murmur with the music that will be a voice for
    her, speaking the dreaded change of speech;
And Rosa, the muslin dreamer of satin and cowry-kin, disdaining
    the empty keys; and the young infanta,
Jocunda, who will arrange the roses and rearrange, letting the
    leaves lie on the water-like lacquer;
And that confident one, Marie, the wearer of cheap stones, who
    will have grown still and restless;
And Crispine, the blade, reddened by some touch, demanding
    the most from the phrases
Of the well-thumbed, infinite pages of her masters, who will seem
    old to her, requiting less and less her feeling:
In the days when the mood of love will be swarming for solace
    and sink deeply into the thin stuff of being,
And these long, black instruments will be so little to them that
    will be needing so much, seeking so much in their music.

## THE INDIGO GLASS IN THE GRASS

Which is real—
This bottle of indigo glass in the grass,
Or the bench with the pot of geraniums, the stained

mattress and the washed overalls drying in
        the sun?
Which of these truly contains the world?

Neither one, nor the two together.

◇◇◇◇◇◇◇◇◇◇◇◇◇◇◇◇◇◇◇◇◇◇◇◇◇◇◇◇◇◇◇◇◇◇◇◇◇◇◇◇◇◇◇◇◇◇◇◇◇◇◇◇◇◇◇

## ANECDOTE OF THE ABNORMAL

He called hydrangeas purple. And they were.
Not fixed and deadly, (like a curving line
That merely makes a ring).
It was a purple changeable to see.
And so hydrangeas came to be.

The common grass is green.
But there are regions where the grass
Assumes a pale, Italianate sheen—
Is almost Byzantine.
And there the common grass is never seen.

And in those regions one still feels the rose
And feels the grass
Because new colors make new things
And new things make old things again . . .
And so with men.

Crispin-valet, Crispin-saint!
The exhausted realist beholds
His tattered manikin arise,
Tuck in the straw,
And stalk the skies.

## ROMANCE FOR A DEMOISELLE
## LYING IN THE GRASS

It is grass.
It is monotonous.

The monotony
Is like your port which conceals
All your characters
And their desires.

I might make many images of this
And twang nobler notes
Of larger sentiment.

But I invoke the monotony of monotonies
Free from images and change.

Why should I savor love
With tragedy or comedy?

Clasp me,
Delicatest machine.

## LULU GAY

Lulu sang of barbarians before the eunuchs
Of gobs, who called her orchidean,
Sniffed her and slapped heavy hands
Upon her.
She made the eunuchs ululate.
She described for them
The manners of the barbarians

44

What they did with their thumbs.
The eunuchs heard her
With continual ululation.
She described how the barbarians kissed her
With their wide mouths
And breaths as true
As the gum of the gum-tree.
"Olu" the eunuchs cried. "Ululalu."

## LULU MOROSE

Is there a sharp edge?
Is there a sharp edge?
On which to lean
Like a belly puckered by a spear.

The cliffs are rough.
Are rough
And not all birds sing cuck
Sing coo, sing cuck, cuckoo.

Oh! Sal, the butcher's wife ate clams
And died amid uproarious damns.
And mother nature sick of silk
Shot lightning at the kind cow's milk.

And father nature, full of butter
Made the maelstrom oceans mutter.
Stabbing at his teat-like corns
From an ottoman of thorns.

# FROM THE JOURNAL OF CRISPIN

### THE WORLD WITHOUT IMAGINATION

Nota: Man is the intelligence of his soil,
The sovereign ghost. As such, the Socrates
Of snails, musician of pears, principium
And lex. Sed quaeritur: Is this same wig
Of things, this nincompated pedagogue,
The sceptre of the unregenerate sea?
Crispin at sea creates a touch of doubt.
An eye most apt in gelatines and jupes,
Berries of villages, a barber's eye,
This eye of land, of simple salad-beds,
Of honest quilts, the eye of Crispin, hangs
On porpoises, that hung on apricots,
And on silentious porpoises, whose snouts
Dibble in waves that are mustachios,
Inscrutable hair in an inscrutable world.

One eats one paté, even of salt, quotha.
It is not so much that one's mythology
Is blotched by the sea. It was a boresome book,
From which one trilled orations of the west,
Based on the prints of Jupiter. Rostrum.
A snug hibernal from this sea and salt,
This century of wind in a single puff.
What counts is the mythology of self.
That's blotched beyond unblotching. Crispin,
The lutanist of fleas, the knave, the thane,
The ribboned stick, the bellowing breeches, cloak
Of China, cap of Spain, imperative haw
Of hum, inquisitorial botanist,
And general lexicographer of mute
And maidenly greenhorns, now beholds himself,

A skinny sailor peering in sea-glass.
What word split up in clickering syllables
And storming under multitudinous tones
Is name for this short-shanks in all this brunt?
Crispin is washed away by magnitude.
The whole of life that still remains in him
Dwindles to one sound strumming in his ear,
Ubiquitous concussion, slap and sigh,
Polyphony beyond his baton's thrust.

Can Crispin stem verboseness in the sea,
The old age of a watery realist,
Triton, dissolved in shifting diaphanes
Of blue and green? A wordy, watery age
That whispers to the sun's compassion, makes
A convocation, nightly, of the sea-stars,
And on the clopping foot-ways of the moon
Lies grovelling. Triton incomplicate with that
Which made him Triton, nothing left of him,
Except in faint, memorial gesturings,
That are like arms and shoulders in the waves,
Here, something in the rise and fall of wind,
That seems hallucinating horn, and here,
And everywhere upon the deep, in caves,
And down the long sea-eddies, his despair,
That is a voice, both of remembering
And of forgetfulness, in alternate strain.
Just so an ancient Crispin is dissolved.
The valet in the tempest is annulled.
Bordeaux to Yucatan, Havana next,
And then to Carolina. Simple jaunt.
Yet Crispin, mere minuscule in the gales,
Appoints his manner to the turbulence.
The salt hangs on his spirit like a frost,
The dead brine melts within him like a dew
Of winter, until nothing of himself
Remains, except some starker, barer self
In a starker, barer world, in which the sun
Is not the sun because it never shines
With bland complaisance on pale parasols,

Beetles, in chapels, on the chaste bouquets.
Against the shepherds' pipes a trumpet brays
Celestial sneering boisterously. Crispin
Becomes an introspective voyager.

Here is the veritable ding an sich, at last.
Crispin confronting it. A vocable thing,
But with a voice belched out of hoary darks
Noway resembling his. A visible thing,
And excepting negligible Triton, free
From the inescapable shadow of himself,
That lies elsewhere around him. Severance
Is clear. The last distortion of romance
Deserts the insatiable egotist. The sea
Severs not only lands but also selves.
Here is no help before reality.
Crispin beholds and Crispin is made new.
The imagination, here, no more evades,
In poems of plums, the strict austerity
Of one vast, subjugating, final tone.
The drenching of stale lives no more descends.
What is this gaudy, gusty panoply?
Out of what swift destruction does it spring?
It is caparison of wind and cloud
And something given to make whole among
The ruses that are shattered by the large.

II

CONCERNING THE THUNDERSTORMS OF YUCATAN

They say they still scratch sonnets in the south,
The bards of Capricorn. Medicaments
Against the weather. Useful laxatives.
Petrarch is the academy of youth
In Yucatan. The Maya sonneteers
Of the Caribbean amphitheatre,
In spite of hawk and falcon, green toucan,
And jay, still to the bulbul make their plea,

48

As if raspberry tanagers in palms,
High up in orange air, were barbarous.

But Crispin is too destitute to find
In any book the succor that he needs.
He is not padre in a curricle,
Thumbing opuscules, brooding on their musk.
He is a man made vivid by the sea,
A man come out of luminous traversing,
Much trumpeted, made desperately clear,
Fresh from discoveries of tidal skies,
To whom oracular rockings give no rest.
Into a savage color he goes on.

How greatly has he grown in his demesne,
This auditor of insects! He that saw
The stride of vanishing autumn in a park
By way of decorous melancholy; he
That wrote his couplet yearly to the spring,
As dissertation of profound delight,
Stopping, on voyage, in the land of snakes,
Finds his vicissitudes have much enlarged
His apprehension, made him intricate
In moody rucks, and difficult and strange
In all desires, his destitution's mark.
Qua interludo: Crispin, if he could,
Would chant assuaging Virgil and recite
In the oratory of his breast, the rhymes
That drop down Ariosto's benison.
And be in this as other freemen are,
Sonorous nutshells. This he cannot do.
His violence is for aggrandizement
And not for stupor, such as music makes
For sleepers halfway waking. He perceives
That coolness for his heat comes suddenly,
And only, in the fables he would write
With his own quill, in its indigenous dew,
Of an aesthetic tough, diverse, untamed,
Incredible to prudes, the mint of dirt,
Green barbarism turning paradigm.

Crispin foresees a curious promenade
Or, nobler, senses elemental fate,
And elemental potencies and pangs,
And beautiful barenesses, as yet unseen.
These are the snowy fables he would write,
Making the most of savagery of palms,
Of moonlight on the thick, cadaverous bloom
That yuccas breed, and of the panther's tread.
An artful, most affectionate emigrant,
From Cytherea and its learned doves,
Or else nearby, become a loyal scribe.
The fabulous and its intrinsic verse
Come like two spirits parleying, adorned
In radiance from the Atlantic coign,
For Crispin and his quill to catechize.
But they come parleying of such an earth,
So thick with sides and jagged lops of green,
So intertwined with serpent-kin encoiled
Among the purple tufts, the scarlet crowns,
Scenting the jungle in their refuges,
So streaked with yellow, blue and green and red
In beak and bud and fruity gobbet-skins,
That earth is like a jostling festival
Of seeds grown fat, too juicily opulent,
Expanding in the gold's maternal warmth.

So much for that. For one compelled to nose
Through much locution for the savory sense,
Crispin is tireless at the task. He hears
A new reality in parrot-squawks.
But let that pass, since Crispin aims at more,
An umbelliferous fact. Now, as this droll
Discoverer walks round the harbor streets
Inspecting the cabildo, the façade
Of the cathedral, making notes, he hears
A rumbling, west of Mexico, it seems,
Approaching like a gasconade of drums.
The white cabildo darkens, the façade,
As sullen as the sky, is swallowed up
In swift, successive shadows, dolefully.

The rumbling broadens as it falls. The wind
Tempestuous clarion, with heavy cry,
Comes bluntly thundering, more terrible
Than the revenge of music on bassoons.
Gesticulating lightning, mystical,
Makes pallid flitter. Crispin, here, takes flight.
An annotator has his scruples, too.
He kneels in the cathedral with the rest,
This connoisseur of elemental fate,
Aware of exquisite thought. The storm is one
Of many proclamations of the kind,
Proclaiming something harsher than he learned
From hearing signboards whimper in cold nights
Or seeing the midsummer artifice
Of heat upon his pane. This is the span
Of force, the umbelliferous fact, the note
Of Vulcan, that a valet seeks to own,
The thing that sanctions his most eloquent phrase.

And while the torrent on the roof still drones
Crispin arraigns the Mexican sonneteers,
Because his soul feels the Andean breath.
Can fourteen laboring mules, like theirs,
In spite of gorgeous leathers, gurgling bells,
Convey his being through the land? A more condign
Contraption must appear. Crispin is free,
And more than free, elate, intent, profound
And studious of a self possessing him,
That was not in him in the crusty town,
From which he sailed. Beyond him, westward, lie
The mountainous ridges, purple balustrades,
In which the thunder lapsing in its clap,
Lets down gigantic quavers of its voice,
For Crispin to vociferate again.

## III

APPROACHING CAROLINA

The book of moonlight is not written yet,
Nor half begun, but, when it is, leave room
For Crispin, fagot in the lunar fire,
Who, in the hubbub of his pilgrimage
Through sweating changes, never can forget
That wakefulness, or meditating sleep,
In which the sulky strophes willingly
Bear up, in time, the somnolent, deep songs.
Leave room, therefore, in that unwritten book
For the legendary moonlight that once burned
In Crispin's mind above a continent.
America was always north to him,
A northern west or western north, but north,
And thereby polar, polar-purple, chilled
And lank, rising and slumping from a sea
Of hardy foam, receding flatly, spread
In endless ledges, glittering, submerged
And cold in a boreal mistiness of the moon.
The spring came there in clinking pannicles
Of half-dissolving frost, the summer came,
If ever, whisked and wet, not ripening
Before the winter's vacancy returned.
The myrtle, if the myrtle ever bloomed,
Was like a glacial pink upon the air,
The green palmettoes in crepuscular ice
Clipped frigidly blue-black meridians,
Morose chiaroscuro, gauntly drawn.
A feverish conception that derived
From early writs and marginal heraldry.

The poet, seeking the true poem, seeks,
As Crispin seeks, the simplifying fact,
The common truth. Crispin, however, sees
How many poems he denies himself
In his observant progress, lesser things
Than the relentless contact he desires,

How many sea-masks he ignores, what sounds
He closes from his tempering ear, what thoughts,
Like jades affecting the sequestered bride,
He banishes, what descants he foregoes.
Perhaps the Arctic moonlight really gave
The liaison, the blissful liaison,
Between himself and his environment,
Which was, and is, chief motive, first delight,
For him, and not for him alone. It seemed
Illusive, faint, more mist than moon, perverse,
Wrong as a divagation to Pekin,
One more frustration, beautiful, perhaps,
To beauty's exorcist, who postulates
The vulgar as his theme, his hymn and flight,
A passionately niggling nightingale.
Moonlight is an evasion, or, if not,
A minor meeting, facile, delicate,
Chanson evoking vague, inaudible words.
Crispin is avid for the strenuous strokes
That clang from a directer touch, the clear
Vibration rising from a daylight bell,
Minutely traceable to the latest reach.
Imagination soon exhausts itself
In artifice too tenuous to sustain
The vaporous moth upon its fickle wings.
Crispin conceives his Odyssey to be
An up and down in these two elements,
A fluctuating between sun and moon,
A sally into gold and scarlet forms,
As on this voyage, out of goblinry,
And then retirement like a sinking down
To sleep, among its violet feints and rest
And turning back to the indulgences
That in the moonlight have their habitude.
But let these backward lapses, if they will,
Grind their seductions on him, Crispin knows
It is a flourishing tropic he requires
For his refreshment, an abundant zone,
Prickly and obdurate, dense, harmonious
Yet with a harmony not rarefied

Nor fined for the inhibited instruments
Of over-civil stops. And thus he tossed
Between a Carolina of old time,
A little juvenile, an ancient whim,
And the visible, circumspect presentment drawn
From what he saw across his vessel's prow.

He comes. The poetic hero without palms
Or jugglery, without regalia.
And as he comes he sees that it is spring,
A time abhorrent to the nihilist
Or searcher for the fecund minimum.
The moonlight fiction vanishes and spring,
Although contending featly in its veils,
Irised in dew and early fragrancies
Is gemmy marionette to him that seeks
A sinewy nakedness. A river bears
The vessel inward. Crispin tilts his nose
To inhale the rancid rosin, burly smells
Of dampened lumber, emanations blown
From warehouse doors, the gustiness of ropes,
Decays of sacks, and all the arrant stinks
That help him round his rude aesthetic out.
He savors rankness like a sensualist.
He notes the marshy ground around the dock,
The crawling railroad spur, the rotten fence
That makes enclosure, a periphery
Of bales, machines and tools and tanks and men,
Directing whistles, puffing engines, cranes,
Provocative paraphernalia to his mind.
A short way off the city starts to climb,
At first in alleys which the lilacs line,
Abruptly, then, to the cobbled merchant streets,
The shops of chandlers, tailors, bakers, cooks,
The Coca Cola-bars, the barber-poles,
The Strand and Harold Lloyd, the lawyers' row,
The Citizens' Bank, two tea rooms, and a church.
Crispin is happy in this metropole.
If the lilacs give the alleys a young air
Of sentiment, the alleys in exchange

54

Make gifts of no less worthy ironies.
If poems are transmutations of plain shops,
By aid of starlight, distance, wind, war, death,
Are not these doldrums poems in themselves,
These trophies of wind and war? At just what point
Do barber-poles become burlesque or cease
To be? Are bakers what the poets will,
Supernal artisans or muffin men,
Or do they have, on poets' minds, more influence
Than poets know? Are they one moment flour,
Another pearl? The Citizens' Bank becomes
Palladian and then the Citizens' Bank
Again. The flimsiest tea room fluctuates
Through crystal changes. Even Harold Lloyd
Proposes antic Harlequin. The bars infect
The sensitive. Crispin revitalized
Makes these researches faithfully, a wide
Curriculum for the marvelous sophomore.
They purify. They make him see how much
Of what he sees he never sees at all.
He grips more closely the essential prose
As being, in a world so falsified,
The one integrity for him, the one
Discovery still possible to make,
To which all poems are incident, unless
That prose should wear a poem's guise at last.


IV


THE IDEA OF A COLONY


Nota: His soil is man's intelligence.
That's better. That's worth crossing seas to find.
Crispin in one laconic phrase lays bare
His cloudy drift and plans a colony.
Exit the mental moonlight, exit lex,
Rex and principium, exit the whole
Shebang. Exeunt omnes. Here is prose
More exquisite than any tumbling verse,

A still new continent in which to dwell.
What was the purpose of his pilgrimage,
Whatever shape it took in Crispin's mind,
If not, when all is said, to drive away
The shadow of his fellows from the skies,
And, from their stale intelligence released,
To make a new intelligence prevail.
Hence his despite of Mexican sonneteers,
Evoking lauras in the thunderstorms.
Hence the reverberations in the words
Of his first central hymns. Hence his intent
Analysis of barber-poles and shops,
Invaluable trivia, tests of the strength,
Of his aesthetic, his philosophy,
The more invidious, the more desired.
The florist asking aid from cabbages,
The rich man going bare, the paladin
Afraid, the blind man as astronomer,
The appointed power unwielded from disdain.

His western voyage ends and it begins.
The torment of fastidious thought abates,
Another, still more bellicose, comes on.
Crispin delineates his progeny:
A race of natives in a primitive land,
But primitive because it is more true
To its begetting than its patriarch,
A race obedient to its origins
And from the obstinate scrutiny of its land,
And in its land's own wit and mood and mask,
Evolving the conjectural resonance
Of voice, the flying youthfulness of form,
Of a spirit to be singer of the song
That Crispin formulates but cannot sing.
It comes to that. This late discoverer
Discovers for himself what idler men
And less ambitious sires have dawdled with.
He, therefore, writes his prolegomena
And, being full of the caprice, inscribes
Commingled souvenirs and prophecies.

56

He makes a singular collation. Thus:
The natives of the rain are rainy men.
Although they paint effulgent, azure lakes,
And April hillsides wooded white and pink,
Their azure has a cloudy edge, their white
And pink, the water bright that dogwood bears.
And in their music showering sounds intone.
This is as certain as their cherry-ripe
Pips in the fruit-men in the month of May.
Virgins on Volcan del Fuego wear
That Volcan in their bosoms as they wear
Its nibs upon their fingers. They adorn
Their weavings with its iridescent threads.
They shut its fury in each bangle-blaze.
On what strange froth does the gross Indian dote
What Eden sapling gum, what honeyed gore,
What pulpy dram distilled of innocence,
That streaking gold should speak in him
Or bask within his images and words?
If these rude instances impeach themselves
By force of rudeness, let the burgher say
If he is burgher by his will. Burgher,
He is, by will, but not his own. He dwells
A part of wilful dwellings that impose
Alike his morning and his evening prayer.
His town exhales its mother breath for him
And this he breathes, a candid bellows-boy,
According to canon. Let the principle
Be plain. For application Crispin strives,
Abhorring Turk as Esquimau, the lute
As the marimba, the magnolia as rose.

Upon these premises Crispin propounds
And propagates. His colony extends
From the big-rimmed snow-star over Canada,
To the dusk of a whistling south below the south,
A comprehensive island hemisphere.
And here he plants his colonists. The man
In Mississippi, waking among pines,
Shall be pine-spokesman. The responsive man,

Planting his pristine cores in Florida,
Shall prick thereof, not on the psaltery,
But on the banjo's categorical gut,
Tuck tuck, while the flamingos flap his bays.
Sepulchral señors, bibbing pale mescal,
Oblivious to the Aztec almanacs,
Shall make the intricate Sierra scan
In polysyllabled vernacular.
The dark Brazilian in his red café,
Musing immaculate, pampean dits,
Shall scrawl a vigilant anthology,
Not based on Camoëns, but flushed and full,
For surfeit in his leaner, lusting years,
For something to make answer when he calls
And be to him his lucent paramour.
These are the broadest instances. Crispin,
Progenitor of such extensive scope,
Is not indifferent to smart detail.
The melon shall have apposite ritual,
Performed in verd apparel, and the peach,
When its black branches germinate, belle day,
Shall have an incantation, and again,
When piled on salvers its aroma steeps
The summer, it shall have a sacrament
And celebration. Shrewd novitiates
Shall be the clerks of our experience.

These bland excursions into time to come,
Related in romance to backward flights,
However prodigal, however proud,
Contain in their afflatus the reproach
That first drove Crispin to his wandering.
He could not be content with counterfeit,
With masquerade of thought, with hapless words
That must belie the racking masquerade,
With fictive flourishes that preordained
His passions' permit, hang of coat, degree
Of buttons, measure of his salt. Such trash
Might help the blind, not him, serenely sly.
It irked beyond his patience. Hence it was,

Preferring text to gloss, he humbly served
Grotesque apprenticeship to chance event,
A clown, perhaps, but an aspiring clown.
There is a monotonous babbling in our dreams
That makes them our dependent heirs, the heirs
Of dreamers buried in our sleep, and not
The oncoming fantasies of better birth.
The apprentice knows these dreamers. If he dreams
Their dreams, he does it in a gingerly way.
All dreams are vexing. Let them be expunged.
But let the rabbit run, the cock declaim.
His colony may not arrive. The site
Exists. So much is sure. And what is sure
In our abundance is his seignory.
His journal, at the best, concerns himself,
Nudging and noting, wary to divulge
Without digression, so that when he comes
To search himself, in the familiar glass
To which the lordliest traveler returns,
Crispin may take the tableau cheerfully.
Trinket pasticcio, flaunting skyey sheets,
With Crispin as the tiptoe cozener?
No, no: veracious page on page, exact.
As Crispin in his attic shapes the book
That will contain him, he requires this end:
The book shall discourse of himself alone,
Of what he was, and why, and of his place,
And of its fitful pomp and parentage.
Thereafter he may stalk in other spheres.

# THIS VAST INELEGANCE

This vast inelegance may seem the blankest desolation,
Beginning of a green Cockaigne to be, disliked, abandoned,

In which the bliss of clouds is mark of an intended meeting
Between the matin air and color, goldenest generating,

Soother and lustier than this vexed, autumnal exhalation,
So sullen with sighing and surrender to marauding ennui.

Which choir makes the most faultless medley in its celebration?
The choir that choirs the first fatigue in deep bell of canzoni?

Or this, whose music, sweeping irradiation of a sea-night,
Piercing the tide by which it moves, is constantly within us?

Or this, whose jingling glorias, importunate of perfection,
Are the fulfilling rhapsodies that hymn it to creation?

Is any choir the whole voice of this fretful habitation,
This parlor of farcical dames, this clowns' colonnade, this kites'
    pavilion?

See, now, the ways beleaguered by black, dropsical duennas,
Young weasels racing steep horizons in pursuit of planets . . .

# SATURDAY NIGHT AT THE CHIROPODIST'S

*Histoire*

For simple pleasure, he beheld,
The rotting man for pleasure saw,
The new spring tumble in the sky.

The wry of neck and the wry of heart
Stood by him when the tumbler fell,
And the mighty, musty belly of tears.

Did they behold themselves in this
And see themselves as once they were,
O spirit of bones, O mountain of graves?

Take counsel, all hierophants
And sentimental roisterers,
They did not so. But in their throats

They pied and chuckled like a flock,
They were so glad to see the spring.
The rotting man was first to sing.

## MANDOLIN AND LIQUEURS

La-la! The cat is in the violets
And the awnings are let down.
The cat should not be where she is
And the awnings are too brown,
Emphatically so.

If awnings were celeste and gay,
Iris and orange, crimson and green,
Blue and vermilion, purple and white,
And not this tinsmith's galaxy,
Things would be different.

The sun is gold, the moon is silver.
There must be a planet that is copper
And in whose light the roses
Would have a most singular appearance,
Or nearly so.

I love to sit and read the *Telegraph,*
That vast confect of telegrams,
And to find how much that really matters
Does not really matter
At all.

◇◇◇◇◇◇◇◇◇◇◇◇◇◇◇◇◇◇◇◇◇◇◇◇◇◇◇◇◇◇◇◇◇◇◇◇◇◇◇◇◇◇◇◇◇◇◇◇◇◇◇◇◇◇

## THE SHAPE OF THE CORONER

It was the morn
And the palms were waved
And the brass was played.
Then the coroner came
In his limpid shoes.

The palms were waved
For the beau of illusions.
The termagant fans
Of his orange days
Fell, famous and flat,
And folded him round,

Folded and fell
And the brass grew cold
And the coroner's hand
Dismissed the band.

It was the coroner
Poured this elixir
Into the ground,
And a shabby man,
An eye too sleek,
And a biscuit cheek.

And the coroner bent
Over the palms.
The elysium lay
In a parlor of day.

# RED LOVES KIT

### I

Your yes her no, your no her yes. The words
Make little difference, for being wrong
And wronging her, if only as she thinks,
You never can be right. You are the man.
You brought the incredible calm in ecstasy.
Which, like a virgin visionary spent
In this spent world, she must possess. The gift
Came not from you. Shall the world be spent again,
Wasted in what would be an ultimate waste,
A deprivation muffled in eclipse,
The final theft? That you are innocent
And love her still, still leaves you in the wrong.
Where is that calm and where that ecstasy?
Her words accuse you of adulteries
That sack the sun, though metaphysical.

### II

A beautiful thing, milord, is beautiful
Not only in itself but in the things
Around it. Thus it has a large expanse,
As the moon has in its moonlight, worlds away,
As the sea has in its coastal clamorings.
So she, when in her mystic aureole
She walks, triumphing humbly, should express
Her beauty in your love. She should reflect
Her glory in your passion and be proud.
Her music should repeat itself in you,
Impelled by a compulsive harmony.
Milord, I ask you, though you will to sing,
Does she will to be proud? True, you may love
And she have beauty of a kind, but such
Unhappy love reveals vast blemishes.

63

Rest, crows, upon the edges of the moon,
Cover the golden altar deepest black,
Fly upward thick in numbers, fly across
The blueness of the half-night, fill the air
And darken it, make an unbroken mat
Out of the whirl and denseness of your wings,
Spread over heaven shutting out the light.
Then turn your heads and let your spiral eyes
Look backward. Let your swiftly-flying flocks
Look suddenly downward with their shining eyes
And move the night by their intelligent motes.
Make a sidereal splendor as you fly.
And you, good galliard, to enchant black thoughts
Beseech them for an overwhelming gloom.
It will be fecund in rapt curios.

## METROPOLITAN MELANCHOLY

A purple woman with a lavender tongue
Said hic, said hac,
Said ha.

To dab things even nicely pink
Adds very little,
So I think.
Oh ha, Oh ha.

The silks they wear in all the cities
Are really much a million pities.

## ANNUAL GAIETY

In the morning in the blue snow
The catholic sun, its majesty,
Pinks and pinks the ice-hard melanchole.

Wherefore those prayers to the moon?
Or is it that alligators lie
Along the edges of your eye
Basking in desert Florida?

Père Guzz, in heaven, thumb your lyre
And chant the January fire
And joy of snow and snow.

## GOOD MAN, BAD WOMAN

You say that spite avails her nothing, that
You rest intact in conscience and intact
In self, a man of longer time than days,
Of larger company than one. Therefore,
Pure scientist, you look with nice aplomb
At this indifferent experience,
Deploring sentiment. When May came last,
And equally as scientist you walked
Among the orchards in the apple-blocks
And saw the blossoms, snow-bred pink and white,
Making your heart of brass to intercept
The childish onslaughts of such innocence,
Why was it that you cast the brass away
And bared yourself, and bared yourself in vain?
She can corrode your world, if never you.

# THE WOMAN WHO BLAMED LIFE
## ON A SPANIARD

### I

You do not understand her evil mood.
You think that like the moon she is obscured
But clears and clears until an open night
Reveals her, rounded in beneficence,
Pellucid love; and for that image, like
Some merciful divination, you forgive.
And you forgive dark broachings growing great
Night after night because the hemisphere
And still the final quarter, still the rim,
And still the impassioned place of it remain.
If she is like the moon, she never clears
But spreads an evil lustre whose increase
Is evil, crisply bright, disclosing you
Stooped in a night of vast inquietude.
Observe her shining in the deadly trees.

### II

That tragic prattle of the fates, astute
To bring destruction, often seems high-pitched.
The babble of generations magnifies
A mot into a dictum, communal,
Of inescapable force, itself a fate.
How, then, if nothing more than vanity
Is at the bottom of her as pique-pain
And picador? Be briny-blooded bull.
Flutter her lance with your tempestuous dust,
Make melic groans and tooter at her strokes,
Rage in the ring and shake the corridors.
Perhaps at so much mastery, the bliss
She needs will come consolingly. Alas,

66

It is a most spectacular role, and yet
Less than contending with fictitious doom.

The choice twixt dove and goose is over-close.
The fowl of Venus may consist of both
And more. It may have feathery color-frets,
A paragon of lustre; may have voice
Like the mother of all nightingales; be wise
As a seraglio-parrot; feel disdain
In concert with the eagle's valiance.
Let this be as it may. It must have tears
And memory and claws: a paragon
Well-wetted; a decoying voice that sings
Arpeggi of celestial souvenirs,
A skillful apprehension and eye proud
In venting lacerations. So composed,
This hallowed visitant, chimerical,
Sinks into likeness blessedly beknown.

## SECRET MAN

The sounds of rain on the roof
Are like the sound of doves.
It is long since there have been doves
On any house of mine.

It is better for me
In the rushes of autumn wind
To embrace autumn, without turning
To remember summer.

Besides, the world is a tower.
Its winds are blue.

The rain falls at its base,
Summers sink from it.

The doves will fly round.
When morning comes
The high clouds will move,
Nobly as autumn moves.

The man of autumn,
Behind its melancholy mask,
Will laugh in the brown grass,
Will shout from the tower's rim.

✿◆✿◆✿◆✿◆✿◆✿◆✿◆✿◆✿◆✿◆✿◆✿◆✿◆✿◆✿◆✿◆✿◆✿◆✿◆✿◆✿◆✿◆✿◆✿◆✿◆✿◆✿◆✿◆

## WHAT THEY CALL RED CHERRY PIE

Meyer is a bum. He eats his pie.
He eats red cherry pie and never says—
He makes no choice of words—

Cherries are ri . . . He would never say that.
He could not. Neither of us could ever say that.
But Meyer is a bum.

He says "That's what I call red cherry pie."
And that's his way. And that's my way as well.
We two share that at least.

What is it that we share? Red cherry pie
When cherries are in season, or, at least
The way we speak of it.

Meyer has my five senses. I have his.
This matters most in things that matter least.
And that's red cherry pie.

## HIEROGLYPHICA

People that live in the biggest houses
Often have the worst breaths.
Hey-di-ho.

Even if I had nothing else to do
I could look at flowers.
Hey-di-ho.

The humming-bird is the national bird
Of the humming-bird.
Hey-di-ho.

X understands Aristotle
Instinctively, not otherwise.
Hey-di-ho.

Let wise men piece the world together with wisdom
Or poets with holy magic.
Hey-di-ho.

## THE DRUM-MAJORS IN THE
## LABOR DAY PARADE

If each of them wasn't a prig
And didn't care a fig,
They would show it.

They would throw their batons far up
To return in a glittering wheel
And make the Dagoes squeal.

But they are empty as balloons
The trombones are like baboons,
The parade's no good.

Are they really mechanical bears,
Toys of the millionaires,
Morbid and bleak?

They ought to be muscular men,
Naked and stamping the earth,
Whipping the air.

The banners should brighten the sun.
The women should sing as they march.
Let's go home.

---

## POLO PONIES PRACTICING

The constant cry against an old order,
An order constantly old,
Is itself old and stale.

Here is the world of a moment,
Fitted by men and horses
For hymns,

In a freshness of poetry by the sea,
In galloping hedges,
In thudding air:

Beyond any order,
Beyond any rebellion,
A brilliant air

On the flanks of horses,
On the clear grass,
On the shapes of the mind.

## LYTTON STRACHEY, ALSO,
## ENTERS INTO HEAVEN

I care for neither fugues nor feathers.
What interests me most is the people
Who have always interested me most,
To see them without their passions
And to understand them.

Perhaps, without their passions, they will be
Men of memories explaining what they meant.
One man opposing a society
If properly misunderstood becomes a myth.
I fear the understanding.

Death ought to spare their passions.
Memory without passion would be better lost.
But memory and passion, and with these
The understanding of heaven, would be bliss,
If anything would be bliss.

How strange a thing it was to understand
And how strange it ought to be again, this time
Without the distortions of the theatre,
Without the revolutions' ruin,
In the presence of the barefoot ghosts!

Perception as an act of intelligence
And perception as an act of grace
Are two quite different things, in particular
When applied to the mythical.
As for myself, I feel a doubt:

I am uncertain whether the perception
Applied on earth to those that were myths
In every various sense, ought not to be preferred
To an untried perception applied
In heaven. But I have no choice.

71

In this apologetic air, one well
Might muff the mighty spirit of Lenin.
That sort of thing was always rather stiff.
Let's hope for Mademoiselle de Lespinasse,
Instead, or Horace Walpole or Mrs. Thrale.

He is nothing, I know, to me nor I to him.
I had looked forward to understanding. Yet
An understanding may be troublesome.
I'd rather not. No doubt there's a quarter here,
Dixhuitième and Georgian and serene.

◇◇◇◇◇◇◇◇◇◇◇◇◇◇◇◇◇◇◇◇◇◇◇◇◇◇◇◇◇◇◇◇◇◇◇◇◇◇◇◇◇◇◇◇◇◇◇◇◇◇◇

## AGENDA

Whipped creams and the Blue Danube,
The lin-lan-lone of Babson,
And yet the damned thing doesn't come right.

Boston should be in the keys
Painting the saints among palms.
Charleston should be New York.

And what a good thing it would be
If Shasta roared up in Nassau,
Cooling the sugary air.

Perhaps if the orchestras stood on their heads
And dancers danced ballets on top of their beds—
We haven't tried that.

Those early centuries were full
Of very haphazard people and things,
The whole of them turning black;

Yet in trees round the College of Heralds,
No doubt, the well-tuned birds are singing,
Slowly and sweetly.

## TABLE TALK

Granted, we die for good.
Life, then, is largely a thing
Of happens to like, not should.

And that, too, granted, why
Do I happen to like red bush,
Gray grass and green-gray sky?

What else remains? But red,
Gray, green, why those of all?
That is not what I said:

Not those of all. But those.
One likes what one happens to like.
One likes the way red grows.

It cannot matter at all.
Happens to like is one
Of the ways things happen to fall.

## A ROOM ON A GARDEN

O stagnant east-wind, palsied mare,
Giddap! The ruby roses' hair
Must blow.

Behold how order is the end
Of everything. The roses bend
As one.

Order, the law of hoes and rakes,
May be perceived in windy quakes
And squalls.

The gardener searches earth and sky
The truth in nature to espy
In vain.

He well might find that eager balm
In lilies' stately-statued calm;
But then

He well might find it in this fret
Of lilies rusted, rotting, wet
With rain.

# OWL'S CLOVER

◈◈◈◈◈◈

## THE OLD WOMAN AND THE STATUE

### I

Another evening in another park,
A group of marble horses rose on wings
In the midst of a circle of trees, from which the leaves
Raced with the horses in bright hurricanes.

### II

So much the sculptor had foreseen: autumn,
The sky above the plaza widening
Before the horses, clouds of bronze imposed
On clouds of gold, and green engulfing bronze,
The marble leaping in the storms of light.
So much he had devised: white forelegs taut
To the muscles' very tip for the vivid plunge,
The heads held high and gathered in a ring
At the center of the mass, the haunches low,
Contorted, staggering from the thrust against
The earth as the bodies rose on feathery wings,
Clumped carvings, circular, like blunted fans,
Arranged for phantasy to form an edge
Of crisping light along the statue's rim.
More than his muddy hand was in the manes,
More than his mind in the wings. The rotten leaves
Swirled round them in immense autumnal sounds.

75

## III

But her he had not foreseen: the bitter mind
In a flapping cloak. She walked along the paths
Of the park with chalky brow scratched over black
And black by thought that could not understand
Or, if it understood, repressed itself
Without any pity in a somnolent dream.
The golden clouds that turned to bronze, the sounds
Descending, did not touch her eye and left
Her ear unmoved. She was that tortured one,
So destitute that nothing but herself
Remained and nothing of herself except
A fear too naked for her shadow's shape.
To search for clearness all an afternoon
And without knowing, and then upon the wind
To hear the stroke of one's certain solitude,
What sound could comfort away the sudden sense?
What path could lead apart from what she was
And was to be? Could it happen to be this,
This atmosphere in which the horses rose,
This atmosphere in which her musty mind
Lay black and full of black misshapen? Wings
And light lay deeper for her than her sight.

## IV

The mass of stone collapsed to marble hulk,
Stood stiffly, as if the black of what she thought
Conflicting with the moving colors there
Changed them, at last, to its triumphant hue,
Triumphant as that always upward wind
Blowing among the trees its meaningless sound.
The space above the trees might still be bright
Yet the light fell falsely on the marble skulls,
Manes matted of marble across the air, the light
Fell falsely on the matchless skeletons,

A change so felt, a fear in her so known,
Now felt, now known as this. The clouds of bronze
Slowly submerging in flatness disappeared.
If the sky that followed, smaller than the night,
Still eked out luminous wrinklings on the leaves,
Whitened, again, forms formless in the dark,
It was as if transparence touched her mind.
The statue stood in stars like water-spheres,
Washed over by their green, their flowing blue.
A mood that had become so fixed it was
A manner of the mind, a mind in a night
That was whatever the mind might make of it,
A night that was that mind so magnified
It lost the common shape of night and came
To be the sovereign shape in a world of shapes.
A woman walking in the autumn leaves,
Thinking of heaven and earth and of herself
And looking at the place in which she walked,
As a place in which each thing was motionless
Except the thing she felt but did not know.


v


Without her, evening like a budding yew
Would soon be brilliant, as it was, before
The harridan self and ever-maladive fate
Went crying their desolate syllables, before
Their voice and the voice of the tortured wind were one,
Each voice within the other, seeming one,
Crying against a need that pressed like cold,
Deadly and deep. It would become a yew
Grown great and grave beyond imagined trees,
Branching through heavens heavy with the sheen
And shadowy hanging of it, thick with stars
Of a lunar light, dark-belted sorcerers
Dazzling by simplest beams and soothly still,
The space beneath it still, a smooth domain,

Untroubled by suffering, which fate assigns
To the moment. There the horses would rise again,
Yet hardly to be seen and again the legs
Would flash in air, and the muscular bodies thrust
Hoofs grinding against the stubborn earth, until
The light wings lifted through the crystal space
Of night. How clearly that would be defined!

# MR. BURNSHAW AND THE STATUE

I

The thing is dead . . . Everything is dead
Except the future. Always everything
That is is dead except what ought to be.
All things destroy themselves or are destroyed.

These are not even Russian animals.
They are horses as they were in the sculptor's mind.
They might be sugar or paste or citron-skin
Made by a cook that never rode the back
Of his angel through the skies. They might be mud
Left here by moonlit muckers when they fled
At the burst of day, crepuscular images
Made to remember a life they never lived
In the witching wilderness, night's witchingness,
Made to affect a dream they never had,
Like a word in the mind that sticks at artichoke
And remains inarticulate, horses with cream.
The statue seems a thing from Schwarz's, a thing
Of the dank imagination, much below

Our crusted outlines hot and huge with fact,
Ugly as an idea, not beautiful
As sequels without thought. In the rudest red
Of autumn, these horses should go clattering
Along the thin horizons, nobly more
Than this jotting-down of the sculptor's foppishness
Long after the worms and the curious carvings of
Their snouts.

II

Come, all celestial paramours,
Whether in-dwelling haughty clouds, frigid
And crisply musical, or holy caverns temple-toned,
Entwine your arms and moving to and fro,
Now like a ballet infantine in awkward steps,
Chant sibilant requiems for this effigy.
Bring down from nowhere nothing's wax-like blooms,
Calling them what you will but loosely-named
In a mortal lullaby, like porcelain.
Then, while the music makes you, make, yourselves,
Long autumn sheens and pittering sounds like sounds
On pattering leaves and suddenly with lights,
Astral and Shelleyan, diffuse new day;
And on this ring of marble horses shed
The rainbow in its glistening serpentines
Made by the sun ascending seventy seas.
Agree: the apple in the orchard, round
And red, will not be redder, rounder then
Than now. No: nor the ploughman in his bed
Be free to sleep there sounder, for the plough
And the dew and the ploughman still will best be one.
But this gawky plaster will not be here.

79

The stones
That will replace it shall be carved, *"The Mass
Appoints These Marbles Of Itself To Be
Itself."* No more than that, no subterfuge,
No memorable muffing, bare and blunt.

IV

Mesdames, one might believe that Shelley lies
Less in the stars than in their earthy wake,
Since the radiant disclosures that you make
Are of an eternal vista, manqué and gold
And brown, an Italy of the mind, a place
Of fear before the disorder of the strange,
A time in which the poets' politics
Will rule in a poets' world. Yet that will be
A world impossible for poets, who
Complain and prophesy, in their complaints,
And are never of the world in which they live.
Disclose the rude and ruddy at their jobs
And if you weep for peacocks that are gone
Or dance the death of doves, most sallowly,
Who knows? The ploughman may not live alone
With his plough, the peacock may abandon pride,
The dove's adagio may lose its depth
And change. If ploughmen, peacocks, doves alike
In vast disorder live in the ruins, free,
The charts destroyed, even disorder may,
So seen, have an order of its own, a peace
Not now to be perceived yet order's own.

V

A solemn voice, not Mr. Burnshaw's says:
At some gigantic, solitary urn,

A trash can at the end of the world, the dead
Give up dead things and the living turn away.
There buzzards pile their sticks among the bones
Of buzzards and eat the bellies of the rich,
Fat with a thousand butters, and the crows
Sip the wild honey of the poor man's life,
The blood of his bitter brain; and there the sun
Shines without fire on columns intercrossed,
White slapped on white, majestic, marble heads,
Severed and tumbled into seedless grass,
Motionless, knowing neither dew nor frost.
There lies the head of the sculptor in which the thought
Of lizards, in its eye, is more acute
Than the thought that once was native to the skull;
And there are the white-maned horses' heads, beyond
The help of any wind or any sky:
Parts of the immense detritus of a world
That is completely waste, that moves from waste
To waste, out of the hopeless waste of the past
Into a hopeful waste to come. There even
The colorless light in which this wreckage lies
Has faint, portentous lustres, shades and shapes
Of rose, or what will once more rise to rose,
When younger bodies, because they are younger, rise
And chant the rose-points of their birth, and when
For a little time, again, rose-breasted birds
Sing rose-beliefs. Above that urn two lights
Commingle, not like the commingling of sun and moon
At dawn, nor of summer-light and winter-light
In an autumn afternoon, but two immense
Reflections, whirling apart and wide away.


VI


Mesdames, it is not enough to be reconciled
Before the strange, having wept and having thought
And having said farewell. It is not enough
That the vista retain ploughmen, peacocks, doves,

However tarnished, companions out of the past,
And that, heavily, you move with them in the dust.
It is not enough that you are indifferent,
Because time moves on columns intercrossed
And because the temple is never quite composed,
Silent and turquoised and perpetual,
Visible over the sea. It is only enough
To live incessantly in change. See how
On a day still full of summer, when the leaves
Appear to sleep within a sleeping air,
They suddenly fall and the leafless sound of the wind
Is no longer a sound of summer. So great a change
Is constant. The time you call serene descends
Through a moving chaos that never ends. Mesdames,
Leaves are not always falling and the birds
Of chaos are not always sad nor lost
In melancholy distances. You held
Each other moving in a chant and danced
Beside the statue, while you sang. Your eyes
Were solemn and your gowns were blown and grief
Was under every temple-tone. You sang
A tragic lullaby, like porcelain.
But change composes, too, and chaos comes
To momentary calm, spectacular flocks
Of crimson and hoods of Venezuelan green
And the sound of z in the grass all day, though these
Are chaos and of archaic change. Shall you,
Then, fear a drastic community evolved
From the whirling, slowly and by trial; or fear
Men gathering for a mighty flight of men,
An abysmal migration into a possible blue?

VII

Dance, now, and with sharp voices cry, but cry
Like damsels daubed and let your feet be bare
To touch the grass and, as you circle, turn
Your backs upon the vivid statue. Then,
Weaving ring in radiant ring and quickly, fling

Yourselves away and at a distance join
Your hands held high and cry again, but cry,
This time, like damsels captured by the sky,
Seized by that possible blue. Be maidens formed
Of the most evasive hue of a lesser blue,
Of the least appreciable shade of green
And despicable shades of red, just seen,
And vaguely to be seen, a matinal red,
A dewy flashing blanks away from fire,
As if your gowns were woven of the light
Yet were not bright, came shining as things come
That enter day from night, came mirror-dark,
With each fold sweeping in a sweeping play.
Let your golden hands wave fastly and be gay
And your braids bear brightening of crimson bands.
Conceive that while you dance the statue falls,
The heads are severed, topple, tumble, tip
In the soil and rest. Conceive that marble men
Serenely selves, transfigured by the selves
From which they came, make real the attitudes
Appointed for them and that the pediment
Bears words that are the speech of marble men.
In the glassy sound of your voices, the porcelain cries,
The alto clank of the long recitation, in these
Speak, and in these repeat: *To Be Itself*,
Until the sharply-colored glass transforms
Itself into the speech of the spirit, until
The porcelain bell-borrowings become
Implicit clarities in the way you cry
And are your feelings changed to sound, without
A change, until the waterish ditherings turn
To the tense, the maudlin, true meridian
That is yourselves, when, at last, you are yourselves,
Speaking and strutting broadly, fair and bloomed,
No longer of air but of the breathing earth,
Impassioned seducers and seduced, the pale
Pitched into swelling bodies, upward, drift
In a storm blown into glittering shapes, and flames
Wind-beaten into freshest, brightest fire.

83

# THE GREENEST CONTINENT

### I

Large-leaved and many-footed shadowing,
What god rules over Africa, what shape,
What avuncular cloud-man beamier than spears?

### II

The heaven of Europe is empty, like a Schloss
Abandoned because of taxes . . . It was enough:
It made up for everything, it was all selves
Become rude robes among white candle lights,
Motions of air, robes moving in torrents of air,
And through the torrents a jutting, jagged tower,
A broken wall—and it ceased to exist, became
A Schloss, an empty Schlossbibliothek, the books
For sale in Vienna and Zurich to people in Maine,
Ontario, Canton. It was the way
Things jutted up, the way the jagged stacks,
The foul immovables, came through the clouds,
Colossal blacks that leaped across the points
Of Boucher pink, the sheens of Venetian gray.
That's what did it. Everything did it at last.
The binders did it with armorial books.
And the cooks, the cooks, the bar-men and the maids,
The churches and their long parades, Seville
At Easter on a London screen, the seeds
Of Vilmorin, Verhaeren in his grave,
The flute on the gramophone, the Daimlers that
Dissolved the woods, war and the fatal farce

84

Of war, the rust on the steeples, these jutted up,
These streaked the mother-of-pearl, the lunar cress.
Everything did.

III

          There was a heaven once,
But not that Salzburg of the skies. It was
The spirit's episcopate, hallowed and high,
To which the spirit ascended, to increase
Itself, beyond the utmost increase come
From youngest day or oldest night and far
Beyond thought's regulation. There each man,
Through long cloud-cloister-porches, walked alone,
Noble within perfecting solitude,
Like a solitude of the sun, in which the mind
Acquired transparence and beheld itself
And beheld the source from which transparence came;
And there he heard the voices that were once
The confusion of men's voices, intricate
Made extricate by meanings, meanings made
Into a music never touched to sound.
There, too, he saw, since he must see, the domes
Of azure round an upper dome, brightest
Because it rose above them all, stippled
By waverings of stars, the joy of day
And its immaculate fire, the middle dome,
The temple of the altar where each man
Beheld the truth and knew it to be true.

IV

That was never the heaven of Africa, which had
No heaven, had death without a heaven, death
In a heaven of death. Beneath the heavy foils,

Beneath the spangling greens, fear might placate
And the serpent might become a god, quick-eyed,
Rising from indolent coils. If the statue rose,
If once the statue were to rise, if it stood,
Thinly, among the elephantine palms,
Sleekly the serpent would draw himself across.
The horses are a part of a northern sky
Too starkly pallid for the jaguar's light,
In which he and the lion and the serpent hide
Even in sleep, deep in the grass of sleep,
Deep grass that totters under the weight of light.
There sleep and waking fill with jaguar-men
And lion-men and the flicking serpent-kin
In flowery nations, crashing and alert.
No god rules over Africa, no throne,
Single, of burly ivory, inched of gold,
Disposed upon the central of what we see,
That purges the wrack or makes the jungle shine,
As brilliant as mystic, as mystic as single, all
In one, except a throne raised up beyond
Men's bones, beyond their breaths, the black sublime,
Toward which, in the nights, the glittering serpents climb,
Dark-skinned and sinuous, winding upwardly,
Winding and waving, slowly, waving in air,
Darting envenomed eyes about, like fangs,
Hissing, across the silence, puissant sounds.
Death, only, sits upon the serpent throne:
Death, the herdsman of elephants,
To whom the jaguars cry and lions roar
Their petty dirges of fallen forest-men,
Forever hunting or hunted, rushing through
Endless pursuit or endlessly pursued,
Until each tree, each evil-blossomed vine,
Each fretful fern drops down a fear like dew
And Africa, basking in antiquest sun,
Contains for its children not a gill of sweet.

Forth from their tabernacles once again
The angels come, armed, gloriously to slay
The black and ruin his sepulchral throne.
Hé quoi! Angels go pricking elephants?
Wings spread and whirling over jaguar-men?
Angels tiptoe upon the snowy cones
Of palmy peaks sighting machine-guns? These,
Seraphim of Europe? Pouring out of dawn,
Fresh from the sacred clarities, chanters
Of the pith of mind, cuirassiers against
The milkiest bowmen. This makes a new design,
Filleted angels over flapping ears,
Combatting bushmen for a patch of gourds,
Loosing black slaves to make black infantry,
Angels returning after war with belts
And beads and bangles of gold and trumpets raised,
Racking the world with clarion puffs. This must
Be merely a masquerade or else a rare
Tractatus, of military things, with plates,
Miraculously preserved, full fickle-fine,
Of an imagination flashed with irony
And by a hand of certitude to cut
The heavenly cocks, the bowmen, and the gourds,
The oracular trumpets round and roundly hooped,
In Leonardo's way, to magnify
Concentric bosh. To their tabernacles, then,
Remoter than Athos, the effulgent hordes
Return, affecting roseate aureoles,
To contemplate time's golden paladin
And purpose, to hear the wild bee drone, to feel
The ecstasy of sense in a sensuous air.

But could the statue stand in Africa?
The marble was imagined in the cold.

Its edges were taken from tumultous wind
That beat out slimmest edges in the ear,
Made of the eye an insatiable intellect.
Its surfaces came from distant fire; and it
Was meant to stand, not in a tumbling green,
Intensified and grandiose, but among
The common-places of which it formed a part
And there, by feat extenuations, to make
A visible clear cap, a visible wreath
To men, to houses, streets and the squalid whole.
There it would be of the mode of common dreams,
A ring of horses rising from memory
Or rising in the appointments of desire,
The spirit's natural images, carriers,
The drafts of gay beginnings and bright ends,
Majestic bearers or solemn haulers trapped
In endless elegies. But in Africa
The memory moves on leopards' feet, desire
Appoints its florid messengers with wings
Wildly curvetted, color-scarred, so beaked,
With tongues unclipped and throats so stuffed with thorns,
So clawed, so sopped with sun, that in these things
The message is half-borne. Could marble still
Be marble after the drenching reds, the dark
And drenching crimsons, or endure? It came
If not from winter, from a summer like
A winter's noon, in which the colors sprang
From snow, and would return again to snow,
As summer would return to weazened days.

VII

The diplomats of the cafés expound:
Fromage and coffee and cognac and no gods.
It was a mistake to paint the gods. The gold
Of constellations on the beachy air
Is difficult. It blights in the studios.
Magnificence most shiningly expressed

88

Is, after all, draped damask pampeluned,
Color and color brightening into one,
A majestic weavers' job, a summer's sweat.
It was a mistake to think of them. They have
No place in the sense of colonists, no place
In Africa. The serpent's throne is dust
At the unbeliever's touch. Cloud-cloisters blow
Out of the eye when the loud wind gathers up
And blows, with heaped-up shoulders loudly blows
And bares an earth that has no gods, and bares
The gods like marble figures fallen, left
In the streets. There will always be cafés and cards
And the obese proprietor, who has a son
In Capricorn. The statue has a form
That will always be and will be everywhere.
Why should it fail to stand? Victoria Platz,
To make its factories content, must have
A cavernous and a cruel past, tropic
Benitia, lapis Ville des Pins must soothe
The impoverished waste with dewy vibrancies
Of April here and May to come. Champagne
On a hot night and a long cigar and talk
About the weather and women and the way
Of things, why bother about the back of stars?
The statue belongs to the cavernous past, belongs
To April here and May to come. Why think,
Why feel the sun or, feeling, why feel more
Than purple paste of fruit, to taste, or leaves
Of purple flowers, to see? The black will still
Be free to sing, if only a sorrowful song.


VIII


Fatal Ananke is the common god.
He looks upon the statue, where it is,
And the sun and the sun-reek piled and peaked above
The jostled ferns, where it might be, having eyes

Of the shape of eyes, like blunt intaglios,
And nothing more. He sees but not by sight.
He does not hear by sound. His spirit knows
Each look and each necessitous cry, as a god
Knows, knowing that he does not care, and knows,
Knowing and meaning that he cannot care.
He sees the angel in the nigger's mind
And hears the nigger's prayer in motets, belched
From pipes that swarm clerestory walls. The voice
In the jungle is a voice in Fontainebleau.
The long recessional at parish eves wails round
The cuckoo trees and the widow of Madrid
Weeps in Segovia. The beggar in Rome
Is the beggar in Bogotá. The kraal
Chants a death that is a medieval death . . .
Fateful Ananke is the final god.
His hymn, his psalm, his cithern song of praise
Is the exile of the disinherited,
Life's foreigners, pale aliens of the mud,
Those whose Jerusalem is Glasgow-frost
Or Paris-rain. He thinks of the noble lives
Of the gods and, for him, a thousand litanies
Are like the perpetual verses in a poet's mind.
He is that obdurate ruler who ordains
For races, not for men, powerful beyond
A grace to nature, a changeless element.
His place is large and high, an ether flamed
By his presence, the seat of his ubiquitous will.
He, only, caused the statue to be made
And he shall fix the place where it will stand.
Be glory to this unmerciful pontifex,
Lord without any deviation, lord
And origin and resplendent end of law,
Sultan of African sultans, starless crown.

[OWL'S CLOVER]

# A DUCK FOR DINNER

### I

The Bulgar said, "After pineapple with fresh mint
We went to walk in the park; for, after all,
The workers do not rise, as Venus rose,
Out of a violet sea. They rise a bit
On summer Sundays in the park, a duck
To a million, a duck with apples and without wine.
They rise to the muddy, metropolitan elms,
To the camellia-chateaux and an inch beyond,
Forgetting work, not caring for angels, hunting a lift,
The triumph of the arcs of heaven's blue
For themselves, and space and time and ease for the duck.
If you caricature the way they rise, yet they rise.
True, only an inch, but an inch at a time, and inch
By inch, Sunday by Sunday, many men.
At least, conceive what these hands from Sweden mean,
These English noses and edged, Italian eyes,
Massed for a head they mean to make for themselves,
From which their grizzled voice will speak and be heard."

### II

O buckskin, O crosser of snowy divides,
For whom men were to be ends in themselves,
Are the cities to breed as mountains bred, the streets
To trundle children like the sea? For you,
Day came upon the spirit as life comes
And deep winds flooded you; for these, day comes,
A penny sun in a tinsel sky, unrhymed,
And the spirit writhes to be wakened, writhes
To see, once more, this hacked-up world of tools,

The heart in slattern pinnacles, the clouds,
Which were their thoughts, squeezed into shapes, the sun
Streamed white and stoked and engined wrick-a-wrack.
In your cadaverous Eden, they desire
The same down-dropping fruit in yellow leaves,
The same return at heavy evening, love
Without any horror of the helpless loss.
The scholar's outline that you had, the print
Of London, the paper of Paris magnified
By poets, the Italian lives preserved
For poverty are gaudy bosh to these.
Their destiny is just as much machine
As death itself, and never can be changed
By print or paper, the trivial chance foregone,
And only an agony of dreams can help,
Not the agony of a single dreamer, but
The wide night mused by tell-tale muttering,
Time's fortune near, the sleepless sleepers moved
By the torture of things that will be realized,
Will, will, but how and all of them asking how
And sighing. These lives are not your lives, O free,
O bold, that rode your horses straight away.


III


Again the Bulgar said, "There are more things
Than poodles in Pomerania. This man
Is all the birds he ever heard and that,
The admiral of his race and everyman,
Infected by unreality, rapt round
By dense unreason, irreproachable force,
Is cast in pandemonium, flittered, howled
By harmonies beyond known harmony.
These bands, these swarms, these motions, what of them?
They keep to the paths of the skeleton architect
Of the park. They obey the rules of every skeleton.
But of what are they thinking, of what, in spite of the duck,
In spite of the watch-chains aus Wien, in spite
Of the Balkan shoes, the bonnets from Moldau, beards

From the steppes, are they being part, feeling the strength,
Seeing the fulgent shadows upward heaped,
Spelling out pandects and haggard institutes?
Is each man thinking his separate thoughts or, for once,
Are all men thinking together as one, thinking
Each other's thoughts, thinking a single thought,
Disclosed in everything, transcended, poised
For the syllable, poised for the touch? But that
Apocalypse was not contrived for parks,
Geranium budgets, pay-roll water-falls,
The clank of the carrousel and, under the trees,
The sheep-like falling-in of distances,
Converging on the statue, white and high."


IV


Then Basilewsky in the band-stand played
"Concerto for Airplane and Pianoforte,"
The newest Soviet réclame. Profound
Abortion, fit for the enchanting of basilisks.
They chanced to think. Suppose the future fails.
If platitude and inspiration are alike
As evils, and if reason, fatuous fire,
Is only another egoist wearing a mask,
What man of folk-lore shall rebuild the world,
What lesser man shall measure sun and moon,
What super-animal dictate our fates?
As the man the state, not as the state the man,
Perennial doctrine and most florid truth;
But man means more, means the million and the duck.
It cannot mean a sea-wide country strewn
With squalid cells, unless New York is Cocos
Or Chicago a Kaffir kraal. It means this mob.
The man in the band-stand could be orator.
It may be the future depends on an orator,
Some pebble-chewer practiced in Tyrian speech,
An apparition, twanging instruments
Within us hitherto unknown, he that
Confounds all opposites and spins a sphere

93

Created, like a bubble, of bright sheens,
With a tendency to bulge as it floats away.
Basilewsky's bulged before it floated, turned
Caramel and would not, could not float. And yet
In an age of concentric mobs would any sphere
Escape all deformation, much less this,
This source and patriarch of other spheres,
This base of every future, vibrant spring,
The volcano Apostrophe, the sea Behold?
Suppose, instead of failing, it never comes,
This future, although the elephants pass and the blare,
Prolonged, repeated and once more prolonged,
Goes off a little on the side and stops.
Yet to think of the future is a genius,
To think of the future is a thing and he
That thinks of it is inscribed on walls and stands
Complete in bronze on enormous pedestals.

v

The statue is white and high, white brillianter
Than the color white and high beyond any height
That rises in the air. The sprawlers on the grass
See more than marble in their eyes, see more
Than the horses quivering to be gone, flashed through
With senses chiseled on bright stone. They see
The metropolitan of mind, they feel
The central of the composition, in which
They live. They see and feel themselves, seeing
And feeling the world in which they live. The manes,
The leaping bodies, come from the truculent hand,
The stubborn eye, of the conformer who conforms
The manes to his image of the flying wind,
The leaping bodies to his strength, convulsed
By tautest pinions lifted through his thought.
The statue is the sculptor not the stone.
In this he carved himself, he carved his age,
He carved the feathery walkers standing by,
Twitching a little with crude souvenirs

Of young identities, Aprilian stubs.
Exceeding sex, he touched another race,
Above our race, yet of ourselves transformed,
Don Juan turned furious divinity,
Ethereal compounder, pater patriae,
Great mud-ancestor, oozer and Abraham,
Progenitor wearing the diamond crown of crowns,
He from whose beard the future springs, elect.
More of ourselves in a world that is more our own,
For the million, perhaps, two ducks instead of one;
More of ourselves, the mood of life made strong
As by a juicier season; and more our own
As against each other, the dead, the phantomesque.

VI

If these were theoretical people, like
Small bees of spring, sniffing the coldest buds
Of a time to come—A shade of horror turns
The bees to scorpions blackly-barbed, a shade
Of fear changes the scorpions to skins
Concealed in glittering grass, dank reptile skins.
The civil fiction, the calico idea,
The Johnsonian composition, abstract man,
All are evasions like a repeated phrase,
Which, by its repetition, comes to bear
A meaning without a meaning. These people have
A meaning within the meaning they convey,
Walking the paths, watching the gilding sun,
To be swept across them when they are revealed,
For a moment, once each century or two.
The future for them is always the deepest dome,
The darkest blue of the dome and the wings around
The giant Phosphor of their earliest prayers.
Once each century or two. But then so great,
So epical a twist, catastrophe
For Isaac Watts: the diverting of the dream
Of heaven from heaven to the future, as a god,
Takes time and tinkering, melodious

95

And practical. The envoi to the past
Is largely another winding of the clock.
The tempo, in short, of this complicated shift,
With interruptions by vast hymns, blood odes,
Parades of whole races with attendant bands,
And the bees, the scorpions, the men that think,
The summer Sundays in the park, must be
A leaden ticking circular in width.
How shall we face the edge of time? We walk
In the park. We regret we have no nightingale.
We must have the throstle on the gramophone.
Where shall we find more than derisive words?
When shall lush chorals spiral through our fire
And daunt that old assassin, heart's desire?

[OWL'S CLOVER]

## SOMBRE FIGURATION

### I

There is a man whom rhapsodies of change,
Of which he is the cause, have never changed
And never will, a subman under all
The rest, to whom in the end the rest return,
The man below the man below the man,
Steeped in night's opium, evading day.

### II

We have grown weary of the man that thinks.
He thinks and it is not true. The man below
Imagines and it is true, as if he thought
By imagining, anti-logician, quick
With a logic of transforming certitudes.

96

It is not that he was born in another land,
Powdered with primitive lights, and lives with us
In glimpses, on the edge or at the tip,
Playing a crackled reed, wind-stopped, in bleats.
He was born within us as a second self,
A self of parents who have never died,
Whose lives return, simply, upon our lips,
Their words and ours; in what we see, their hues
Without a season, unstinted in livery,
And ours, of rigid measure, a miser's paint;
And most in what we hear, sound brushed away,
A mumbling at the elbow, turgid tunes,
As of insects or cloud-stricken birds, away
And away, dialogues between incognitos.
He dwells below, the man below, in less
Than body and in less than mind, ogre,
Inhabitant, in less than shape, of shapes
That are dissembled in vague memory
Yet still retain resemblances, remain
Remembrances, a place of a field of lights,
As a church is a bell and people are an eye,
A cry, the pallor of a dress, a touch.
He turns us into scholars, studying
The masks of music. We perceive each mask
To be the musician's own and, thence, become
An audience to mimics glistening
With meanings, doubled by the closest sound,
Mimics that play on instruments discerned
In the beat of the blood.
                              Green is the path we take
Between chimeras and garlanded the way,
The down-descent into November's void.
The spontaneities of rain or snow
Surprise the sterile rationalist who sees
Maidens in bloom, bulls under sea, the lark
On urns and oak-leaves twisted into rhyme.
The man, but not the man below, for whom
The pheasant in a field was pheasant, field,
Until they changed to eagle in white air,
Lives in a fluid, not on solid rock.

The solid was an age, a period
With appropriate, largely English, furniture,
Barbers with charts of the only possible modes,
Cities that would not wash away in the mist,
Each man in his asylum maundering,
Policed by the hope of Christmas. Summer night,
Night gold, and winter night, night silver, these
Were the fluid, the cat-eyed atmosphere, in which
The man and the man below were reconciled,
The east wind in the west, order destroyed,
The cycle of the solid having turned.

III

High up in heaven a sprawling portent moves,
As if it bears all darkness in its bulk.
But this we cannot see. The shaggy top
Broods in tense meditation, constantly,
On the city, on which it leans, the people there,
Its shadow on their houses, on their walls,
Their beds, their faces drawn in distant sleep.
This is invisible. The supporting arms
Reach from the horizons, rim to rim,
While the shaggy top collects itself to do
And the shoulders turn, breathing immense intent.
All this is hidden from sight.
                              It is the form
Of a generation that does not know itself,
Still questioning if to crush the soaring stacks,
The churches, like dalmatics stooped in prayer,
And the people suddenly evil, waked, accused,
Destroyed by a vengeful movement of the arms,
A mass overtaken by the blackest sky,
Each one as part of the total wrath, obscure
In slaughter; or if to match its furious wit
Against the sleepers to re-create for them,
Out of their wilderness, a special fane,
Midmost in its design, the arms grown swift,
The body bent, like Hercules, to build.

If the fane were clear, if the city shone in mind,
If more than the wished-for ruin racked the night,
If more than pity and despair were sure,
If the flashy extravaganzas of the lean
Could ever make them fat, these are delays
For ponderous revolving, without help.
And, while revolving, ancient hyacinths
And fragrant fomentations of the spring
Come, baffling discontent. These, too, must be
Revolved.
            Which counts for most, the anger borne
In anger; or the fear that from the death
Of evil, evil springs; or catholic hope,
Young catechumen answering the worms?
The man below beholds the portent poised,
An image of his making, beyond the eye,
Poised, but poised as the mind through which a storm
Of other images blows, images of time
Like the time of the portent, images like leaves,
Except that this is an image of black spring
And those the leaves of autumn-afterwards,
Leaves of the autumns in which the man below
Lived as the man lives now, and hated, loved,
As the man hates now, loves now, the self-same things.
The year's dim elongations stretch below
To rumbled rock, its bright projections lie
The shallowest iris on the emptiest eye.
The future must bear within it every past,
Not least the pasts destroyed, magniloquent
Syllables, pewter on ebony, yet still
A board for bishops' grapes, the happy form
That revolution takes for connoisseurs:
The portent may itself be memory;
And memory may itself be time to come
And must be, when the portent, changed, takes on
A mask up-gathered brilliantly from the dirt,
And memory's lord is the lord of prophecy
And steps forth, priestly in severity,
Yet lord, a mask of flame, the sprawling form
A wandering orb upon a path grown clear.

99

IV

High up in heaven the sprawling portent moves.
The statue in a crow's perspective of trees
Stands brimming white, chiaroscuro scaled
To space. To space? The statue scaled to space
Would be a ring of heads and haunches, torn
From size, backs larger than the eye, not flesh
In marble, but marble massive as the thrust
Of that which is not seen and cannot be.
The portent would become man-haggard to
A race of dwarfs, the meditative arms
And head a shadow trampled under hoofs,
Man-misty to a race star-humped, astride
In a clamor thudding up from central earth.
Not the space in camera of the man below,
Immeasurable, the space in which he knows
The locust's titter and the turtle's sob.
The statue stands in true perspective. Crows
Give only their color to the leaves. The trees
Are full of fanfares of farewell, as night
And the portent end in night, composed, before
Its wheel begins to turn.

                                  The statue stands
In hum-drum space, farewell, farewell, by day
The green, white, blue of the ballad-eye, by night
The mirror of other nights combined in one.
The spring is hum-drum like an instrument,
That a man without passion plays in an aimless way.
Even imagination has an end,
When the statue is not a thing imagined, a stone
That changed in sleep. It is, it is, let be
The way it came, let be what it may become.
Even the man below, the subverter, stops
The flight of emblemata through his mind,
Thoughts by descent. To flourish the great cloak we wear
At night, to turn away from the abominable
Farewells and, in the darkness, to feel again
The reconciliation, the rapture of a time

100

Without imagination, without past
And without future, a present time, is that
The passion, indifferent to the poet's hum,
That we conceal? A passion to fling the cloak,
Adorned for a multitude, in a gesture spent
In the gesture's whim, a passion merely to be
For the gaudium of being, Jocundus instead
Of the black-blooded scholar, the man of the cloud, to be
The medium man among other medium men,
The cloak to be clipped, the night to be re-designed,
Its land-breath to be stifled, its color changed,
Night and the imagination being one.

❀◇❀◇❀◇❀◇❀◇❀◇❀◇❀◇❀◇❀◇❀◇❀◇❀◇❀◇❀◇❀◇❀◇❀◇❀◇❀◇❀◇❀◇❀◇❀◇❀◇❀◇❀◇❀◇❀◇❀◇❀◇

## STANZAS FOR "THE MAN WITH THE BLUE GUITAR"

### III

The parrot in its balmy boughs
Repeats the farmer's almanac.

A duckling of the wildest blood
Convinces Athens with its quack.

Much too much thought, too little thought,
No thought at all: a guttural growl,

A snort across the silver-ware,
The rose-leaves flying through the air.

### VII

The day is green and the wind is young.
The world is young and I play my guitar.

The skeletons sit on the wall. They drop
Red mango peels and I play my guitar.

The gate is not jasper. It is not bone.
It is mud, and mud long baked in the sun,

An eighteenth century fern or two
And the dewiest beads of insipid fruit

And honey from thorns and I play my guitar.
The negress with laundry passes me by.

The boatman goes humming. He smokes a cigar
And I play my guitar. The vines have grown wild.

The oranges glitter as part of the sky.
A tiara from Cohen's, this summer sea.


IX

A letter for the ignorant.
The dithering goes on. I read.

"The myths in which we recognize
Ourselves, incessantly revealed,

Keep us concealed." Things as they are
Stand jabbering. But to catch the word,

To know completely we have heard,
To pick it on the blue guitar—

I read. "The subject of poetry
Is poetry, things as they are."

We hear them on the blue guitar.
The poet picks them as they are,

But picks them on a blue guitar,
A guitar that makes things as they are.

x

But then things never really are.
How does it matter how I play

Or what I color what I say?
It all depends on inter-play

Or inter-play and inter-say,
Like tweedle-dum and tweedle-dee,

Or ti-ri-la and ti-ri-li
And these I play on my guitar

And leave the final atmosphere
To the imagination of the engineer.

I could not find it if I would.
I would not find it if I could.

I cannot say what things I play,
Because I play things as they are

And since they are not as they are,
I play them on a blue guitar.

XI

I play them on a blue guitar
And then things are not as they are.

The shaping of the instrument
Distorts the shape of what I meant,

Which takes a shape by accident.
Yet what I mean I always say.

103

The accident is how I play.
I still intend things as they are.

The greenish quaverings of day
Quiver upon the blue guitar.

XXI

To ride an old mule round the keys—
Mature emotional gesture, that—

Blond weather. One is born a saint,
Complete in wind-sucked poverty,

In such an air, poor as one's mule.
Here, if there was a peak to climb,

One could watch the blue sea's blueness flow
And blacken into indigo.

But squint and squeak, where no people are:
On such a peak, the blue guitar—

Blond weather. Give the mule his hay.
True, things are people as they are.

◇◇◇◇◇◇◇◇◇◇◇◇◇◇◇◇◇◇◇◇◇◇◇◇◇◇◇◇◇◇◇◇◇◇◇◇◇◇◇◇◇◇◇◇◇◇◇◇◇◇◇◇

# THE WOMAN THAT HAD MORE BABIES THAN THAT

I

An acrobat on the border of the sea
Observed the waves, the rising and the swell
And the first line spreading up the beach; again,
The rising and the swell, the preparation

104

And the first line foaming over the sand; again,
The rising and the swell, the first line's glitter,
Like a dancer's skirt, flung round and settling down.
This was repeated day by day. The waves
Were mechanical, muscular. They never changed,
They never stopped, a repetition repeated
Continually—There is a woman has had
More babies than that. The merely revolving wheel
Returns and returns, along the dry, salt shore.
There is a mother whose children need more than that.
She is not the mother of landscapes but of those
That question the repetition on the shore,
Listening to the whole sea for a sound
Of more or less, ascetically sated
By amical tones.
                    The acrobat observed
The universal machine. There he perceived
The need for a thesis, a music constant to move.


II


Berceuse, transatlantic. The children are men, old men,
Who, when they think and speak of the central man,
Of the humming of the central man, the whole sound
Of the sea, the central humming of the sea,
Are old men breathed on by a maternal voice,
Children and old men and philosophers,
Bald heads with their mother's voice still in their ears.
The self is a cloister full of remembered sounds
And of sounds so far forgotten, like her voice,
That they return unrecognized. The self
Detects the sound of a voice that doubles its own,
In the images of desire, the forms that speak,
The ideas that come to it with a sense of speech.
The old men, the philosophers, are haunted by that
Maternal voice, the explanation at night.
They are more than parts of the universal machine.
Their need in solitude: that is the need,
The desire, for the fiery lullaby.

105

                              If her head
Stood on a plain of marble, high and cold;
If her eyes were chinks in which the sparrows built;
If she was deaf with falling grass in her ears—
But there is more than a marble, massive head.
They find her in the crackling summer night,
In the *Duft* of towns, beside a window, beside
A lamp, in a day of the week, the time before spring,
A manner of walking, yellow fruit, a house,
A street. She has a supernatural head.
On her lips familiar words become the words
Of an elevation, an elixir of the whole.

## LIFE ON A BATTLESHIP

### I

The rape of the bourgeoisie accomplished, the men
Returned on board *The Masculine*. That night,
The captain said,
                    "The war between classes is
A preliminary, a provincial phase,
Of the war between individuals. In time,
When earth has become a paradise, it will be
A paradise full of assassins. Suppose I seize
The ship, make it my own and, bit by bit,
Seize yards and docks, machinery and men,
As others have, and then, unlike the others,
Instead of building ships, in numbers, build
A single ship, a cloud on the sea, the largest
Possible machine, a divinity of steel,
Of which I am captain. Given what I intend,
The ship would become the centre of the world.

My cabin as the centre of the ship and I
As the centre of the cabin, the centre of
The divinity, the divinity's mind, the mind
Of the world would have only to ring and ft!
It would be done. If, only to please myself,
I said that men should wear stone masks and, to make
The word respected, fired ten thousand guns
In mid-Atlantic, bellowing, to command,
It would be done. And once the thing was done,
Once the assassins wore stone masks and did
As I wished, once they fell backward when my breath
Blew against them or bowed from the hips, when I turned
My head, the sorrow of the world, except
As man is natural, would be at an end."


II


So posed, the captain drafted rules of the world,
*Regulæ mundi,* as apprentice of
Descartes:
        First. The grand simplifications reduce
Themselves to one.
           Of this the captain said,
"It is a lesser law than the one itself,
Unless it is the one itself, or unless
*The Masculine,* much magnified, that cloud
On the sea, is both law and evidence in one,
As the final simplification is meant to be.
It is clear that it is not a moral law.
It appears to be what there is of life compressed
Into its own illustration, a divinity
Like any other, rex by right of the crown,
The jewels in his beard, the mystic wand,
And imperator because of death to oppose
The illustrious arms, the symbolic horns, the red
For battle, the purple for victory. But if
It is the absolute why must it be
This immemorial grandiose, why not

107

A cockle-shell, a trivial emblem great
With its final force, a thing invincible
In more than phrase? There's the true masculine,
The spirit's ring and seal, the naked heart."
It was a rabbi's question. Let the rabbis reply.
It implies a flaw in the battleship, a defeat
As of a make-believe.


III


                       Second. The part
Is the equal of the whole.
                              The captain said,
"The ephebi say that there is only the whole,
The race, the nation, the state. But society
Is a phase. We approach a society
Without a society, the politicians
Gone, as in Calypso's isle or in Citare,
Where I or one or the part is the equal of
The whole. The sound of a dozen orchestras
May rush to extinguish the theme, the basses thump
And the fiddles smack, the horns yahoo, the flutes
Strike fire, but the part is the equal of the whole,
Unless society is a mystical mass.
This is a thing to twang a philosopher's sleep,
A vacuum for the dozen orchestras
To fill, the grindstone of antiquest time,
Breakfast in Paris, music and madness and mud,
The perspective squirming as it tries to take
A shape, the vista twisted and burning, a thing
Kicked through the roof, caressed by the river-side.
On *The Masculine* one asserts and fires the guns.
But one lives to think of this growing, this pushing life,
The vine, at the roots, this vine of Key West, splurging,
Covered one morning with blue, one morning with white,
Coming from the East, forcing itself to the West,
The jungle of tropical part and tropical whole."

The first and second rules are reconciled
In a third: The whole cannot exist without
The parts. Thus: Out of the number of his thoughts
The thinker knows. The gunman of the commune
Kills the commune.
                              Captain, high captain, how is it, now,
With our affair, our destiny, our hash?
Your guns are not rhapsodic strophes, red
And true. The good, the strength, the sceptre moves
From constable to god, from earth to air,
The circle of the sceptre growing large
And larger as it moves, moving toward
A hand that fails to seize it. High captain, the grand
Simplifications approach but do not touch
The ultimate one, though they are parts of it.
Without them it could not exist. That's our affair,
That's this grandiose battleship of yours and your
*Regulæ mundi* . . . That much is out of the way.
If the sceptre returns to earth, still moving, still
Precious from the region of the hand, still bright
With saintly imagination and the stains
Of martyrs, to be arrogant in our need,
It will be all we have. Our fate is our own:
Our good, from this the rhapsodic strophes flow,
Through prophets and succeeding prophets, whose prophecies
Grow large and larger. Our fate is our own. The hand,
It must be the hand of one, it must be the hand
Of a man, that seizes our strength, will seize it to be
Merely the sceptre over long desire,
Merely the centre of a circle, spread
To the final full, an end without rhetoric.

# STANZAS FOR "EXAMINATION OF THE HERO IN A TIME OF WAR"

### I

An immense drum rolls through a clamor of people.
The women with eyes like opals vanish
And men look inwardly, for the emblem:
The star-yplaited, visible sanction,
The strength of death or triumph. Oheu!
That the choice should come on them so early.
They had hardly grown to know the sunshine,
Before the sun brought them that destruction
And with it, the antiquest wishing
To bear virile grace before their fellows,
Regardless of gods that were praised in goldness
And triple chime . . . The self-same rhythm
Moves in lamenting and the fatal,
The bold, obedience to Ananke.

### II

The words are in the way and thoughts are.
Forgetful of death in war, there rises
From the middens of life, rotten and acrid,
A race that is a hero, entirely
Without heroic words, heroic
Hybrids impossible to the wardens
Within us. False hybrids and false heroes,
Half men and half new, modern monsters . . .
The hero is the man who is himself, who
As a man among other men, divested
Of attributes, naked of myth, true,
Not true to this or that, but true, knows
The frame of the hero. Yet, willingly, he
Becomes the hero without heroics.

It is the common man against evil,
Now. War as a punishment. The hero
As hangman, a little sick of blood, of
The deep sigh with which the hanging ends, close
To his gorge, hangman, once helmet-maker
And headsman and trumpeteer and feather
In casque and scaffold orator, fortified
By gestures of a mortal perfection.
What misanthrope, impugning heroica,
Maligning his costumes and disputing
His roles, would leave to the clouds the righting,
The immediate and intolerable need
Of the very body instinctively crying
A challenge to a final solution.

❀◈❀◈❀◈❀◈❀◈❀◈❀◈❀◈❀◈❀◈❀◈❀◈❀◈❀◈❀◈❀◈❀◈❀◈❀◈❀◈❀◈❀◈❀◈❀◈❀◈❀◈❀◈❀◈❀◈❀◈❀◈❀◈❀◈❀◈❀◈❀◈❀◈❀◈❀◈❀◈❀◈❀◈❀◈❀◈❀◈❀◈

## FROM "FIVE GROTESQUE PIECES"

### I

*One of Those Hibiscuses of Damozels*

She was all of her airs and, for all of her airs,
She was all of her airs and ears and hairs,
Her pearly ears, her jeweler's ears
And the painted hairs that composed her hair.

In spite of her airs, that's what she was. She was all
Of her airs, as surely cologne as that she was bone
Was what she was and flesh, sure enough, but airs;
Rather rings than fingers, rather fingers than hands.

How could you ever, how could you think that you saw her,
Knew her, how could you see the woman that wore the beads,
The ball-like beads, the bazzling and the bangling beads
Or hear her step in the way she walked?

This was not how she walked for she walked in a way
And the way was more than the walk and was hard to see.
You saw the eye-blue, sky-blue, eye-blue, and the powdered ears
And the cheeks like flower-pots under her hair.


v


*Outside of Wedlock*


The strong music of hard times,
In a world forever without a plan
For itself as a world,
Must be played on the concertina.


The poor piano forte
Whimpers when the moon above East Hartford
Wakes us to the emotion, grand fortissimo,
Of our sense of evil,


Of our sense that time has been
Like water running in a gutter
Through an alley to nowhere,
Without beginning or the concept of an end.


The old woman that knocks at the door
Is not our grandiose destiny.
It is an old bitch, an old drunk,
That has been yelling in the dark.


Sing for her the seventy-fold Amen,
White February wind,
Through banks and banks of voices,
In the cathedral-shanty,


To the sound of the concertina,
Like the voice of all our ancestors,
The *père* Benjamin, the *mère* Blandenah,
Saying we have forgot them, they never lived.

## DESIRE & THE OBJECT

It is curious that I should have spoken of Raël,
When it never existed, the order
That I desired. It could be—

Curious that I should have spoken of Jaffa
By her sexual name, saying that that high marriage
Could be, it could be.

I had not invented my own thoughts,
When I was sleeping, nor by day,
So that thinking was a madness, and is:

It was to be as mad as everyone was,
And is. Perhaps I had been moved
By feeling the like of thought in sleep,

So that feeling was a madness, and is.
Consider that I had asked
Was it desire that created Raël

Or was it Jaffa that created desire?
The origin could have its origin.
It could be, could be.

It could be that the sun shines
Because I desire it to shine or else
That I desire it to shine because it shines.

## THIS AS INCLUDING THAT

This rock and the dry birds
Fluttering in blue leaves,

113

This rock and the priest,
The priest of nothingness who intones—

It is true that you live on this rock
And in it. It is wholly you.

It is true that there are thoughts
That move in the air as large as air,

That are almost not our own, but thoughts
To which we are related,

In an association like yours
With the rock and mine with you.

The iron settee is cold.
A fly crawls on the balustrades.

◇◇◇◇◇◇◇◇◇◇◇◇◇◇◇◇◇◇◇◇◇◇◇◇◇◇◇◇◇◇◇◇◇◇◇◇◇◇◇◇◇◇◇◇◇◇◇◇◇◇◇◇◇◇◇

## RECITATION AFTER DINNER

A poem about tradition could easily be
A windy thing . . . However, since we are here,
Cousins of the calendar if not of kin,
To be a part of tradition, to identify
Its actual appearance, suppose we begin
By giving it a form. But the character
Of tradition does not easily take form.

It is not a set of laws. Therefore, its form
Is not lean marble, trenchant-eyed. There is
No book of the past in which time's senators
Have inscribed life's do and don't. The commanding codes
Are not tradition. To identify it
Is to define its form, to say: this image
Is its body visible to the important eye.

The bronze of the wise man seated in repose
Is not its form. Tradition is wise but not
The figure of the wise man fixed in sense.
The scholar is always distant in the space
Around him and in that distance meditates
Things still more distant. And tradition is near.
It joins and does not separate. What, then,

Is its true form? Is it the memory
That hears a pin fall in New Amsterdam
Or sees the new North River heaping up
Dutch ice on English boats? The memory
Is part of the classic imagination, posed
Too often to be more than secondhand.
Tradition is much more than the memory.

Is it experience, say, the final form
To which all other forms, at last, return,
The frame of a repeated effect, is it that?
Are we characters in an arithmetic
Or letters of a curious alphabet;
And is tradition an unfamiliar sum,
A legend scrawled in a script we cannot read?

It has a clear, a single, a solid form,
That of the son who bears upon his back
The father that he loves, and bears him from
The ruins of the past, out of nothing left,
Made noble by the honor he receives,
As if in a golden cloud. The son restores
The father. He hides his ancient blue beneath

His own bright red. But he bears him out of love,
His life made double by his father's life,
Ascending the humane. This is the form
Tradition wears, the clear, the single form,
The solid shape, Æneas seen, perhaps,
By Nicolas Poussin, yet nevertheless
A tall figure upright in a giant's air.

The father keeps on living in the son, the world
Of the father keeps on living in the world
Of the son. These survivals out of time and space
Come to us every day. And yet they are
Merely parts of the general fiction of the mind:
Survivals of a good that we have loved,
Made eminent in a reflected seeming-so.

❀◇❀◇❀◇❀◇❀◇❀◇❀◇❀◇❀◇❀◇❀◇❀◇❀◇❀◇❀◇❀◇❀◇❀◇❀◇❀◇❀◇❀◇❀◇❀◇❀◇

## MEMORANDUM

The katy-dids at Ephrata return
But this time at another place.
It is the same sound, the same season,
But it is not Ephrata.

You said the dew falls in the blood.
The dew falls deep in the mind
On life itself and there the katy-dids
Keep whanging their brass wings. . . .

Say this to Pravda, tell the damned rag
That the peaches are slowly ripening.
Say that the American moon comes up
Cleansed clean of lousy Byzantium.

Say that in the clear Atlantic night
The plums are blue on the trees. The katy-dids
Bang cymbals as they used to do.
Millions hold millions in their arms.

# FIRST WARMTH

I wonder, have I lived a skeleton's life,
As a questioner about reality,

A countryman of all the bones in the world?
Now, here, the warmth I had forgotten becomes

Part of the major reality, part of
An appreciation of a reality;

And thus an elevation, as if I lived
With something I could touch, touch every way.

# AS YOU LEAVE THE ROOM

*You speak. You say*: Today's character is not
A skeleton out of its cabinet. Nor am I.

That poem about the pineapple, the one
About the mind as never satisfied,

The one about the credible hero, the one
About summer, are not what skeletons think about.

I wonder, have I lived a skeleton's life,
As a disbeliever in reality,

A countryman of all the bones in the world?
Now, here, the snow I had forgotten becomes

Part of a major reality, part of
An appreciation of a reality

And thus an elevation, as if I left
With something I could touch, touch every way.

And yet nothing has been changed except what is
Unreal, as if nothing had been changed at all.

◇◇◇◇◇◇◇◇◇◇◇◇◇◇◇◇◇◇◇◇◇◇◇◇◇◇◇◇◇◇◇◇◇◇◇◇◇◇◇◇◇◇◇◇◇◇◇◇

## THE SICK MAN

Bands of black men seem to be drifting in the air,
In the South, bands of thousands of black men,
Playing mouth-organs in the night or, now, guitars.

Here in the North, late, late, there are voices of men,
Voices in chorus, singing without words, remote and deep,
Drifting choirs, long movements and turnings of sounds.

And in a bed in one room, alone, a listener
Waits for the unison of the music of the drifting bands
And the dissolving chorals, waits for it and imagines

The words of winter in which these two will come together,
In the ceiling of the distant room, in which he lies,
The listener, listening to the shadows, seeing them,

Choosing out of himself, out of everything within him,
Speech for the quiet, good hail of himself, good hail, good hail,
The peaceful, blissful words, well-tuned, well-sung, well-spoken.

✿◇✿◇✿◇✿◇✿◇✿◇✿◇✿◇✿◇✿◇✿◇✿◇✿◇✿◇✿◇✿◇✿◇✿◇✿◇✿◇✿◇✿◇✿◇✿◇✿◇✿◇✿◇✿◇

## AS AT A THEATRE

Another sunlight might make another world,
Green, more or less, in green and blue in blue,

118

Like taste distasting the first fruit of a vine,
Like an eye too young to grapple its primitive,
Like the artifice of a new reality,
Like the chromatic calendar of time to come.

It might be the candle of another being,
Ragged in unkempt perceptions, that stands
And meditates an image of itself,
Studies and shapes a tallowy image, swarmed
With slight, prismatic reeks not recollected,
A bubble without a wall on which to hang.

The curtains, when pulled, might show another whole,
An azure outre-terre, oranged and rosed,
At the elbow of Copernicus, a sphere,
A universe without life's limp and lack,
Philosophers' end . . . What difference would it make,
So long as the mind, for once, fulfilled itself?

# THE DESIRE TO MAKE LOVE IN A PAGODA

Among the second selves, sailor, observe
The rioter that appears when things are changed,

Asserting itself in an element that is free,
In the alien freedom that such selves degustate:

In the first inch of night, the stellar summering
At three-quarters gone, the morning's prescience,

As if, alone on a mountain, it saw far-off
An innocence approaching toward its peak.

## NUNS PAINTING WATER-LILIES

These pods are part of the growth of life within life:
Part of the unpredictable sproutings, as of

The youngest, the still fuzz-eyed, odd fleurettes,
That could come in a slight lurching of the scene,

A swerving, a tilting, a little lengthening,
A few hours more of day, the unravelling

Of a ruddier summer, a birth that fetched along
The supernatural of its origin.

Inside our queer chapeaux, we seem, on this bank,
To be part of a tissue, a clearness of the air,

That matches, today, a clearness of the mind.
It is a special day. We mumble the words

Of saints not heard of until now, unnamed,
In aureoles that are over-dazzling crests . . .

We are part of a fraicheur, inaccessible
Or accessible only in the most furtive fiction.

## THE ROLE OF THE IDEA IN POETRY

Ask of the philosopher why he philosophizes,
Determined thereto, perhaps by his father's ghost,
Permitting nothing to the evening's edge.

The father does not come to adorn the chant.
One father proclaims another, the patriarchs
Of truth. They stride across and are masters of

The chant and discourse there, more than wild weather
Or clouds that hang lateness on the sea. They become
A time existing after much time has passed.

Therein, day settles and thickens round a form—
Blue-bold on its pedestal—that seems to say,
"I am the greatness of the new-found night."

❀◇❀◇❀◇❀◇❀◇❀◇❀◇❀◇❀◇❀◇❀◇❀◇❀◇❀◇❀◇❀◇❀◇❀◇❀◇❀◇❀◇❀◇❀◇❀◇

## AMERICANA

The first soothsayers of the land, the man
In a field, the man on the side of a hill, all men
In a health of weather, knowing a few, old things,

(Remote from the deadly general of men,
The over-populace of the idea, the voices
Hard to be told from thoughts, the repeated drone

Of other lives becoming a total drone,
A sense separate that receives and holds the rest,
That which is human and yet final, like

A man that looks at himself in a glass and finds
It is the man in the glass that lives, not he.
He is the image, the second, the unreal,

The abstraction. He inhabits another man,
Other men, and not this grass, this valid air.
He is not himself. He is vitally deprived . . .)

These things he thinks of, as the buckskin hoop-la,
In a returning, a seeming of return,
Flaunts that first fortune, which he wanted so much.

## THE SOULS OF WOMEN AT NIGHT

Now, being invisible, I walk without mantilla,
In the much-horned night, as its chief personage.
Owls warn me and with tuft-eared watches keep

Distance between me and the five-times-sensed,
In these stations, in which nothing has been lost,
Sight least, but metaphysical blindness gained,

The blindness in which seeing would be false,
A fantastic irruption. Salute you, cata-sisters,
Ancient amigas, knowing partisans—

Or is it I that, wandering, know, one-sensed,
Not one of the five, and keep a rendezvous,
Of the loftiest amour, in a human midnight?


## A DISCOVERY OF THOUGHT

At the antipodes of poetry, dark winter,
When the trees glitter with that which despoils them,
Daylight evaporates, like a sound one hears in sickness.

One is a child again. The gold beards of waterfalls
Are dissolved as in an infancy of blue snow.
It is an arbor against the wind, a pit in the mist,

A trinkling in the parentage of the north,
The cricket of summer forming itself out of ice.
And always at this antipodes, of leaden loaves

Held in the hands of blue men that are lead within,
One thinks that it could be that the first word spoken,
The desire for speech and meaning gallantly fulfilled,

122

The gathering of the imbecile against his motes
And the wry antipodes whirled round the world away—
One thinks, when the houses of New England catch the first
    sun,

The first word would be of the susceptible being arrived,
The immaculate disclosure of the secret no more obscured.
The sprawling of winter might suddenly stand erect,

Pronouncing its new life and ours, not autumn's prodigal re-
    turned,
But an antipodal, far-fetched creature, worthy of birth,
The true tone of the metal of winter in what it says:

The accent of deviation in the living thing
That is its life preserved, the effort to be born
Surviving being born, the event of life.

$$\diamond\diamond\diamond\diamond\diamond\diamond\diamond\diamond\diamond\diamond\diamond\diamond\diamond\diamond\diamond\diamond\diamond\diamond\diamond\diamond\diamond\diamond\diamond\diamond\diamond\diamond\diamond\diamond\diamond\diamond\diamond\diamond\diamond\diamond\diamond\diamond\diamond\diamond\diamond\diamond\diamond\diamond\diamond\diamond\diamond\diamond\diamond\diamond\diamond\diamond\diamond\diamond$$

## THE COURSE OF A PARTICULAR

Today the leaves cry, hanging on branches swept by wind,
Yet the nothingness of winter becomes a little less.
It is still full of icy shades and shapen snow.

The leaves cry . . . One holds off and merely hears the cry.
It is a busy cry, concerning someone else.
And though one says that one is part of everything,

There is a conflict, there is a resistance involved;
And being part is an exertion that declines:
One feels the life of that which gives life as it is.

The leaves cry. It is not a cry of divine attention,
Nor the smoke-drift of puffed-out heroes, nor human cry.
It is the cry of leaves that do not transcend themselves,

In the absence of fantasia, without meaning more
Than they are in the final finding of the ear, in the thing
Itself, until, at last, the cry concerns no one at all.

## HOW NOW, O, BRIGHTENER . . .

Something of the trouble of the mind
Remains in the sight, and in sayings of the sight,
Of the spring of the year,

Trouble in the spillage and first sparkle of sun,
The green-edged yellow and yellow and blue and blue-edged
    green—
The trouble of the mind

Is a residue, a land, a rain, a warmth,
A time, an apparition and nourishing element
And simple love,

In which the spectra have dewy favor and live
And take from this restlessly unhappy happiness
Their stunted looks.

## THE DOVE IN SPRING

Brooder, brooder, deep beneath its walls—
A small howling of the dove
Makes something of the little there,

The little and the dark, and that
In which it is and that in which
It is established. There the dove

Makes this small howling, like a thought
That howls in the mind or like a man
Who keeps seeking out his identity

In that which is and is established . . . It howls
Of the great sizes of an outer bush
And the great misery of the doubt of it,

Of stripes of silver that are strips
Like slits across a space, a place
And state of being large and light.

There is this bubbling before the sun,
This howling at one's ear, too far
For daylight and too near for sleep.

## FAREWELL WITHOUT A GUITAR

Spring's bright paradise has come to this.
Now the thousand-leaved green falls to the ground.
Farewell, my days.

The thousand-leaved red
Comes to this thunder of light
As its autumnal terminal—

A Spanish storm,
A wide, still Aragonese,
In which the horse walks home without a rider,

Head down. The reflections and repetitions,
The blows and buffets of fresh senses
Of the rider that was,

Are a final construction,
Like glass and sun, of male reality
And of that other and her desire.

# THE SAIL OF ULYSSES

*Under the shape of his sail, Ulysses,*
*Symbol of the seeker, crossing by night*
*The giant sea, read his own mind.*
*He said, "As I know, I am and have*
*The right to be." Guiding his boat*
*Under the middle stars, he said:*

I

"If knowledge and the thing known are one
So that to know a man is to be
That man, to know a place is to be
That place, and it seems to come to that;
And if to know one man is to know all
And if one's sense of a single spot
Is what one knows of the universe,
Then knowledge is the only life,
The only sun of the only day,
The only access to true ease,
The deep comfort of the world and fate.

II

There is a human loneliness,
A part of space and solitude,
In which knowledge cannot be denied,
In which nothing of knowledge fails,
The luminous companion, the hand,
The fortifying arm, the profound
Response, the completely answering voice,
That which is more than anything else
The right within us and about us,
Joined, the triumphant vigor, felt,

The inner direction on which we depend,
That which keeps us the little that we are,
The aid of greatness to be and the force.


### III

This is the true creator, the waver
Waving purpling wands, the thinker
Thinking gold thoughts in a golden mind,
Loftily jingled, radiant,
The joy of meaning in design
Wrenched out of chaos . . . The quiet lamp
For this creator is a lamp
Enlarging like a nocturnal ray
The space in which it stands, the shine
Of darkness, creating from nothingness
Such black constructions, such public shapes
And murky masonry, one wonders
At the finger that brushes this aside
Gigantic in everything but size.


### IV

The unnamed creator of an unknown sphere,
Unknown as yet, unknowable,
Uncertain certainty, Apollo
Imagined among the indigenes
And Eden conceived on Morningside,
The center of the self, the self
Of the future, of future man
And future place, when these are known,
A freedom at last from the mystical,
The beginning of a final order,
The order of man's right to be
As he is, the discipline of his scope
Observed as an absolute, himself.

A longer, deeper breath sustains
The eloquence of right, since knowing
And being are one: the right to know
And the right to be are one. We come
To knowledge when we come to life.
Yet always there is another life,
A life beyond this present knowing,
A life lighter than this present splendor,
Brighter, perfected and distant away,
Not to be reached but to be known,
Not an attainment of the will
But something illogically received,
A divination, a letting down
From loftiness, misgivings dazzlingly
Resolved in dazzling discovery.
There is no map of paradise.
The great Omnium descends on us
As a free race. We know it, one
By one, in the right of all. Each man
Is an approach to the vigilance
In which the litter of truths becomes
A whole, the day on which the last star
Has been counted, the genealogy
Of gods and men destroyed, the right
To know established as the right to be.
The ancient symbols will be nothing then.
We shall have gone behind the symbols
To that which they symbolized, away
From the rumors of the speech-full domes,
To the chatter that is then the true legend,
Like glitter ascended into fire.

VI

Master of the world and of himself,
He came to this by knowledge or

Will come. His mind presents the world
And in his mind the world revolves.
The revolutions through day and night,
Through wild spaces of other suns and moons,
Round summer and angular winter and winds,
Are matched by other revolutions
In which the world goes round and round
In the crystal atmospheres of the mind,
Light's comedies, dark's tragedies,
Like things produced by a climate, the world
Goes round in the climates of the mind
And bears its floraisons of imagery.

The mind renews the world in a verse,
A passage of music, a paragraph
By a right philosopher: renews
And possesses by sincere insight
In the John-begat-Jacob of what we know,
The flights through space, changing habitudes.

In the generations of thought, man's sons
And heirs are powers of the mind,
His only testament and estate.
He has nothing but the truth to leave.
How then shall the mind be less than free
Since only to know is to be free?

VII

The living man in the present place,
Always, the particular thought
Among Plantagenet abstractions,
Always and always, the difficult inch,
On which the vast arches of space
Repose, always, the credible thought
From which the incredible systems spring,
The little confine soon unconfined
In stellar largenesses—these
Are the manifestations of a law

That bends the particulars to the abstract,
Makes them a pack on a giant's back,
A majestic mother's flocking brood,
As if abstractions were, themselves
Particulars of a relative sublime.
This is not poet's ease of mind.
It is the fate that dwells in truth.
We obey the coaxings of our end.

VIII

What is the shape of the sibyl? Not,
For a change, the englistered woman, seated
In colorings harmonious, dewed and dashed
By them: gorgeous symbol seated
On the seat of halidom, rainbowed,
Piercing the spirit by appearance,
A summing up of the loftiest lives
And their directing sceptre, the crown
And final effulgence and delving show.
It is the sibyl of the self,
The self as sibyl, whose diamond,
Whose chiefest embracing of all wealth
Is poverty, whose jewel found
At the exactest central of the earth
Is need. For this, the sibyl's shape
Is a blind thing fumbling for its form,
A form that is lame, a hand, a back,
A dream too poor, too destitute
To be remembered, the old shape
Worn and leaning to nothingness,
A woman looking down the road,
A child asleep in its own life.
As these depend, so must they use.
They measure the right to use. Need makes
The right to use. Need names on its breath
Categories of bleak necessity,
Which, just to name, is to create
A help, a right to help, a right

To know what helps and to attain,
By right of knowing, another plane.
The englistered woman is now seen
In an isolation, separate
From the human in humanity,
A part of the inhuman more,
The still inhuman more, and yet
An inhuman of our features, known
And unknown, inhuman for a little while,
Inhuman for a little, lesser time."

*The great sail of Ulysses seemed,*
*In the breathings of this soliloquy,*
*Alive with an enigma's flittering . . .*
*As if another sail went on*
*Straight forwardly through another night*
*And clumped stars dangled all the way.*

## PRESENCE OF AN EXTERNAL MASTER
## OF KNOWLEDGE

Under the shape of his sail, Ulysses,
Symbol of the seeker, crossing by night
The giant sea, read his own mind.
He said, "As I know, I am and have
The right to be." He guided his boat
Beneath the middle stars and said:

"Here I feel the human loneliness
And that, in space and solitude,
Which knowledge is: the world and fate,
The right within me and about me,
Joined in a triumphant vigor,
Like a direction on which I depend . . .

A longer, deeper breath sustains
This eloquence of right, since knowing

And being are one—the right to know
Is equal to the right to be.
The great Omnium descends on me,
Like an absolute out of this eloquence."

The sharp sail of Ulysses seemed,
In the breathings of that soliloquy,
Alive with an enigma's flittering,
And bodying, and being there,
As he moved, straightly, on and on,
Through clumped stars dangling all the way.

## A CHILD ASLEEP IN ITS OWN LIFE

Among the old men that you know,
There is one, unnamed, that broods
On all the rest, in heavy thought.

They are nothing, except in the universe
Of that single mind. He regards them
Outwardly and knows them inwardly,

The sole emperor of what they are,
Distant, yet close enough to wake
The chords above your bed to-night.

## TWO LETTERS

I

*A Letter From*

Even if there had been a crescent moon
On every cloud-tip over the heavens,
Drenching the evening with crystals' light,

One would have wanted more—more—more—
Some true interior to which to return,
A home against one's self, a darkness,

An ease in which to live a moment's life,
The moment of life's love and fortune,
Free from everything else, free above all from thought.

It would have been like lighting a candle,
Like leaning on the table, shading one's eyes,
And hearing a tale one wanted intensely to hear,

As if we were all seated together again
And one of us spoke and all of us believed
What we heard and the light, though little, was enough.


II

*A Letter To*

She wanted a holiday
With someone to speak her dulcied native tongue,

In the shadows of a wood . . .
Shadows, woods . . . and the two of them in speech,

In a secrecy of words
Opened out within a secrecy of place,

Not having to do with love.
A land would hold her in its arms that day

Or something much like a land.
The circle would no longer be broken but closed.

The miles of distance away
From everything would end. It would all meet.

# CONVERSATION WITH THREE WOMEN
## OF NEW ENGLAND

The mode of the person becomes the mode of the world,
For that person, and, sometimes, for the world itself.
The contents of the mind become solid show
Or almost solid seem show—the way a fly bird
Fixes itself in its inevitable bush . . .
It follows that to change modes is to change the world.

Now, you, for instance, are of this mode: You say
That in that ever-dark central, wherever it is,
In the central of earth or sky or air or thought,
There is a drop that is life's element,
Sole, single source and minimum patriarch,
The one thing common to all life, the human
And inhuman same, the likeness of things unlike.

And you, you say that the capital things of the mind
Should be as natural as natural objects,
So that a carved king found in a jungle, huge
And weathered, should be part of a human landscape,
That a figure reclining among columns toppled down,
Stiff in eternal lethargy, should be,
Not the beginning but the end of artifice,
A nature of marble in a marble world.

And then, finally, it is you that say
That only in man's definitions of himself,
Only encompassed in humanity, is he
Himself. The author of man's canons is man,
Not some outer patron and imaginer.

In which one of these three worlds are the four of us
The most at home? Or is it enough to have seen
And felt and known the differences we have seen
And felt and known in the colors in which we live,

In the excellences of the air we breathe,
The bouquet of being—enough to realize
That the sense of being changes as we talk,
That talk shifts the cycle of the scenes of kings?

## DINNER BELL IN THE WOODS

He was facing phantasma when the bell rang.
The picnic of children came running then,

In a burst of shouts, under the trees
And through the air. The smaller ones

Came tinkling on the grass to the table
Where the fattest women belled the glass.

The point of it was the way he heard it,
In the green, outside the door of phantasma.

## REALITY IS AN ACTIVITY OF THE MOST AUGUST IMAGINATION

Last Friday, in the big light of last Friday night,
We drove home from Cornwall to Hartford, late.

It was not a night blown at a glassworks in Vienna
Or Venice, motionless, gathering time and dust.

There was a crush of strength in a grinding going round,
Under the front of the westward evening star,

The vigor of glory, a glittering in the veins,
As things emerged and moved and were dissolved,

Either in distance, change or nothingness,
The visible transformations of summer night,

An argentine abstraction approaching form
And suddenly denying itself away.

There was an insolid billowing of the solid.
Night's moonlight lake was neither water nor air.

❦◇❦◇❦◇❦◇❦◇❦◇❦◇❦◇❦◇❦◇❦◇❦◇❦◇❦◇❦◇❦◇❦◇❦◇❦◇❦◇❦◇❦◇❦◇❦◇❦◇❦◇❦◇❦◇

## ON THE WAY TO THE BUS

A light snow, like frost, has fallen during the night.
Gloomily, the journalist confronts

Transparent man in a translated world,
In which he feeds on a new known,

In a season, a climate of morning, of elucidation,
A refreshment of cold air, cold breath,

A perception of cold breath, more revealing than
A perception of sleep, more powerful

Than a power of sleep, a clearness emerging
From cold, slightly irised, slightly bedazzled,

But a perfection emerging from a new known,
An understanding beyond journalism,

A way of pronouncing the word inside of one's tongue
Under the wintry trees of the terrace.

# SOLITAIRE UNDER THE OAKS

In the oblivion of cards
One exists among pure principles.

Neither the cards nor the trees nor the air
Persist as facts. This is an escape

To principium, to meditation.
One knows at last what to think about

And thinks about it without consciousness,
Under the oak trees, completely released.


# LOCAL OBJECTS

He knew that he was a spirit without a foyer
And that, in this knowledge, local objects become
More precious than the most precious objects of home:

The local objects of a world without a foyer,
Without a remembered past, a present past,
Or a present future, hoped for in present hope,

Objects not present as a matter of course
On the dark side of the heavens or the bright,
In that sphere with so few objects of its own.

Little existed for him but the few things
For which a fresh name always occurred, as if
He wanted to make them, keep them from perishing,

The few things, the objects of insight, the integrations
Of feeling, the things that came of their own accord,
Because he desired without quite knowing what,

That were the moments of the classic, the beautiful.
These were that serene he had always been approaching
As toward an absolute foyer beyond romance.

## ARTIFICIAL POPULATIONS

The centre that he sought was a state of mind,
Nothing more, like weather after it has cleared—
Well, more than that, like weather when it has cleared
And the two poles continue to maintain it

And the Orient and the Occident embrace
To form that weather's appropriate people,
The rosy men and the women of the rose,
Astute in being what they are made to be.

This artificial population is like
A healing-point in the sickness of the mind:
Like angels resting on a rustic steeple
Or a confect of leafy faces in a tree—

A health—and the faces in a summer night.
So, too, of the races of appropriate people
Of the wind, of the wind as it deepens, and late sleep,
And music that lasts long and lives the more.

## A CLEAR DAY AND NO MEMORIES

No soldiers in the scenery,
No thoughts of people now dead,

As they were fifty years ago:
Young and living in a live air,
Young and walking in the sunshine,
Bending in blue dresses to touch something—
Today the mind is not part of the weather.

Today the air is clear of everything.
It has no knowledge except of nothingness
And it flows over us without meanings,
As if none of us had ever been here before
And are not now: in this shallow spectacle,
This invisible activity, this sense.

## BANJO BOOMER

The mulberry is a double tree.
Mulberry, shade me, shade me awhile.

A white, pink, purple berry tree,
A very dark-leaved berry tree.
Mulberry, shade me, shade me awhile.

A churchyard kind of bush as well,
A silent sort of bush, as well.
Mulberry, shade me, shade me awhile.

It is a shape of life described
By another shape without a word.
Mulberry, shade me, shade me awhile—

With nothing fixed by a single word.
Mulberry, shade me, shade me awhile.

## JULY MOUNTAIN

We live in a constellation
Of patches and of pitches,
Not in a single world,
In things said well in music,
On the piano, and in speech,
As in a page of poetry—
Thinkers without final thoughts
In an always incipient cosmos,
The way, when we climb a mountain,
Vermont throws itself together.


## THE REGION NOVEMBER

It is hard to hear the north wind again,
And to watch the treetops, as they sway.

They sway, deeply and loudly, in an effort,
So much less than feeling, so much less than speech,

Saying and saying, the way things say
On the level of that which is not yet knowledge:

A revelation not yet intended.
It is like a critic of God, the world

And human nature, pensively seated
On the waste throne of his own wilderness.

Deeplier, deeplier, loudlier, loudlier,
The trees are swaying, swaying, swaying.

## "A MYTHOLOGY REFLECTS ITS REGION . . ."

A mythology reflects its region. Here
In Connecticut, we never lived in a time
When mythology was possible—But if we had—
That raises the question of the image's truth.
The image must be of the nature of its creator.
It is the nature of its creator increased,
Heightened. It is he, anew, in a freshened youth
And it is he in the substance of his region,
Wood of his forests and stone out of his fields
Or from under his mountains.

## OF MERE BEING

The palm at the end of the mind,
Beyond the last thought, rises
In the bronze decor,

A gold-feathered bird
Sings in the palm, without human meaning,
Without human feeling, a foreign song.

You know then that it is not the reason
That makes us happy or unhappy.
The bird sings. Its feathers shine.

The palm stands on the edge of space.
The wind moves slowly in the branches.
The bird's fire-fangled feathers dangle down.

## MOMENT OF LIGHT

I feel an apparition,
at my back,
an ebon wrack,
of more than man's condition,
that leans upon me there;
and then in back, one more;
and then, still farther back,
still other men aligned;
and then, toujours plus grands, immensities of night,
who, less and less defined
by light,
stretch off in the black:

ancestors from the first days of the world.

Before me, I know more,
one smaller at the first, and then one smaller still,
and more and more, that are my son and then his sons.

They lie buried in dumb sleep,
or bury themselves in the future.

And for the time, just one exists:
I.
Just one exists and I am time,
the whole of time.
I am the whole of light.

My flesh alone, for the moment, lives,
my heart alone gives,
my eyes alone have sight.
I am emblazoned, the others, all, are black.
I am the whole of light!
And those behind and those before
are only routineers of rounding time.

In back, they lie perdu in the black: the breachless grime,
(just one exists and I am time)
in front, they lie in the ruddyings
of an incalculable ether that burns and stings.
My will alone commands me: I am time!
Behind they passed the point of man,
before they are not embryo—I, only, touch with prime.
And that will last long length of time,
think what you will!

I am between two infinite states
on the mid-line dividing,
between the infinite that waits
and the long-abiding,
at the golden spot, where the mid-line swells
and yields to a supple, quivering, deep
inundation.

What do we count? All is for us that live!
Time, even time, and the day's strength and beam.
My fellows, you that live around me,
are you not surprised to be supreme,
on the tense line, in this expanse
of dual circumstance?
And are you not surprised to be the base
on which the eternal poising turns?
To know that, without you, the scale of lives
would sink upon death's pitty under-place?
And are you not surprised to be the very poles?

Let us make signals in the air and cry aloud.
We must leave a wide noise tolling
in the night;
and, in the deep of time,
set the wide wind rolling.

# THREE PARAPHRASES FROM
# LÉON-PAUL FARGUE

I should like to close this program by turning, now, for a very few minutes, to the work of someone else, a Frenchman, Léon-Paul Fargue, who lived as a poet all his life in Paris and died there two or three years ago. As a boy of eight or nine he was a member of Mallarmé's class in English at the Collège Rollin and ten years or more thereafter became one of those that were accustomed to gather in Mallarmé's apartment. He was a friend of Paul Valéry for fifty years. I suppose it could be said that during the greater part of the last half-century he knew everyone in Paris having to do with poetry. It is not possible to comment on his work beyond saying that most of his poems were prose poems. Claudine Chonez in a study that she made of him for the series, Poètes d'Aujourd'hui, Poets of To-Day, speaks (p. 66) of the solemnity of his strophe, of its somewhat ritual, not to say theatrical character. I shall read paraphrases of two of the poems contained in Poèmes (1912), his first book of importance, and the one best liked, and also of a page of his prose from Portraits de famille (1947). I call these translations paraphrases because, in order to carry over the sense of cadence, paraphrase seemed more useful than literal translation.

I

In a quarter made drowsy by the odor of its gardens and of its trees, the ramp of dreams, in the distance, accelerates and retards its chords, a little, in the autumn weather . . .

What gorgeous aspects cluster over their pale Calvary! What gestures evoke the chants of latent and unrealized dreams! What hands have opened penetrations into landscapes where things remembered come to sight like the perspectives of roofs seen by lightning . . .

A road lamp bides its time at the end of the gravel walk that leads to the villa lost beneath the leaves, in which a light rain still drips.

The angel is there, no doubt, at the keyboard, under the plume of the shade; and his noble visage, and his hands, on which the rings put forth touches toward the light, are bright with a steadfast flame.

The bird troubled by some secret of the Islands, and yet concealing it, picks up its song, in its basketry of gold!

A terrace of autumn. A white villa placed like something on the watch

144

at the terminal of the walk in the bitter odor. A thought as of gold falls down with sad descent. The blinds have been drawn in the rooms in which the idylls are dead.

"Dans un quartier," Poèmes (1912)

## II

A fragrance of night, not to be defined, that brings on an obscure doubt, exquisite, tender, comes by the open window into the room where I am at work . . .

My cat watches the darkness, as rigid as a jug. A fortune of subtle seeing looks at me through its green eyes . . .

The lamp sings its slight song quietly, subdued as the song one hears in a shell. The lamp reaches out its placating hands. In its aureole, I hear the litanies, the choruses and the responses of flies. It lights up the flowers at the edge of the terrace. The nearest ones come forward timidly to see me, like a troop of dwarfs that discover an ogre . . .

The minute violin of a mosquito goes on and on. One could believe that a person was playing alone in a house at a remote distance . . . Insects fall with a sidewise fall and writhe gently on the table. A butterfly yellow as a wisp of straw drags itself along the little yellow valley that is my book . . .

A big clock outdoors intones drearily. Memories take motion like children dancing in a ring . . .

The cat stretches itself to the uttermost. Its nose traces in the air an imperceptible evolution. A fly fastens its scissors in the lamp . . .

Kitchen clatter mounts in a back-yard. Argumentative voices play at pigeon-vole. A carriage starts up and away. A train chugs at the next station. A long whistle rises far-off . . .

I think of someone whom I love, who is so little to be so separated, perhaps beyond the lands covered by the night, beyond the profundities of water. I am not able to engage her glance . . .

"Un Odeur nocturne," Poèmes (1912)

## III

Between the things of these twenty years, between the sensations of these twenty years and the eye of Segonzac, there have been exchanges, secret, puissant, unerring, which he has inscribed in lasting stone. His faces, his portraits, his Morin, whom he loves like a son, his strolls around circuses, his bathers of Saint-Tropez, his heads of calves, his willows and his harvests sometimes, for me, finish by having the documentary value of postage-stamps. What I want to say is that they illustrate messages of precise origin, well-defined sensations, about which it is impossible to be mistaken. For me, the true artist appears to be like that: he is a witness. Sometimes a guide. Through him should shine the time that inspired him, of which he has disengaged in traits of fire the special symbols, the forms, the views, the spiritual habit as well as the positions of trees or of villages that belong to this time round the carrousel. That the National Library has now hastened to recognize in Segonzac this social role and this talent compounded of instinct and authority, shows that our poor old country is far from being down and out.

I read recently in a review these lines over which I meditated: "What is left today of the misty sheets of water of Corot, of those glades where the gold of the sun filtered, rich and clear, through the foliage woven by Courbet, and of these celebrated slopes of the Seine, so Second Empire, of Renoir, of Manet, and of Monet? What is left of the rose and blue snows of Monet?

Yes: but where are last year's snows?"

What is left? Well, for one thing, men like Segonzac, who carry on, quite simply, who lead tradition by the hand, up to the point where it meets what is modern. A modernity which they pass through without becoming too splashed up, always to find again, on the appointed day, the durable, the classic, the incontestable.

"Segonzac, ou l'artiste," *Portraits de famille* (1947)

# PLAYS

# THREE TRAVELERS WATCH A SUNRISE

*The characters are three Chinese, two negroes and a girl.*

*The scene represents a forest of heavy trees on a hilltop in eastern Penn-sylvania. To the right is a road, obscured by bushes. It is about four o'clock of a morning in August, at the present time.*

*When the curtain rises, the stage is dark. The limb of a tree creaks. A negro carrying a lantern passes along the road. The sound is repeated. The negro comes through the bushes, raises his lantern and looks through the trees. Discerning a dark object among the branches, he shrinks back, crosses stage, and goes out through the wood to the left.*

*A second negro comes through the bushes to the right. He carries two large baskets, which he places on the ground just inside of the bushes. Enter three Chinese, one of whom carries a lantern. They pause on the road.*

SECOND CHINESE

    All you need,
    To find poetry,
    Is to look for it with a lantern.
            [*The Chinese laugh.*]

THIRD CHINESE

    I could find it without,
    On an August night,
    If I saw no more
    Than the dew on the barns.
            [*The Second Negro makes a sound to attract their attention. The three Chinese come through the bushes. The first is short, fat, quizzical, and of middle age. The second is of middle height, thin and turning gray; a man of sense and sympathy. The third is a young man, intent, detached. They wear European clothes.*]

149

SECOND CHINESE [*glancing at the baskets*]

> Dew is water to see,
> Not water to drink:
> We have forgotten water to drink.
> Yet I am content
> Just to see sunrise again.
> I have not seen it
> Since the day we left Pekin.
> It filled my doorway,
> Like whispering women.

FIRST CHINESE

> And I have never seen it.
> If we have no water,
> Do find a melon for me
> In the baskets.

> > [*The Second Negro, who has been opening the baskets, hands the First Chinese a melon.*]

FIRST CHINESE

> Is there no spring?

> > [*The negro takes a water bottle of red porcelain from one of the baskets and places it near the Third Chinese.*]

SECOND CHINESE [*to Third Chinese*]

> Your porcelain water bottle.

> > [*One of the baskets contains costumes of silk, red, blue and green. During the following speeches, the Chinese put on these costumes, with the assistance of the negro, and seat themselves on the ground.*]

THIRD CHINESE

> This fetches its own water.

> > [*Takes the bottle and places it on the ground in the center of the stage.*]

> I drink from it, dry as it is,
> As you from maxims, [*to Second Chinese*]
> Or you from melons. [*to First Chinese*]

FIRST CHINESE

> Not as I, from melons.
> Be sure of that.

SECOND CHINESE

> Well, it is true of maxims.

[*He finds a book in the pocket of his costume, and reads from it.*]

"The court had known poverty and wretchedness; humanity had invaded its seclusion, with its suffering and its pity."

[*The limb of the tree creaks.*]

Yes: it is true of maxims,
Just as it is true of poets,
Or wise men, or nobles,
Or jade.

FIRST CHINESE

Drink from wise men? From jade?
Is there no spring?

[*Turning to the negro, who has taken a jug from one of the baskets.*]

Fill it and return.

[*The negro removes a large candle from one of the baskets and hands it to the First Chinese; then takes the jug and the lantern and enters the trees to the left. The First Chinese lights the candle and places it on the ground near the water bottle.*]

THIRD CHINESE

There is a seclusion of porcelain
That humanity never invades.

FIRST CHINESE [*with sarcasm*]

Porcelain!

THIRD CHINESE

It is like the seclusion of sunrise,
Before it shines on any house.

FIRST CHINESE

Pooh!

SECOND CHINESE

This candle is the sun;
This bottle is earth:
It is an illustration
Used by generations of hermits.
The point of difference from reality
Is this:
That, in this illustration,
The earth remains of one color—
It remains red,

It remains what it is.
But when the sun shines on the earth,
In reality
It does not shine on a thing that remains
What it was yesterday.
The sun rises
On whatever the earth happens to be.

THIRD CHINESE

And there are indeterminate moments
Before it rises,
Like this,

[*with a backward gesture*]

Before one can tell
What the bottle is going to be—
Porcelain, Venetian glass,
Egyptian . . .
Well, there are moments
When the candle, sputtering up,
Finds itself in seclusion,

[*He raises the candle in the air.*]

And shines, perhaps, for the beauty of shining.
That is the seclusion of sunrise
Before it shines on any house.

[*replacing the candle*]

FIRST CHINESE [*wagging his head*]

As abstract as porcelain.

SECOND CHINESE

Such seclusion knows beauty
As the court knew it.
The court woke
In its windless pavilions,
And gazed on chosen mornings,
As it gazed
On chosen porcelain.
What the court saw was always of the same color,
And well shaped,
And seen in a clear light.

[*He points to the candle.*]

It never woke to see,
And never knew,

152

The flawed jars,
The weak colors,
The contorted glass.
It never knew
The poor lights.
                [*He opens his book significantly.*]
When the court knew beauty only,
And in seclusion,
It had neither love nor wisdom.
These came through poverty
And wretchedness,
Through suffering and pity.
                [*He pauses.*]
It is the invasion of humanity
That counts.

                [*The limb of the tree creaks. The First Chinese turns,
                for a moment, in the direction of the sound.*]

FIRST CHINESE [*thoughtfully*]
        The light of the most tranquil candle
        Would shudder on a bloody salver.
SECOND CHINESE [*with a gesture of disregard*]
        It is the invasion
        That counts.
        If it be supposed that we are three figures
        Painted on porcelain
        As we sit here,
        That we are painted on this very bottle,
        The hermit of the place,
        Holding this candle to us,
        Would wonder;
        But if it be suppposed
        That we are painted as warriors,
        The candle would tremble in his hands;
        Or if it be supposed, for example,
        That we are painted as three dead men,
        He could not see the steadiest light
        For sorrow.
        It would be true
        If the emperor himself
        Held the candle.

He would forget the porcelain
For the figures painted on it.

THIRD CHINESE [*shrugging his shoulders*]

Let the candle shine for the beauty of shining.
I dislike the invasion
And long for the windless pavilions.
And yet it may be true
That nothing is beautiful
Except with reference to ourselves,
Nor ugly,
Nor high,

[*pointing to the sky*]

Nor low.

[*pointing to the candle*]

No: not even sunrise.
Can you play of this

[*mockingly to First Chinese*]

For us?

[*He stands up.*]

FIRST CHINESE [*hesitatingly*]

I have a song
Called *Mistress and Maid.*
It is of no interest to hermits
Or emperors,
Yet it has a bearing;
For if we affect sunrise,
We affect all things.

THIRD CHINESE

It is a pity it is of women.
Sing it.

[*He takes an instrument from one of the baskets and hands it to the First Chinese, who sings the following song, accompanying himself, somewhat tunelessly, on the instrument. The Third Chinese takes various things out of the basket for tea. He arranges fruit. The First Chinese watches him while he plays. The Second Chinese gazes at the ground. The sky shows the first signs of morning.*]

FIRST CHINESE

The mistress says, in a harsh voice,

154

"He will be thinking in strange countries
   Of the white stones near my door,
   And I—I am tired of him."
She says, sharply, to her maid,
   "Sing to yourself no more."

Then the maid says, to herself,
   "He will be thinking in strange countries
   Of the white stones near her door;
   But it is me he will see
   At the window, as before.

   "He will be thinking in strange countries
   Of the green gown I wore.
   He was saying good-by to her."
The maid drops her eyes and says to her mistress,
   "I shall sing to myself no more."

THIRD CHINESE
   That affects the white stones,
   To be sure.
                    [*They laugh.*]

FIRST CHINESE
   And it affects the green gown.

SECOND CHINESE
   Here comes our black man.
                    [*The Second Negro returns, somewhat agitated, with
                    water but without his lantern. He hands the jug to
                    the Third Chinese. The First Chinese from time to
                    time strikes the instrument. The Third Chinese, who
                    faces the left, peers in the direction from which the
                    negro has come.*]

THIRD CHINESE
   You have left your lantern behind you.
   It shines, among the trees,
   Like evening Venus in a cloud-top.
                    [*The Second Negro grins but makes no explanation.
                    He seats himself behind the Chinese to the right.*]

FIRST CHINESE
   Or like a ripe strawberry
   Among its leaves.

[*They laugh.*]
I heard tonight
That they are searching the hill
For an Italian.
He disappeared with his neighbor's daughter.
SECOND CHINESE [*confidingly*]
I am sure you heard
The first eloping footfall,
And the drum
Of pursuing feet.
FIRST CHINESE [*amusedly*]
It was not an elopement.
The young gentleman was seen
To climb the hill
In the manner of a tragedian
Who sweats.
Such things happen in the evening.
He was
*Un misérable.*
SECOND CHINESE
Reach the lady quickly.

> [*The First Chinese strikes the instrument twice as a prelude to his narrative.*]

FIRST CHINESE
There are as many points of view
From which to regard her
As there are sides to a round bottle.

> [*pointing to the water bottle*]

She was represented to me
As beautiful.

> [*They laugh. The First Chinese strikes the instrument, and looks at the Third Chinese, who yawns.*]

FIRST CHINESE [*reciting*]
She was as beautiful as a porcelain water bottle.

> [*He strikes the instrument in an insinuating manner.*]

FIRST CHINESE
She was represented to me
As young.
Therefore my song should go
Of the color of blood.

[*He strikes the instrument. The limb of the tree creaks. The First Chinese notices it and puts his hand on the knee of the Second Chinese, who is seated between him and the Third Chinese, to call attention to the sound. They are all seated so that they do not face the spot from which the sound comes. A dark object, hanging to the limb of the tree, becomes a dim silhouette. The sky grows constantly brighter. No color is to be seen until the end of the play.*]

SECOND CHINESE [*to First Chinese*]

     It is only a tree
     Creaking in the night wind.

THIRD CHINESE [*shrugging his shoulders*]

     There would be no creaking
     In the windless pavilions.

FIRST CHINESE [*resuming*]

     So far the lady of the present ballad
     Would have been studied
     By the hermit and his candle
     With much philosophy;
     And possibly the emperor would have cried,
     "More light!"
     But it is a way with ballads
     That the more pleasing they are
     The worse end they come to;
     For here it was also represented
     That the lady was poor—
     The hermit's candle would have thrown
     Alarming shadows,
     And the emperor would have held
     The porcelain in one hand . . .
     She was represented as clinging
     To that sweaty tragedian,
     And weeping up the hill.

SECOND CHINESE [*with a grimace*]

     It does not sound like an elopement.

FIRST CHINESE

     It is a doleful ballad,
     Fit for keyholes.

THIRD CHINESE

Shall we hear more?

SECOND CHINESE
Why not?

THIRD CHINESE
We came for isolation,
To rest in sunrise.

SECOND CHINESE [*raising his book slightly*]
But this will be a part of sunrise,
And can you tell how it will end?—
Venetian,
Egyptian,
Contorted glass . . .

> [*He turns toward the light in the sky to the right,
> darkening the candle with his hands.*]

In the meantime, the candle shines,

> [*indicating the sunrise*]

As you say,

> [*to the Third Chinese*]

For the beauty of shining.

FIRST CHINESE [*sympathetically*]
Oh! it will end badly.
The lady's father
Came clapping behind them
To the foot of the hill.
He came crying,
"Anna, Anna, Anna!"

> [*imitating*]

He was alone without her,
Just as the young gentleman
Was alone without her:
Three beggars, you see,
Begging for one another.

> [*The First Negro, carrying two lanterns, approaches
> cautiously through the trees. At the sight of him, the
> Second Negro, seated near the Chinese, jumps to his
> feet. The Chinese get up in alarm. The Second Negro
> goes around the Chinese toward the First Negro. All
> see the body of a man hanging to the limb of the tree.
> They gather together, keeping their eyes fixed on it.
> The First Negro comes out of the trees and places*]

*the lanterns on the ground. He looks at the group and
then at the body.*]

FIRST CHINESE [*moved*]

    The young gentleman of the ballad.

THIRD CHINESE [*slowly, approaching the body*]

    And the end of the ballad.

    Take away the bushes.

        [*The negroes commence to pull away the bushes.*]

SECOND CHINESE

    Death, the hermit,

    Needs no candle

    In his hermitage.

        [*The Second Chinese snuffs out the candle. The First
Chinese puts out the lanterns. As the bushes are
pulled away, the figure of a girl, sitting half stupefied
under the tree, suddenly becomes apparent to the
Second Chinese and then to the Third Chinese. They
step back. The negroes move to the left. When the
First Chinese sees the girl, the instrument slips from
his hands and falls noisily to the ground. The girl
stirs.*]

SECOND CHINESE [*to the girl*]

    Is that you, Anna?

        [*The girl starts. She raises her head, looks around
slowly, leaps to her feet and screams.*]

SECOND CHINESE [*gently*]

    Anna.

        [*She turns quickly toward the body, looks at it fixedly
and totters up the stage.*]

ANNA [*bitterly*]

    Go.

    Tell my father:

    He is dead.

        [*The Second and Third Chinese support her. The
First Negro whispers to the First Chinese, then takes
the lanterns and goes through the opening to the road,
where he disappears in the direction of the valley.*]

FIRST CHINESE [*to Second Negro*]

    Bring us fresh water

    From the spring.

[*The Second Negro takes the jug and enters the trees to the left. The girl comes gradually to herself. She looks at the Chinese and at the sky. She turns her back toward the body, shuddering, and does not look at it again.*]

ANNA

It will soon be sunrise.

SECOND CHINESE

One candle replaces
Another.

[*The First Chinese walks toward the bushes to the right. He stands by the roadside, as if to attract the attention of anyone passing.*]

ANNA [*simply*]

When he was in his fields,
I worked in ours—
Wore purple to see;
And when I was in his garden
I wore gold ear-rings.
Last evening I met him on the road.
He asked me to walk with him
To the top of the hill.
I felt the evil,
But he wanted nothing.
He hanged himself in front of me.

[*She looks for support. The Second and Third Chinese help her toward the road. At the roadside, the First Chinese takes the place of the Third Chinese. The girl and the two Chinese go through the bushes and disappear down the road. The stage is empty except for the Third Chinese. He walks slowly across the stage, pushing the instrument out of his way with his foot. It reverberates. He looks at the water bottle.*]

THIRD CHINESE

Of the color of blood ...
Seclusion of porcelain ...
Seclusion of sunrise ...

[*He picks up the water bottle.*]

The candle of the sun

160

Will shine soon
On this hermit earth.
            [*indicating the bottle*]
It will shine soon
Upon the trees,
And find a new thing
            [*indicating the body*]
Painted on this porcelain,
            [*indicating the trees*]
But not on this.
            [*indicating the bottle*]
            [*He places the bottle on the ground. A narrow cloud
            over the valley becomes red. He turns toward it, then
            walks to the right. He finds the book of the Second
            Chinese lying on the ground, picks it up and turns
            over the leaves.*]
Red is not only
The color of blood,
Or
            [*indicating the body*]
Of a man's eyes,
Or
            [*pointedly*]
Of a girl's.
And as the red of the sun
Is one thing to me
And one thing to another,
So it is the green of one tree
            [*indicating*]
And the green of another,
Which without it would all be black.
Sunrise is multiplied,
Like the earth on which it shines,
By the eyes that open on it,
Even dead eyes,
As red is multiplied by the leaves of trees.
            [*Toward the end of this speech, the Second Negro
            comes from the trees to the left, without being seen.
            The Third Chinese, whose back is turned toward the
            negro, walks through the bushes to the right and*]

161

*disappears on the road. The negro looks around at the objects on the stage. He sees the instrument, seats himself before it and strikes it several times, listening to the sound. One or two birds twitter. A voice, urging a horse, is heard at a distance. There is the crack of a whip. The negro stands up, walks to the right and remains at the side of the road. The curtain falls slowly.]*

# CARLOS AMONG THE CANDLES

*The stage is indistinguishable when the curtain rises.*

*The room represented is semi-circular. In the center, at the back, is a large round window, covered by long curtains. There is a door at the right and one at the left. Farther forward on the stage there are two long, low, wooden tables, one at the right and one at the left. The walls and the curtains over the window are of a dark reddish-purple, with a dim pattern of antique gold.*

*Carlos is an eccentric pedant of about forty. He is dressed in black. He wears close-fitting breeches and a close-fitting, tightly-buttoned, short coat with long tails. His hair is rumpled. He leaps upon the stage through the door at the right. Nothing is visible through the door. He has a long thin white lighted taper, which he holds high above his head as he moves, fantastically, over the stage, examining the room in which he finds himself.*

*When he has completed examining the room, he tip-toes to the table at the right and lights a single candle at the edge of the table nearest the front of the stage. It is a thin black candle, not less than two feet high. All the other candles are like it. They give very little light.*

*He speaks in a lively manner, but is over-nice in sounding his words.*

*As the candle begins to burn, he steps back, regarding it. Nothing else is visible on the table.*

CARLOS:

How the solitude of this candle penetrates me! I light a candle in the darkness. It fills the darkness with solitude, which becomes my own. I become a part of the solitude of the candle . . . of the darkness flowing over the house and into it . . . This room . . . and the profound room outside . . . Just to go through a door, and the change . . . the becoming a part, instantly, of that profounder room . . . and equally to feel it communicating, with the same persistency, its own mood, its own influence . . . and there, too, to feel the lesser influences of the shapes of things, of exhalations, sounds . . . to feel the mood of the candle vanishing and the mood of the special night coming to take its place . . .

> [*He sighs. After a pause he pirouettes, and then continues.*]

I was always affected by the grand style. And yet I have been thinking neither of mountains nor of morgues . . . To think of this light and of myself . . . it is a duty . . . Is it because it makes me think of myself in other places in such a light . . . or of other people in other places in such a light? How true that is: other people in other places in such a light . . . If I looked in at that window and saw a single candle burning in an empty room . . . but if I saw a figure . . . If, now, I felt that there was someone outside . . . The vague influence . . . the influence that clutches . . . But it is not only here and now . . . It is in the morning . . . the difference between a small window and a large window . . . a blue window and a green window . . . It is in the afternoon and in the evening . . . in effects, so drifting, that I know myself to be incalculable, since the causes of what I am are incalculable . . .

> [*He springs toward the table, flourishing his taper. At the end farthest from the front of the stage, he discovers a second candle, which he lights. He goes back to his former position.*]

The solitude dissolves . . . The light of two candles has a meaning different from the light of one . . . and an effect different from the effect of one . . . And the proof that that is so, is that I feel the difference . . . The associations have drifted a little and changed, and I have followed in this change . . . If I see myself in other places in such a light, it is not as I saw myself before. If I see other people in other places in such a light, the people and places are different from the people and places I saw before. The solitude is gone. It is as if a company of two or three people had just separated, or as if they were about to gather. These candles are too far apart.

> [*He flourishes his taper above the table and finds a third candle in the center of it, which he lights.*]

And yet with only two candles it would have been a cold and respectable company; for the feeling of coldness and respectability persists in the presence of three, modified a little, as if a kind of stateliness had modified into a kind of elegance . . . How far away from the isolation of the single candle, as arrogant of the vacancy around it as three are arrogant of association . . . It is no longer as if a company had just separated. It is only as if it were about to gather . . . as if one were soon to forget the room because of the people in the room . . . people tempered by the lights around

164

them, affected by the lights around them . . . sensible that one more candle would turn this formative elegance into formative luxury.

[*He lights a fourth candle. He indulges his humor.*]

And the suggestion of luxury into the suggestion of magnificence.

[*He lights a fifth candle.*]

And the beginning of magnificence into the beginning of splendor.

[*He lights a sixth candle. He sighs deeply.*]

In how short a time have I been solitary, then respectable—in a company so cold as to be stately, then elegant, then conscious of luxury, even magnificence; and now I come, gradually, to the beginning of splendor. Truly, I am a modern.

[*He dances around the room.*]

To have changed so often and so much . . . or to have been changed . . . to have been carried by the lighting of six candles through so many lives and to have been brought among so many people . . . This grows more wonderful. Six candles burn like an adventure that has been completed. They are established. They are a city . . . six common candles . . . seven . . .

[*He lights another and another, until he has lighted twelve, saying after them, in turn:*]

Eight, nine, ten, eleven, twelve.

[*Following this, he goes on tip-toe to the center of the stage, where he looks at the candles. Their brilliance has raised his spirits to the point of gaiety. He turns from the lighted table to face the dark one at the left. He holds his taper before him.*]

Darkness again . . . as if a night wind had come blowing . . . but too weakly to fling the cloth of darkness.

[*He goes to the window, draws one of the curtains a little and peers out. He sees nothing.*]

I had as lief look into night as look into the dark corner of a room. Darkness expels me.

[*He goes forward, holding his taper high above him, until he comes to the table at the left. He finds this covered with candles, like the table at the right, and lights them, with whimsical motions, one by one. When all the candles have been lighted, he runs to the center of the stage, holding his hands over his eyes. Then he returns to the window and flings aside the curtains. The light from the window falls on the*]

*tall stalks of flowers outside. The flowers are like holly-*
*hocks, but they are unnaturally large, of gold and*
*silver. He speaks excitedly.*]

Where now is my solitude and the lonely figure of solitude? Where now are the two stately ones that left their coldness behind them? They have taken their bareness with them. Their coldness has followed them. Here there will be silks and fans . . . the movement of arms . . . rumors of Renoir . . . coiffures . . . hands . . . scorn of Debussy . . . communications of body to body . . . There will be servants, as fat as plums, bearing pineapples from the Azores . . . because of twenty-four candles, burning together, as if their light had dispelled a phantasm, falling on silks and fans . . . the movement of arms . . . The pulse of the crowd will beat out the shallow pulses . . . it will fill me.

[*A strong gust of wind suddenly blows into the room,*
*extinguishing several of the candles on the table at*
*the left. He runs to the table at the left and looks, as*
*if startled, at the extinguished candles. He buries his*
*head in his arms.*]

That, too, was phantasm . . . The night wind came into the room . . . The fans are invisible upon the floor.

[*In a burst of feeling, he blows out all the candles*
*that are still burning on the table at the left. He*
*crosses the stage and stands before the table at the*
*right. After a moment he goes slowly to the back*
*of the stage and draws the curtains over the window.*
*He returns to the table at the right.*]

What is there in the extinguishing of light? It is like twelve wild birds flying in autumn.

[*He blows out one of the candles.*]

It is like an eleven-limbed oak tree, brass-colored in frost . . . Regret . . .

[*He blows out another candle.*]

It is like ten green sparks of a rocket, oscillating in air . . . The extinguishing of light . . . how closely regret follows it.

[*He blows out another candle.*]

It is like the diverging angles that follow nine leaves drifting in water, and that compose themselves brilliantly on the polished surface.

[*He blows out another candle.*]

It is like eight pears in a nude tree, flaming in twilight . . . The extinguishing of light is like that. The season is sorrowful. The air is cold.

[*He blows out another candle.*]

It is like the six Pleiades, and the hidden one, that makes them seven.

[*He blows out another candle.*]

It is like the seven Pleiades, and the hidden one, that makes them six.

[*He blows out another candle.*]

The extinguishing of light is like the five purple palmations of cinquefoil withering . . . It is full of the incipiencies of darkness . . . of desolation that rises as a feeling rises . . . Imagination wills the five purple palmations of cinquefoil. But in this light they have the appearance of withering . . . To feel and, in the midst of feeling, to imagine . . .

[*He blows out another candle.*]

The extinguishing of light is like the four posts of a cadaver, two at its head and two at its feet, to-wit: its arms and legs.

[*He blows out another candle.*]

It is like three peregrins, departing.

[*He blows out another candle.*]

It is like heaven and earth in the eye of the disbeliever.

[*He blows out another candle. He dances around the room. He returns to the single candle that remains burning.*]

The extinguishing of light is like that old Hesper, clapped upon by clouds.

[*He stands in front of the candle, so as to obscure it.*]

The spikes of his light bristle around the edge of the bulk. The spikes bristle among the clouds and behind them. There is a spot where he was bright in the sky . . . It remains fixed a little in the mind.

[*He opens the door at the right. Outside, the night is as blue as water. He crosses the stage and opens the door at the left. Once more he flings aside the curtains. He extinguishes his taper. He looks out. He speaks with elation.*]

Oh, ho! Here is matter beyond invention.

[*He springs through the window. Curtain.*]

# BOWL, CAT AND BROOMSTICK

*Two figures sit in the circle of a spotlight, on a white bench, before a golden curtain. The rest of the stage is obscure. Their shadows are strongly reflected on the curtain. One, at the right, wears a gown falling below his knees. It is black covered with a faded silver pattern. Flat hat. Jewel in the hat. Black stockings. Small silver buckles on his shoes. He is gaunt. He is reading aloud from a book which is bound in yellow paper, like a French book. The other figure is smaller and more supple. Tight green costume. He is listening closely. The floor of the stage has a violet covering.*

BOWL [*with finical importance*]: She says — m — m — she says — m. [*patronizing Cat*] I shall continue to translate this for you. Fleurs — des fleurs — full of flowers — full of tawny flowers —

CAT [*a little bored*]: Tawny? What is the word for tawny?

BOWL: *Rouges.*

CAT: But, Bowl, *rouges* means red.

BOWL [*coolly*]: No doubt, when it refers to something red. But when, as here, it refers to something tawny, then it means tawny.

> [*Broomstick saunters on the stage at the left. Heavily built. Hard-looking. Elderly. He uses a stick. Blue blouse, red sash, white trousers, like a French peasant. Bowl studies his book. Cat is interested in Broomstick's appearance.*]

BROOMSTICK [*brusquely*]: Bibliophiles!

CAT [*very politely*]: Bowl is reading from the poems of Claire Dupray.

BROOMSTICK: Charming!

> [*He seats himself on the bench.*]

CAT: What was the line you read last, Bowl?

BOWL [*with chilly diffidence*]: Le jardin est si plein de fleurs rouges ... The garden is so full of tawny flowers.

BROOMSTICK: Remarkable!

CAT: He translates *fleurs rouges* by tawny flowers.

168

BROOMSTICK: Why not?

CAT: But, of course, *rouges* means red.

BROOMSTICK: A man with so firm a faith in the meaning of words should not listen to poetry.

CAT: Broomstick!

> [*Bowl turns to the frontispiece of his book. Cat looks furtively at the portrait there.*]

BOWL: I say tawny because it is obvious that Claire Dupray means tawny.

BROOMSTICK: Her portrait tells you that?

BOWL: Yes; and her age tells me. She cannot be more than twenty-two.

CAT: And at twenty-two one does not like red flowers?

BOWL: At twenty-two, with eyes as large as those of Claire Dupray, with hair combed as a girl combs her hair—concealing in its arrangement the things it begins to disclose to her—and then, most of all, with the look she has here, one goes in for things that go with one's own mystery.

BROOMSTICK: And, of course, red flowers and one's own mystery—

BOWL: Are incongruous.

CAT: You see.

BOWL: They are incongruous at that age. It is an age when red becomes tawny, when blue becomes aerial—and when a girl, at least, when a girl like Claire Dupray, becomes a poetess.

CAT: Say poet—poet. I hate poetess.

BROOMSTICK: Oh, poetess is just the word at twenty-two! What you are thinking of is forty-two.

CAT: You are right, old Broomstick. May I see the portrait?

> [*Bowl hands him the book.*]

You speak of her hair because her head is bare.

BROOMSTICK: It is only the poetess of forty-two that sits for a portrait covered.

BOWL: I speak of her hair because in the case of a poetess, in the sense in which that word is just and beautiful, the speaking of it means so much to the portrait of her.

CAT: More than her nose or her chin? She has a delicate nose. She has a good chin.

BROOMSTICK: She has a good chin! Oh, ho! She has a good chin. Has she?

BOWL: Her hair reveals her. Three things live in the portrait of a poetess: her hair, her eyes and her mouth. These make it possible to discover something of what she is from the image of her. Claire Dupray has black hair. It is arranged simply, but, for all that, it remains full of the long

169

motions of her bare arms. Is not that a part of her? What are we to expect from such a poetess? Waxen odes? Skimped meditations? Let me have the book.

[*Cat hands him the book.*]

Take this poem on twilight. What does she see in twilight? Not the commonplace end of daily momentum. She sees the light continuing to burn in stars. She says that the sun burns all night. And, in that, she sees the incessant momentum that tranquillizes because of the knowledge that it is immortal. The sun burns all night. She says that she will love as long as she lives.

CAT [*fascinated*]: She is glorious.

BROOMSTICK: How little it would take to turn the poets into the only true comedians! There's no truer comedy than this hodge-podge of men and sunlight, women and moonlight, houses and clouds, and so on.

BOWL: Nor any truer tragedy.

BROOMSTICK: No one believes in tragedy.

CAT: At twenty-two—

BROOMSTICK: That brings us to her eyes.

BOWL: But her eyes are nothing unless you believe in tragedy.

CAT: I believe.

BROOMSTICK: Poor sensualist! You think you believe. The truth is, you believe in eyes.

CAT: Have you seen the portrait?

[*He hands Broomstick the book.*]

Now, we shall have Broomstick on eyes.

BROOMSTICK: I concede that these eyes are capable of tragedy. But that is not the same thing as tragedy itself: and it is tragedy itself that we were speaking of.

BOWL: Then let me amend what I said: and say, instead, that her eyes are nothing unless you believe in eyes.

BROOMSTICK: A very proper amendment. But I am rather old, don't you think, to believe in eyes? I have reached the point where I don't believe in much of anything except legs. And one cannot be too sure even of legs.

CAT: Legs are art, not literature.

BROOMSTICK: They were always intended to be.

CAT: They are still intended to be.

BOWL: All the more reason for saying no more about them. It is a new thing that the eyes of a poetess should bring us to this.

BROOMSTICK [*drily*]: Possibly. And yet it may not be so new, after all. [*He pauses.*] We are not living in the seventeenth century for nothing.

[*He pauses.*] Moreover, just as the relations of man and moonlight, women and moonlight, man and mountains, women and waves, and so on, are undefined, so the relations of eyes and legs, lips and cheeks, and that kind of thing, are equally undefined. It is all part of the universal comedy, which the poets ignore, because they continue to believe in tragedy. You see tragedy in these eyes. They are capable of tragedy. Does the voice of tragedy dwell in this mouth?

BOWL: I was not thinking of that. I was thinking merely of the expression it gives to the portrait. That expression is vitally biographical.

BROOMSTICK: Vitally biographical? The book has the usual preface. Is that not biographical enough?

CAT: We shall come to that in time.

BOWL [*making a point*]: We had agreed to skip it, for the moment, and to form our own idea of Claire Dupray from her portrait, and from her poetry. That is what we are doing.

CAT: Bowl is an idealist, you know.

BROOMSTICK: An idealist has nothing to fear from a preface.

CAT: That she has heavy, black hair, large eyes, capable of tragedy, as you say, which means, I hope, that they are brilliant and mysterious, for so I see them, and that her mouth is expressive, this seemed preface enough.

BROOMSTICK: It is the kind of preface you yourself would write and that is why you think it preface enough.

CAT [*offended*]: What do you mean?

BROOMSTICK [*putting him down*]: I assume that in what Bowl has been saying of this portrait he has been intending to derive from ink and paper a vivid impression of the sensibility of his poetess. You have seen only her beauty.

CAT [*as if justified*]: I make no bones about that. There is a special power in the poetry of a beauty.

BROOMSTICK: For you: yes.

CAT: For you, too.

BROOMSTICK [*maliciously*]: Pathos, perhaps; not power. But Bowl's portrait is a failure.

BOWL: A failure?

BROOMSTICK [*sarcastically*]: You might have been describing one of the many dark-haired and dark-eyed Peloponnesians. And what you say of the expressive quality of the mouth has been trite for a long time.

BOWL: And true for a long time.

BROOMSTICK: If it has been true for a long time, then I doubt if it is true any longer. The fact remains that your young poetess is an old poetess.

171

BOWL [*querulously*]: Ought her hair to be cropped?

BROOMSTICK: Unquestionably. Something of the sort.

CAT: Adieu, Dupray!

BROOMSTICK: I do not insist on the cropped hair.

CAT: But on something of the sort. Poor Claire!

BROOMSTICK: You judge her poetry by her portrait. Very well. I judge her portrait by her poetry.

BOWL: You are prejudiced by the cant of the moment that she should be of her day.

BROOMSTICK: That is far from being the cant of the moment. It will still be the cant of the moment in the eighteenth century, and in the nineteenth century, too.

BOWL: Broomstick, it galls me to agree with you. If I submit, will you go no farther?

BROOMSTICK: I shall go as far as possible. Take the book again.

[*He hands the book to Bowl.*]

Would it have any effect if she wore black pendants in her ears? It should have. Test her poetry by that. They are wearing black pendants, you know.

[*Cat snatches the book out of Bowl's hands.*]

CAT: Would it have any effect?

[*He laughs heartily.*]

Confound it, Bowl! What was that poem about? The incessant momentum that tranquillizes because of the knowledge that it is immortal. Tranquillity and long, black pendants!

[*Bowl recovers the book from him.*]

BOWL: As you like. My portrait is not a failure. Broomstick is right. A poetess should be of her day. But he is thinking of the poetess of forty-two: the sophisticated poetess. I am thinking of the unsophisticated poetess of twenty-two. If she happens to look like one of the dark-haired and dark-eyed Peloponnesians, that is not a rococo pose. It is an unaffected disclosure of her relationship.

CAT: Dupray returns, a little.

BOWL: And besides, Broomstick, what you mean, no doubt, by being of one's day is being one's self in one's day.

BROOMSTICK: Well, Bowl, I submit to that, provided you, in turn, go no farther.

BOWL: Only to the extent of saying that Claire Dupray is simply herself in this portrait. It is true that she is not of the long, black pendant type. Nevertheless, she is of her day, in the sense in which you used that phrase.

CAT [*succulently*]: And I may be tempted by her again?

BOWL: In the long run, you would have been tempted by her regardless of these, or any other, considerations; so that your question is not honest.

CAT [*brazenly*]: It is honest enough. I am still a little harrowed by the poem on twilight.

BROOMSTICK: It haunts my own mind.

BOWL [*to Cat*]: You said that there was a special power in the poetry of a beauty.

CAT [*alarmed*]: I said it. But I am not so certain of the beauty now.

BOWL: Then let me see.

[*He turns over the pages of the book rapidly.*]
"Banal Sojourn." "Old Catamaran"—an amazing thing in the way it designs the catamaran on the surface of the sea: one of the poems in which by the description of the thing seen, she makes an image of the greatest intensity. Nothing in nature could have revealed what her imagination and sensibility have revealed. How true that is to my conception of Claire Dupray! She is beautiful. Her poems are beautiful. Here are similar poems: "Les Dahlias"— "The Dahlias"—What an extraordinary effect one gets from seeing things as they are, that is to say: from looking at ordinary things intensely!

BROOMSTICK: But to look at ordinary things intensely, is not to see things as they are. However, go on.

BOWL: Here, in another division of her book, is a group of poems in which she studies herself—not the individual Claire Dupray, but the racial Claire—

CAT: Ah! The racial Claire.

BOWL: When you think of what the study of self used to mean, and then read these clear and thoughtful pages—

BROOMSTICK [*impatiently*]: Read them, read them. Please do.

BOWL: I thought you might like me to explain.

BROOMSTICK: I may, by and by; but if these pages are as clear as you say they are, then I am content to have you read them first.

BOWL [*translating à la mode*]: In the motion of trees, m — m— that is, in the movement of trees, I find my own agitation. If it be morning, the mood of poplars, filled with sunlight, glistening in the dark west-wind, is already my own. If it be noon, the tossing of the elm trees in the golden sky has an identity with my own exulting. And if it be evening, the forms of trees, moving not at all, defining their beauty through the obscure air, m — m — m— These things are atrociously difficult in English. In French, they seem almost pellucid. Let me see: the forms of trees, moving not at all,

173

outlining their beauty across the dim air, or in the midst of the dim air—the forms of trees are the only images in my mind. She means that the images in her mind are of the forms of trees and that there are no other images there.

> [*Cat takes the book from Bowl, turns to the portrait, looks at it, as if impressed, and then returns the book to Bowl, marking his place.*]

BOWL: Does not such a poem, so young, so communicative, warrant the definition of the poetess made by her portrait? How new she is!

BROOMSTICK [*astonished*]: New? But read another.

BOWL: One of "The Dahlias," this time. "Le Bouquet"—"The Bouquet." She tries to stimulate the sense of color and, therefore, her poem consists of nothing more than the names of colors. You read these rapidly and so produce in the mind a visual impression like that produced by the actual sight of dahlias.

BROOMSTICK: And that is a poem?

CAT [*apprehensively*]: Read just as rapidly as you can.

BOWL: Are you ready?

CAT: I am.

BROOMSTICK: I am ready.

BOWL: Green, green, green—no doubt, this indicates the stalks—green, green, green, green, green, yellow, green, yellow, green, green, gray, green, yellow, yellow, white, white, white, green—

BROOMSTICK: We ought to be getting to the flowers soon.

BOWL: We're right in them now. The white, white, white indicates white flowers, white dahlias.

BROOMSTICK: I am sorry. I was thinking of a white holder. I thought we had come up the stalks and were going around the edge of the holder.

CAT [*like a knowing person*]: This is really very promising; but not for Broomstick, I'm afraid.

BROOMSTICK: There might be some advantage in getting along.

BOWL: Shall I read another?

BROOMSTICK [*striking the floor with his cane*]: Provided I select it.

BOWL: Nothing would please me more.

> [*He hands the book to Broomstick, who refers to the index at the back.*]

BROOMSTICK [*with the hopeful manner of one consulting an index*]: "The Shadow in the Trees."

BOWL: That is the one I read you a moment ago, the one beginning, "In the movement of trees, I find my own agitation."

174

BROOMSTICK [*with disgust*]: An index is full of pit-falls.

CAT: Why do you say that? I thought "The Shadow in the Trees" rather lovely.

BROOMSTICK [*energetically*]: Pshaw! And imagine Bowl's thinking it new. Only because he wanted to think well of his poetess. She is young. Therefore she is new. Or therefore her poetry is young. That is one of the most persistent of all fallacies. Her poetry is young if her spirit is young— or whatever it is that poetry springs from. Not otherwise. This emotional waste, like the first poem, the one about twilight, this stale monism like "The Shadow in the Trees," this sophisticated green, green, green—it is all thirty years old at the least. Thirty years at the very least. I might even put it in the last century. But aside from the poems we have actually heard— and I dare say the book is full of others just like them—what I hold against Claire Dupray, above everything else, is just that she is not herself in her day. To be herself she must be free. She looks free [*looking at the portrait*]. But she is not free in spirit, and therefore her portrait fails.

BOWL: Free from what? I regarded "The Shadow in the Trees" as an instance of good seventeenth century work. And "Le Bouquet" seemed fairly advanced. Such things are not myths.

BROOMSTICK: The most fascinating myths in the world. To be free, Claire Dupray must be as free from to-day as from yesterday.

CAT: Rather difficult.

BROOMSTICK: Indescribably so. Look at people the world over. The extent and degree of imitation is appalling.

CAT: Necessarily, as a matter of convenience.

BROOMSTICK: Oh, but convenience is impossible in poetry. It is bad enough that Claire Dupray imitates at all. But it is fatal that she imitates the point of view and the feelings of a generation ago. Let her portrait be ever so charming. When all is said and done, she is a poetess in the old-maidenly sense of the word, not the brilliant and vivid creature you conceive her to be.

BOWL: In what year was her book published?

[*Broomstick examines the title page.*]

BROOMSTICK: In sixteen hundred and sixty.

CAT: If Bowl was right in supposing her to be twenty-two then, she would be twenty-nine or thirty now.

[*Cat makes a wry face. Bowl seems shocked. Broomstick turns a page or two.*]

BROOMSTICK [*with zest*]: Avant-Propos. You must help me with this, Bowl. My knowledge of French is not absolutely penetrating.

BOWL: Well, *avant-propos* means preface.

BROOMSTICK [*imitating Bowl*]: Claire Madeleine Colombier Dupray, the writer of the—m—the extraordinary poems gathered together in this volume, was born—m—in Geneva, of French parents. During the first fifteen years of her life she lived with her parents in Geneva, receiving instruction from her mother, a Calvinist, a woman of pronounced devotional character, and of wide reading.

> [*Cat goes behind Broomstick and looks over his shoulder. Bowl paces up and down the stage.*]

BROOMSTICK: It will interest my readers—What a nice old touch that is!—It will interest my readers to know that Madame Dupray—

BOWL [*with force*]: Madame?

> [*Cat puts his finger on the word over Broomstick's shoulder.*]

CAT: Mademoiselle, mademoiselle.

BROOMSTICK: I always confuse them. It will interest my readers to know that Mademoiselle Dupray still has in her possession some of the books from which she first became acquainted with—m—literature, in her early years.

BOWL [*protesting*]: Still has? Her early years?

CAT: Jeunesse. Youth.

BROOMSTICK: The abbot of Bellozane's translation of Plutarch's Lives, Florio's Dictionary, a volume of Du Bellay . . . There is a list of twenty or thirty in all. I shall skip them.

> [*Bowl is visibly affected.*]

BROOMSTICK: I gather that the books were selected by her mother. Piquant reading for a young French poetess.

> [*Cat takes the book from Broomstick and runs with it to Bowl.*]

CAT: Here is something about the portrait. Translate it, Bowl.

> [*Bowl looks at the preface. He seems incredulous. He looks at the portrait and then at the preface, and again at the portrait. He throws the book on the floor.*]

BOWL: What a fool I have been!

> [*He hurries off the stage. Cat is dumbfounded. Broomstick laughs loudly. Cat picks up the book and returns it to Broomstick.*]

CAT: What does it say about the portrait?

BROOMSTICK: Well, just here, skipping a few lines, the sentence you saw reads as follows: The frontispiece of this volume was etched in Amsterdam, from life, after Mademoiselle Dupray, at the age of twenty-three, in the year—

[He pauses.]

CAT: At the age of twenty-three, in the year—

BROOMSTICK: Sixteen hundred and thirty-seven.

CAT: Sixteen hundred and thirty-seven! If she was twenty-three in sixteen hundred and thirty-seven, she was forty-six in sixteen hundred and sixty when her poems were published. She is more than fifty now—fifty-three. She will love as long as she lives.

BROOMSTICK [cavalierly]: I think you are right, after all, in your translation of rouges.

CAT: Oh, red, red! Acutely red! Damn all portraits of poets and poetesses.

[Cat collapses. Broomstick laughs again, turning over the pages of the book.]

BROOMSTICK: One should always read a preface first.

[He helps Cat off the stage.]

## CURTAIN

# A CEREMONY

In the sixteen hundreds, three brothers left Holland to seek their fortunes. One found his way to Ceylon where he took up life with a herd of elephants. In his discourse before the elephants, he said that he was human, believing that this alone would be enough to establish himself among them. But the tradition of men among elephants was not the same as it was among men themselves; and the elephants concluding that man in general was less worthy of his tradition among other men than of his tradition among elephants condemned him and trampled him to death.

The second brother went to Brazil. Leaving the Dutch fort near Belem and pushing up the Amazon to a remote position, he was attacked by Indians, who had never before seen a Dutchman. When taken prisoner, he tried to procure his liberty by indicating, as best he could, that he was not an enemy, that in spite of many differences he and they were or could be friends and allies. The Indians, notwithstanding a tradition among them respecting Spaniards, determined to spare his life. They disarmed him and kept him a prisoner until his death. They held off from him, since they had no single tradition in common; and when they buried him they built a mound for him far from their own.

The third brother came to New Netherland and bought a farm at New Utrecht. He became a neighbor of people who had left Holland when he was a boy, to whom he brought letters and news from home and word of parents and friends. He had come from Leyden and was welcome, as any one from an old land is welcome among those that have left it and know it and know him. His merely being what he was composed of him and for him a tradition that was recognized. On his death he was buried under the altar of his church.

The ghosts of these three men met at dinner a long time later. The first ghost said of his discourse before the elephants that the appeal to tradition is not an appeal that can be made to barbarians, whether elephants or otherwise, since it is predicated on something that is held in common honor; and that it is this holding in common honor that gives it compulsion. The second ghost said of his dumb-show in the presence of the Indians that tradition is not ourselves imitating ourselves. If it was that, it would be what is left of the past and nothing more. Tradition is more than the memory and the customs of the memory. It is life's experiment made knowingly. The third ghost said that tradition is something that awakens a sense not only of that to which it relates but of itself. Thus when he had brought news of the university at Leyden to the fiscaal in New Amsterdam, when he had delivered messages from the many uncles who had stayed at home, when he had described the new banners in the old church, it was not only that the exiles to whom he spoke were back in Holland again, but that they felt a pride in having been, or of being still, a part of that of which such things could be said. The third ghost said that it is that pride, that warmth of feeling about many things, not only great things but also things small and dear to us, things held in common honor by those that have gone before us and by ourselves, that awaken a sense that tradition is like the revelations of an instinct.

At this moment, there entered into the room in which the three ghosts were having their dinner, together with a much larger company of persons dining there, as if they were a single body or society, a group of men carrying a kind of litter, on which they bore an ancient bird of lead, a cock desperate to be abroad with all his feathers fighting the wind. At this gallant sight, the whole company rose to salute the procession waving their napkins in the air in a storm, in the midst of which the three ghosts suddenly vanished.

FANFARE IN THE MODE

OF

MYNHEER VAN DONK

PROCESSION

# APHORISMS

## FROM
### *SUR PLUSIEURS BEAUX SUJECTS*

Success as the result of industry is a peasant ideal.

Success is to be happy with the wise.

Suppose any man whose spirit has survived had consulted his contemporaries as to what to do, or what to think, or what music to write, and so on.

In the long run the truth does not matter.

It should be said of poetry that it is essentially romantic as if one were recognizing the truth about poetry for the first time. Although the romantic is referred to, most often, in a pejorative sense, this sense attaches, or should attach, not to the romantic in general but to some phase of the romantic that has become stale. Just as there is always a romantic that is potent, so there is always a romantic that is impotent.

Ex Divina Pulchritudine esse omnium Derivatur, and, above all, poetry. And in reflecting on this think of it in connection with the association of poetry and pleasure and, also, in connection with l'instinct du bonheur. If happiness is in our selves, divine pulchritude is in our selves and poetry is a revelation or a contact.

Poetry creates a fictitious existence on an exquisite plane. This definition must vary as the plane varies, an exquisite plane being merely illustrative.

An objection to originality in poetry is an objection to poetry itself because originality is of the essence of the thing. Renard wrote to Rostand that one of his books was "jeune, surprenant, émouvant et joli." The original is the surprenant, even the émouvant.

◇◇◇◇◇◇◇◇◇◇◇◇◇◇◇◇◇◇◇◇◇◇◇◇◇◇◇◇◇◇◇◇◇◇◇◇◇◇◇◇◇◇◇◇◇◇◇◇◇◇◇◇

# ADAGIA

I

Happiness is an acquisition.

Progress in any aspect is a movement through changes of terminology.

The highest pursuit is the pursuit of happiness on earth.

L'art d'être heureuse.

Goethe's *General-Beichte* was written of another who "spake three thousand proverbs, and his songs were a thousand and five. From Goethe proverbs poured incessantly."
  *Goethe*: Felkin O. Univ. P. 1932.

Each age is a pigeon-hole.

The stream of consciousness is individual; the stream of life is total. Or, the stream of consciousness is individual; the stream of life, total.

To give a sense of the freshness or vividness of life is a valid purpose for poetry. A didactic purpose justifies itself in the mind of the teacher; a philosophical purpose justifies itself in the mind of the philosopher. It is not that one purpose is as justifiable as another but that some purposes are pure others impure. Seek those purposes that are purely the purposes of the pure poet.

The poet makes silk dresses out of worms.

The public of the poet. The public of the organist is the church in which he improvises.

Merit in poets is as boring as merit in people.

Authors are actors, books are theatres.

184

An attractive view: The aspects of earth of interest to a poet are the casual ones, as light or color, images.

Definitions are relative. The notion of absolutes is relative.

Life is an affair of people not of places. But for me life is an affair of places and that is the trouble.

Wisdom asks nothing more.

Parfait Martinique: coffee mousse, rum on top, a little cream on top of that.

Literature is the better part of life. To this it seems inevitably necessary to add provided life is the better part of literature.

Thought is an infection. In the case of certain thoughts it becomes an epidemic.

It is life that we are trying to get at in poetry.

After one has abandoned a belief in god, poetry is that essence which takes its place as life's redemption.

Art, broadly, is the form of life or the sound or color of life. Considered as form (in the abstract) it is often indistinguishable from life itself.

The poet seems to confer his identity on the reader. It is easiest to recognize this when listening to music—I mean this sort of thing: the transference.

Accuracy of observation is the equivalent of accuracy of thinking.

A poem is a meteor.

An evening's thought is like a day of clear weather.

The loss of a language creates confusion or dumbness.

The collecting of poetry from one's experience as one goes along is not the same thing as merely writing poetry.

The relation of art to life is of the first importance especially in a skeptical age since, in the absence of a belief in God, the mind turns to its own creations and examines them, not alone from the aesthetic point of view, but for what they reveal, for what they validate and invalidate, for the support that they give.

A grandiose subject is not an assurance of a grandiose effect but, most likely, of the opposite.

Art involves vastly more than the sense of beauty.

Life is the reflection of literature.

As life grows more terrible, its literature grows more terrible.

Poetry and materia poetica are interchangeable terms.

Usage is everything. (Les idées sont destinées à être déformées à l'usage. Reconnaître ce fait est une preuve de désintéressement. Georges Braque, Verve No. 2).

The imagination wishes to be indulged.

A new meaning is the equivalent of a new word.

Poetry is not personal.

The earth is not a building but a body.

Manner is an additional element.

A dead romantic is a falsification.

The romantic cannot be seen through: it is for the moment willingly not seen through.

Poetry is a means of redemption.

Poetry is a form of melancholia. Or rather, in melancholy it is one of the "aultres choses solatieuses."

The poet must come at least as the miraculous beast and, at his best, as the miraculous man.

(Poet,) feed my lambs.

The real is only the base. But it is the base.

Life cannot be based on a thesis, since, by nature, it is based on instinct. A thesis, however, is usually present and living is the struggle between thesis and instinct.

The poem reveals itself only to the ignorant man.

The relation between the poetry of experience and the poetry of rhetoric is not the same thing as the relation between the poetry of reality and that of the imagination. Experience, at least in the case of a poet of any scope, is much broader than reality.

To a large extent, the problems of poets are the problems of painters and poets must often turn to the literature of painting for a discussion of their own problems.

Weather is a sense of nature. Poetry is a sense.

Abstraction is a part of idealism. It is in that sense that it is ugly.

There are two opposites: the poetry of rhetoric and the poetry of experience.

In poetry at least the imagination must not detach itself from reality.

Not all objects are equal. The vice of imagism was that it did not recognize this.

The poet must put the same degree of intentness into his poetry as, for example, the traveller into his adventure, the painter into his painting.

All poetry is experimental poetry.

The bare image and the image as a symbol are the contrast: the image without meaning and the image as meaning. When the image is used to suggest something else, it is secondary. Poetry, as an imaginative thing, consists of more than lies on the surface.

Politics is the struggle for existence.

One has a sensibility range beyond which nothing really exists for one. And in each this is different.

In poetry, you must love the words, the ideas and images and rhythms with all your capacity to love anything at all.

The individual partakes of the whole. Except in extraordinary cases he never adds to it.

It is the belief and not the god that counts.

A journey in space equals a journey in time.

Things seen are things as seen. Absolute real.

Not all objects are equal.

What we see in the mind is as real to us as what we see by the eye.

Poetry must be irrational.

The purpose of poetry is to make life complete in itself.

Poetry increases the feeling for reality.

The mind is the most powerful thing in the world.

There is nothing in life except what one thinks of it.

A new future is good business.

Poetry is a form of melancholia.

There is nothing beautiful in life except life.

There is no wing like meaning.

Poetry is not a personal matter.

Poetry is a means of redemption.

Consider
I
That the whole world is material for poetry.
II
That there is not a specifically poetic material.

One reads poetry with one's nerves.

The poet is the intermediary between people and the world in which they live and, also, between people as between themselves; but not between people and some other world.

Sentimentality is a failure of feeling.

The imagination is the romantic.

Poetry is not the same thing as the imagination taken alone. Nothing is itself taken alone. Things are because of interrelations or interactions.

The final belief is to believe in a fiction, which you know to be a fiction, there being nothing else. The exquisite truth is to know that it is a fiction and that you believe in it willingly.


I
All of our ideas come from the natural world: Trees = umbrellas.
II
There is nothing so offensive to a man of intellectual principle as unprincipled thinking.

Wine and music are not good until afternoon. But poetry is like prayer in that it is most effective in solitude and in the times of solitude as, for example, in the earliest morning.

Intolerance respecting other people's religion is toleration itself in comparison with intolerance respecting other people's art.

The great objective is the truth not only of the poem but of poetry.

Poetry is a poetic conception, however expressed. A poem is poetry expressed in words. But in a poem there is a poetry of words. Obviously, a poem may consist of several poetries.

That part of the truth of the world that has its origin in the feelings.

The exposition of a theory of poetry involves comparison with other theories and the analysis of all.

Ethics are no more a part of poetry than they are of painting.

Poetry is the expression of the experience of poetry.

Values other than those merely of the eye and ear.

Seelenfriede durch Dichtung.

The ideal is the actual become anaemic. The romantic is often pretty much the same thing.

As the reason destroys, the poet must create.

The exquisite environment of fact. The final poem will be the poem of fact in the language of fact. But it will be the poem of fact not realized before.

We live in the mind.

A poet must have something by nature and he must know more about the world by reason thereof.

The poet feels *abundantly* the poetry of everything.

To live in the world but outside of existing conceptions of it.

It is the explanations of things that we make to ourselves that disclose our character:
The subjects of one's poems are the symbols of one's self or of one of one's selves.

Poetry has to be something more than a conception of the mind. It has to be a revelation of nature. Conceptions are artificial. Perceptions are essential.

A poem should be part of one's sense of life.

To read a poem should be an experience, like experiencing an act.

There is no difference between god and his temple.

War is the periodical failure of politics.

Money is a kind of poetry.

Poetry is an effort of a dissatisfied man to find satisfaction through words, occasionally of the dissatisfied thinker to find satisfaction through his emotions.

It is not every day that the world arranges itself in a poem.

The death of one god is the death of all.

In the presence of extraordinary actuality, consciousness takes the place of imagination.

Everything tends to become real; or everything moves in the direction of reality.

There is an intensely pejorative aspect of the idea of the real. The opposite should be the case. Its own poetry is actual.

One does not write for any reader except one.

Every man dies his own death.

The writer who is content to destroy is on a plane with the writer who is content to translate. Both are parasites.

The thing said must be the poem not the language used in saying it. At its best the poem consists of both elements.

A poet looks at the world somewhat as a man looks at a woman.

To have nothing to say and to say it in a tragic manner is not the same thing as to have something to say.

The poem is a nature created by the poet.

The aesthetic order includes all other orders but is not limited to them.

Religion is dependent on faith. But aesthetics is independent of faith. The relative positions of the two might be reversed. It is possible to establish aesthetics in the individual mind as immeasurably a greater thing than religion. Its present state is the result of the difficulty of establishing it except in the individual mind.

La vie est plus belle que les idées.

Perhaps there is a degree of perception at which what is real and what is imagined are one: a state of clairvoyant observation, accessible or possibly accessible to the poet or, say, the acutest poet.

The ultimate value is reality.

Realism is a corruption of reality.

Perhaps it is of more value to infuriate philosophers than to go along with them.

The world is the only thing fit to think about.

All history is modern history.

Poetry is the sum of its attributes.

I don't think we should insist that the poet is normal or, for that matter, that anybody is.

This happy creature—It is he that invented the Gods. It is he that put into their mouths the only words they have ever spoken.

Poetry is a purging of the world's poverty and change and evil and death. It is a present perfecting, a satisfaction in the irremediable poverty of life.

Poetry is the scholar's art.

The thing seen becomes the thing unseen. The opposite is, or seems to be, impossible.

To study and to understand the fictive world is the function of the poet.

When one is young everything is physical; when one is old everything is psychic.

Hermit of poetry.

Which is correct: whether, if I respect my ancestors I am bound to respect myself or if I respect myself I am bound to respect my ancestors?

Meine Seele muss Prachtung haben.

The most beautiful (the only beautiful) (beautiful is an inadequate and temporizing improvisation) thing in the world is, of course, the world itself. This is so not only logically but categorically.

I believe in the image.

The tongue is an eye.

God is a symbol for something that can as well take other forms, as, for example, the form of high poetry.

The satisfactions of nature.

The time will come when poems like Paradise will seem like very *triste* contraptions.

The poet is a stronger life.

The great conquest is the conquest of reality. It is not to present life, for a moment, as it might have been.

A poem is a pheasant.

How has the human spirit ever survived the terrific literature with which it has had to contend?

The gold dome of things is the perfected spirit.

Reality is a vacuum.

All men are murderers.

Poetry is metaphor.

The word must be the thing it represents otherwise it is a symbol. It is a question of identity.

When the mind is like a hall in which thought is like a voice speaking, the voice is always that of some one else.

In dramatic poetry the imagination attaches itself to a heightened reality. Degrees or planes of reality.

It is necessary to propose an enigma to the mind. The mind always proposes a solution.

There must be something of the peasant in every poet.

Aristotle is a skeleton.

The body is the great poem.

The purpose of poetry is to contribute to man's happiness.

There is a basic literature of which poetry is an essential part.

How things seem now is always a question of sensibility.

Man is an eternal sophomore.

It is necessary to any originality to have the courage to be an amateur.

Life is the elimination of what is dead.

The fundamental difficulty in any art is the problem of the normal.

The poet is the priest of the invisible.

Society is a sea.

Metaphor creates a new reality from which the original appears to be unreal.

The transition from make believe for one's self to make believe for others is the beginning, or the end, of poetry in the individual.

The acquisitions of poetry are fortuitous: trouvailles. (Hence, its disorder.)

Exhibitionism attaches and is not inherent.

Romanticism is to poetry what the decorative is to painting.

The great poem is the disengaging of (a) reality.

The eye sees less than the tongue says. The tongue says less than the mind thinks.

Reality is the motif.

We have to step boldly into man's interior world or not at all.

A living poetry that deals with everything or none.

To touch with the imagination in respect to reality.

The World Reduced to One Thing

Genealogy is the science of correcting other genealogists' mistakes.

The poet must not adapt his experience to that of the philosopher.

It is manner that becomes stale.

Description is an element, like air or water.

The reading of a poem should be an experience. Its writing must be all the more so.

A poem is a café. (Restoration.)

Poets acquire humanity.

Thought tends to collect in pools.

The reason is a part of nature and is controlled by it.

Life is not people and scene but thought and feeling.

In the world of words, the imagination is one of the forces of nature.

Life is not free from its forms.

The poet comes to words as nature comes to dry sticks.

Words are the only melodeon.

Bringing out the music of the eccentric sounds of words is no different in principle from bringing out their form & its eccentricities (Cummings): language as the material of poetry not its mere medium or instrument.

We have made too much of life. A journal of life is rarely a journal of happiness.

Since man made the world, the inevitable god is the beggar.

Poetry sometimes crowns the search for happiness. It is itself a search for happiness.

God is a postulate of the ego.

*Esthétique* is the measure of a civilization: not the sole measure, but a measure.

Poetry must resist the intelligence almost successfully.

The romantic exists in precision as well as in imprecision.

Literature is based not on life but on propositions about life, of which this is one.

Life is a composite of the propositions about it.

A change of style is a change of subject.

Poetry is the statement of a relation between a man and the world.

The feeling or the insight is that which quickens the words, not the other way round.

A man cannot search life for unprecedented experiences.

In children it is not the imitation that pleases us, but our perception of it. In later life, the pejorative aspect of imitation discloses its inherent unpleasantness. To give pleasure an imitation must have been studied as an imitation and then it pleases us as art.

Everything accomplishes itself: fulfills itself.

The imagination is not the only co-relation of reality. Science etc.

The romantic is the first phase of (a non-pejorative) lunacy.

The full flower of the actual, not the California fruit of the ideal.

In the end, the esthetic is completely crushed and destroyed by the inability of the observer who has himself been crushed to have any feeling for it left.

The world is myself. Life is myself.

II

God is in me or else is not at all (does not exist).

The world is a force, not a presence.

Loss of faith is growth.

People take the place of thoughts.

Life lived on the basis of opinion is more nearly life than life lived without opinion.

Thought is life.

Everyone takes sides in social change if it is profound enough.

Poetry is not limited to a single effect, as, for example, overt reality.

Poetry is a search for the inexplicable.

Poems are new subjects.

Ignorance is one of the sources of poetry.

Poetry is a pheasant disappearing in the brush.

We never arrive intellectually. But emotionally we arrive constantly (as in poetry, happiness, high mountains, vistas).

The imagination consumes & exhausts some element of reality.

The poet is a god or The young poet is a god. The old poet is a tramp.

198

If the mind is the most terrible force in the world, it is, also, the only force that defends us against terror. (or)

The mind is the most terrible force in the world principally in this that it is the only force that can defend us against itself. The modern world is based on this pensée.

The poet represents the mind in the act of defending us against itself.

Quaere, whether the residual satisfaction in a poem is the intellectual one.

No man is a hero to anyone that knows him.

On the bearing of the poet:
  1. The prestige of the poet is part of the prestige of poetry.
  2. The prestige of poetry is essential to the prestige of the poet.

The world is at the mercy of the strongest mind in it whether that strength is the strength of sanity or insanity, cunning or good-will.

Every poem is a poem within a poem: the poem of the idea within the poem of the words.

The poetic view of life is larger than any of its poems (a larger thing than any poem); and to recognize this is the beginning of the recognition of the poetic spirit.

On the death of some men the world reverts to ignorance.

Poetry is the gaiety (joy) of language.

Words are everything else in the world.

Only a noble people evolve a noble God.

If the answer is frivolous, the question was frivolous.

Unless life is interesting, there is nothing left (or, unless life is made interesting).

The interest of life is experienced by participating and by being part, not by observing nor by thinking.

Eventually an imaginary world is entirely without interest.

To be at the end of fact is not to be at the beginning of the imagination but it is to be at the end of both.

To sit in a park and listen to the locusts; to sit in a park and hear church-bells—two pasts or one present and one past?

What is meant by interest? Is it a form of liking?

One cannot spend one's time in being modern when there are so many more important things to be.

The man who asks questions seeks only to reach a point where it will no longer be necessary for him to ask questions.

I have no life except in poetry. No doubt that would be true if my whole life was free for poetry.

The more intensely one feels something that one likes the more one is willing for it to be what it is.

The mind is not equal to the demands of oratory, poetry etc.

There is a nature that absorbs the mixedness of metaphors.

The world of the poet depends on the world that he has contemplated.

Poetry is a health.

Poetry is great only as it exploits great ideas or what is often the same thing great feelings.

Imagination applied to the whole world is vapid in comparison to imagination applied to a detail.

It is easier to copy than to think, hence fashion. Besides a community of originals is not a community.

There must be some wing on which to fly.

Poetry is a cure of the mind.

Most modern reproducers of life, even including the camera, really repudiate it. We gulp down evil, choke at good.

We like the world because we do.

The mind that in heaven created the earth and the mind that on earth created heaven were, as it happened, one.

Nothing could be more inappropriate to American literature than its English source since the Americans are not British in sensibility.

Poetry is a response to the daily necessity of getting the world right.

A poem should stimulate the sense of living and of being alive.

Reality is the spirit's true centre.

A poem need not have a meaning and like most things in nature often does not have.

Newness (not novelty) may be the highest individual value in poetry. Even in the meretricious sense of newness a new poetry has value.

There is nothing in the world greater than reality. In this predicament we have to accept reality itself as the only genius.

Man is the imagination or rather the imagination is man.

To "subtilize experience" = to apprehend the complexity of the world, to perceive the intricacy of appearance.

Poetry is often a revelation of the elements of appearance.

Literature is the abnormal creating an illusion of the normal.

Poetry is a renovation of experience. Originality is an escape from repetition.

The theory of poetry is the life of poetry. Christianity is an exhausted culture.

Feed my lambs (on the bread of living) . . . The glory of god is the glory of the world . . . To find the spiritual in reality . . . To be concerned with reality.

The theory of poetry is the theory of life.

Reality is the object seen in its greatest common sense.

Poetry constantly requires a new relation.

Reality is not what it is. It consists of the many realities which it can be made into.

What reality lacks is a *noeud vital* with life.

French and English constitute a single language.

One's ignorance is one's chief asset.

Proposita:
    1. God and the imagination are one.
    2. The thing imagined is the imaginer.
The second equals the thing imagined and the imaginer are one. Hence, I suppose, the imaginer is God.

The greatest piece of fiction: Greek mythology. Classical mythology but Greek above Latin.

Poetry is, (and should be,) for the poet, a source of pleasure and satisfaction, not a source of honors.

# FROM "MATERIA POETICA"

The essential fault of surrealism is that it invents without discovering. To make a clam play an accordion is to invent not to discover. The observation of the unconscious, so far as it can be observed, should reveal things of which we have previously been unconscious, not the familiar things of which we have been conscious plus imagination.

The imagination does not add to reality.

The great well of poetry is not other poetry but prose: reality. However it requires a poet to perceive the poetry in reality.

At the moments when one's terror of life should be greatest (when one is young or old) one is usually insensible to it. Some such thing is true of the most profoundly poetic moments. This is the origin of sentimentality, which is a failure of feeling.

Poetry is reality and thought or feeling.

If one believes in poetry then questions of principle become vital questions. In any case, if there is nothing except reality and art, the mere statement of that fact discloses the significance of art.

The dichotomy is not between realists and artists. There must be few pure realists and few pure artists. We are hybrids absorbed in hybrid literature.

# FROM MISCELLANEOUS NOTEBOOKS

## I

Gaiety in poetry is a precious characteristic but it should be a characteristic of the diction.

Reality is a cliché
From which we escape by metaphor
It is only au pays de la métaphore
Qu'on est poète.

The degrees of metaphor
The absolute object slightly turned
Is a metaphor of the object.

Some objects are less susceptible to metaphor than others. The whole world
is less susceptible to metaphor than a tea-cup is.

There is no such thing as a metaphor of a metaphor. One does not progress
through metaphors. Thus reality is the indispensable element of each metaphor. When I say that man is a god it is very easy to see that if I say also that
a god is something else, god has become reality.

Poetry seeks out the relation of men to facts.

The imagination is man's power over nature. Query

Imagination is the only genius. Query

How to change real objects without the aid of metaphor. By feeling, style etc.

Poetry as manifestation of the relationship that man creates between himself
& reality.

The momentum of the mind is all toward abstraction.

The imagination of the blind man cannot be the extension of an externality
he has never seen. (Berkeley)

The effect of the imagination on the works of artists is a different subject
from that in which I am interested. In art its effect is the production of
qualities: as strength (Pater, Michael Angelo) and its value is a question of
the value of those qualities. In life it produces things and its value is a question of the value of those things as, for example, the value of works of art.

There are two arch-types of poets, of whom it is possible to take Homer as an illustration of the narrative type and Plato, regardless of the consideration that he did not write in verse, as an illustration of the reflective type.

A poem is like a natural object.

# ESSAYS, SPEECHES, NOTES

## CATTLE *KINGS* OF FLORIDA

Saddle bags filled with gold left lying on the front porch or even in the stable!

Coffee cans or kitchen pots filled to the brim with the yellow Spanish coins and left unguarded on kitchen shelves of isolated ranch homes!

Such tales told by the few surviving pioneer cattle kings of Florida contrasts strangely with present day customs. A single gold coin is more or less of a curiosity today while anyone in Atlanta, or Florida either, with a sizable bag of gold would watch it with a shot gun until they could procure an armored car to move it to the deposit vaults of some bank.

And yet the Florida tales are true, as any old time cow hunter who trailed the herds down to Punta Rassa in the '70s and '80s will testify. The little port a few miles from Fort Myers, on the Gulf of Mexico, is only a cable station with a few fishing racks now, but in the early days it saw thousands of Florida's free range cattle rafted out to Spanish ships bound for Havana and in turn saw thousands of Spain's golden coins turned over to the cattle barons who lived on scattered and unfenced ranches in the interior.

Fort Myers itself wasn't much of a town then and didn't offer many facilities for recreation. Some of the early cattlemen, the Tolles and the Hendrys and a few others made their homes there, but most of them poured the gold into their saddle bags and after a few drinks around mounted their shaggy and tired looking ponies and rode northward toward Polk or DeSoto Counties.

Although their mounts had several times the speed and spirit their appearances indicated, it usually took several days to cover the trail back home. Camp was made by the cattlemen wherever nightfall found them and the tired riders would dump their saddle bags wherever it was handiest. If a friend dropped in after camp was made and wanted to borrow money, or if the cattle owner owed him money, the visitor was frequently told to find the saddle bags and count out what he needed or what was due him.

Honesty wasn't questioned in money matters on the range. From all re-

209

ports, the cattle kings would and did steal cows from each other. But stealing money was taboo among the home folks and tourists and other visiting gentry were still practically unknown in Florida below Jacksonville and St. Augustine.

One of the famous cattle kings of this period was Jacob Summerlin, a cowboy philanthropist of the early days whose generosity made him rather a patron saint of the south Florida range, and who left eternal monuments to his credit in Bartow and Orlando.

There are many still living who knew Summerlin personally and he has several descendants still residing in Polk County. Innumerable stories are told of his saddle pockets filled with gold and how any tale of distress or want, particularly on the part of widow or orphan, always found him digging out a handful of coins for the unfortunate one.

Despite his wealth he was said to have always dressed only in the cotton trousers and shirt, leather boots and five-gallon hat of the range. Thus, without any outward manifestation of having any money it was said to be a favorite trick of his to ride into some settler's yard where he was not known and beg a meal for himself and his horse. If the family was hospitable, as practically all pioneer families were, he would keep up his disguise until leaving; then he would give each child a Spanish ten-dollar gold piece; and if he had learned during his visit that the family lacked any particular necessity which money could buy, that would be forthcoming, too.

Summerlin was said to have been an orphan boy and to have had practically no schooling. That he deeply missed his lack of an opportunity for a higher education was shown when he purchased a large tract of land near the heart of Bartow, county seat of Polk County, and deeded it to trustees to sell in city lots and "form a free school for the poor white children." Schools up to that time in south Florida had been largely operated under the fee system, with few but the children of the well-to-do able to attend. Summerlin's donation financed the erection of the first brick school building in the southern portion of the state and initiated the free school system through the entire region, for, although his first intention was only a school for the poor children who could not attend the fee schools, his idea was enlarged upon by the trustees and a public school opened. The main public school in Bartow today is still known as Summerlin Institute, although, of course, it is now supported entirely by tax money.

Summerlin also donated ten-acre tracts of land within the town to each of the then established churches of Bartow and gave the town of Orlando the land surrounding many of the beautiful little lakes, forming the basis of Orlando's present park system around its lake shores—one of its chief claims to fame.

Another instance illustrating conditions when the Cuban cattle trade was booming was related to the writer some years ago by the late T. L. Wilson, of Bartow, who, before his death, became one of the most prominent attorneys and bankers of south Florida and was well known in Atlanta through his activities as a member of the war finance board appointed by President Woodrow Wilson.

Colonel Wilson was the son of a farmer and small cattleman who came from Georgia just after the War Between the States. "Tom" grew up as a pioneer Cracker boy without much book learning but with a pretty thorough knowledge of the out-of-doors. He started out to become a cattle king on his own account and had acquired a herd of a couple of hundred head by the time he was 18.

But one stormy night while he was riding herd down in the cypress flats and palmetto prairies near the present site of Immokalee, in Collier County, one thing went wrong after another. The cattle stampeded at every lightning flash. His horse slipped and fell with him half a dozen times while he was working in the dark. Wet and muddy and cold he stuck it out until daylight and then turned the job over to the cow hand he had riding with him with the brief remark that he was through with bovine playmates forever, or words to that effect.

He rode into Fort Myers, reaching the home of an uncle there after the family had gone to bed. He woke his relative up and after a short explanation of the situation, offered him his herd at the market price, saying he was going to take the money and study law.

The uncle didn't think much of his nephew's decision. In a land where most of the crime concerned shooting matches, and the shootees unable to go to court after it was over as a usual thing, he didn't see much promise in becoming a lawyer. But he agreed to buy the cattle if the boy insisted on selling.

"You'll see my saddle bags on the porch as you go out," he said. "I just sold a bunch at Punta Rassa this morning and am pretty tired, so I won't get up. You count out your money and go ahead, if you're bound you won't spend the night."

Mr. Wilson counted out the nearly two thousand dollars that his cattle came to and left for home. And he stated that there was probably a thousand dollars more still in the bags left on the porch for the night.

The youth never regretted his change of profession from a financial viewpoint at least. He went direct from the range to Washington and Lee University at Lexington, and was said to have been one of the two men ever to complete the law course there in one year, and that without even a complete grammar school education. He was admitted to the bar before he was 21 by a special act of the Florida legislature, and from that time on his success justified his choice of a career.

The old order of cattle raising began to change generally after the Spanish-American war. Cuba settled down under its new regime and began to raise more of its own beef. Florida's own steady growth furnished a constantly increasing home market, but at the same time the new towns and farms and groves springing up all over the former vast open range cut into the pasturage and made it more difficult and costly to handle the big herds.

Many of the cattle kings held on. Most of the big ones had built up very sizable fortunes when the yellow coins from Spain were rolling in so freely. Some of them went into other activities as the changes became more marked. Others who felt that they could not be satisfied with any other life began to alter their methods. Many voluntarily fenced their vast pastures long before the townsfolk and grove owners began to advocate a fence law in the more settled regions.

The old careless days of half a century ago with their easy money will probably never return, but the manner in which the Florida cattle industry is adapting itself to the new conditions indicates that it will be a big business there for a long time to come.

◇◇◇◇◇◇◇◇◇◇◇◇◇◇◇◇◇◇◇◇◇◇◇◇◇◇◇◇◇◇◇◇◇◇◇◇◇◇◇◇◇◇◇◇◇◇◇◇◇◇◇◇◇◇◇◇◇

# ON "THE EMPEROR OF ICE-CREAM"

I think I should select from my poems as my favorite "The Emperor of Ice-Cream." This wears a deliberately commonplace costume, and yet seems to me to contain something of the essential gaudiness of poetry; that is the reason why I like it. I do not remember the circumstances under which this poem was written, unless this means the state of mind from which it came. I dislike niggling, and like letting myself go. Poems of this sort are the pleasantest on which to look back, because they seem to remain fresher than others. This represented what was in my mind at the moment, with the least possible manipulation.

# WILLIAMS

The slightly tobaccoy odor of autumn is perceptible in these pages. Williams is past fifty.

There are so many things to say about him. The first is that he is a romantic poet. This will horrify him. Yet the proof is everywhere. Take the first poem, "All the Fancy Things." What gives this its distinction is the image of the woman, once a girl in Puerto Rico in the old Spanish days, now solitary and growing old, not knowing what to do with herself, remembering. Of course, this is romantic in the accepted sense, and Williams is rarely romantic in the accepted sense.

The man has spent his life in rejecting the accepted sense of things. In that, most of all, his romantic temperament appears. But it is not enough merely to reject: what matters is the reason for rejection. The reason is that Williams has a romantic of his own. His strong spirit makes its own demands and delights to try its strength.

It will be observed that the lonely figure in "All the Fancy Things" and the person addressed in "Brilliant Sad Sun" have been slightly sentimentalized. In order to understand Williams at all, it is necessary to say at once that he has a sentimental side. Except for that, this book would not exist and its character would not be what it is. "The Cod Head" is a bit of pure sentimentalization; so is "The Bull." Sentiment has such an abhorrent name that one hesitates. But if what vitalizes Williams has an abhorrent name, its obviously generative function in his case may help to change its reputation. What Williams gives, on the whole, is not sentiment but the reaction from sentiment, or, rather, a little sentiment, very little, together with acute reaction.

His passion for the anti-poetic is a blood passion and not a passion of the inkpot. The anti-poetic is his spirit's cure. He needs it as a naked man needs shelter or as an animal needs salt. To a man with a sentimental side the anti-poetic is that truth, that reality to which all of us are forever fleeing.

The anti-poetic has many aspects. The aspect to which a poet is addicted is a test of his validity. Its merely rhetorical aspect is valueless. As an affectation it is a commonplace. As a scourge it has a little more meaning. But as a phase of a man's spirit, as a source of salvation, now, in the midst of a baffled generation, as one looks out of the window at Rutherford or Passaic, or as one walks the streets of New York, the anti-poetic acquires an extraordinary potency, especially if one's nature possesses that side so attractive to the Furies.

Something of the unreal is necessary to fecundate the real; something of the sentimental is necessary to fecundate the anti-poetic. Williams, by nature, is more of a realist than is commonly true in the case of a poet. One might, at this point, set oneself up as the Linnæus of aesthetics, assigning a female role to the unused tent in "The Attic Which Is Desire," and a male role to the soda sign; and generally speaking one might run through these pages and point out how often the essential poetry is the result of the conjunction of the unreal and the real, the sentimental and the anti-poetic, the constant interaction of two opposites. This seems to define Williams and his poetry.

All poets are, to some extent, romantic poets. Thus, the poet who least supposes himself to be so is often altogether so. For instance, no one except a *surréaliste* himself would hesitate to characterize that whole school as romantic, dyed through and through with the most authentic purple. What, then, is a romantic poet now-a-days? He happens to be one who still dwells in an ivory tower, but who insists that life there would be intolerable except for the fact that one has, from the top, such an exceptional view of the public dump and the advertising signs of Snider's Catsup, Ivory Soap and Chevrolet Cars; he is the hermit who dwells alone with the sun and moon, but insists on taking a rotten newspaper. While Williams shares a good deal of this with his contemporaries in the manner and for the reason indicated, the attempt to define him and his work is not to be taken as an attempt to define anyone or anything else.

So defined, Williams looks a bit like that grand old plaster cast, Lessing's Laocoön: the realist struggling to escape from the serpents of the unreal.

He is commonly identified by externals. He includes here specimens of abortive rhythms, words on several levels, ideas without logic, and similar minor matters, which, when all is said, are merely the diversions of the prophet between morning and evening song. It will be found that he has made some veritable additions to the corpus of poetry, which certainly is no more sacred to anyone than to him. His special use of the anti-poetic is an example of this. The ambiguity produced by bareness is another. The implied image, as in "Young Sycamore," the serpent that leaps up in one's imagination at his prompting, is an addition to imagism, a phase of realism which Williams has always found congenial. In respect to manner he is a virtuoso. He writes of flowers exquisitely. But these things may merely be mentioned. Williams himself, a kind of Diogenes of contemporary poetry, is a much more vital matter. The truth is that, if one had not chanced to regard him as Laocoön, one could have done very well by him as Diogenes.

## A NOTE ON MARTHA CHAMPION

Miss Champion begins by being an artist. The trouble she takes about small letters in place of capitals and about the relations between her lines and about punctuation; the indifference to what she is writing about as compared to the way in which she writes about it; the pleasure she finds in lines like

> Intent and bright
> Like tenderness

and

> Wave-slap on the shore.
> Grief is slow,
> Which overtakes me here;

these things are manifestly the affairs of an artist. If it is the "Farewell of Meleager" translated by Mackail in *Select Epigrams* (8:XIV):

No longer will I . . . inhabit the hill-tops: what is there sweet, what desirable in the mountains? Daphnis is dead . . . I will dwell here in the city

that is the source of "After Meleager," Miss Champion's paraphrase which changes the tone of the Anthology to the tone of today is again the affair of an artist.

Youngish artists have a way of being melancholy. It may be that this is merely a symptom of the distress they feel at the absence of definition. They have no very distinct outline either of themselves or of the abstractions that bedevil them. They are, in short, likely to be a bit baffled. Thus to Miss Champion the idea of the twisting of love, which might involve all sorts of implications, has exclusively an artistic implication. The elaboration of the metaphor in "Fragmenta I" interests her without regard to its insignificance. In "Fragmenta II," a subject that might have been profoundly felt, there are, in the absence of feeling, the phrases:

215

towering plains

Divides the waves
Like solitude

sweet-crumbling pebbles;

and in "Perseid" the melancholy of what chance have we is confused with

giddy Charlestoning deft houses.

If Miss Champion happened to be setting out to think about the twisting of love, or to think about farewells to Daphnis or Daphne or her Uncle Charles or Mrs. Mistlebacher, or about separation, or grief and its assuaging, or the oddity of man measuring himself against things which the Perseids do so poorly as, say the Hotel Pierre; or if she meant to feel these things to the depths or felt them whether or not she meant to do so; or if she did not mean to think about them or to be moved by them in the least but to use them for the sounds they might provoke, the sensations as of color or the opportunities for strange conjunctions to which they might give rise, as

dark seas,
And silly clouds

and

feeble stars . . .
bent, hatted chimneys;

if she meant to do any one of these things and meant it persistently so that her will involved everything for her, that would be one thing; but if she did not quite know what she meant to do and did a little of all of them, that would be something infinitely more complicated and difficult and defeating and discouraging. None of Miss Champion's themes is a clear theme lustily treated.

Yet there is nothing more delightful in poetry than the sort of sensitiveness that Miss Champion possesses when it is put to the lusty uses to which she seems capable of putting it. The

crooked noises

and

we finger a dead mouse in this house

of "Poem" are fascinating.

# A POET THAT MATTERS

The tall pages of *Selected Poems* by Marianne Moore are the papers of a scrupulous spirit. The merely fastidious spirit *à la mode* is likely to be on the verge of suffocation from hyperaesthesia. But Miss Moore's is an unaffected, witty, colloquial sort of spirit. In "The Fish," for instance, the lines move with the rhythm of sea-fans waving to and fro under water. They are lines of exquisite propriety. Yet in this poem she uses what appears, aesthetically, to be most inapposite language:

> All
> external
>     marks of abuse are present on this
>     defiant edifice—
>         all the physical features of.

Everywhere in the book there is this enhancing diversity. In consequence, one has more often than not a sense of invigoration not usually communicated by the merely fastidious.

That Miss Moore is scrupulous, the lines just quoted demonstrate. *All* and *external* are rhymes enough for anyone that finds full rhymes to be crude. The same thing is true of *this* and *edifice*. Thus, the lines which at first glance appeared to contain no rhymes whatever, have on a second look a more intricate appearance. Moreover, the units of the lines are syllables and not feet; the first line contains one syllable; the second three; the third nine; the fourth six; the last eight. This scheme is repeated with exactness throughout the poem. It is this scheme that requires Miss Moore to end the stanza with *of*, and that occasionally requires her to pass, elsewhere, from one line to the next in the middle of a word. If the verse is not to be free, its alternative is to be rigid. Finally, in printing the lines, the first two have been set well to the left, the next two have been set in a little to the right and the last has been set in still farther to the right. Now, all these things contribute to the effect of the stanza. The light rhymes please one unconsciously. The exactness with which the syllables are repeated, the larger recurrences as the stanzas are repeated, the indentations which arrest the eye, even if slightly: all these things assist in creating and in modulating the rhythm. In addition, Miss Moore instinctively relates sounds. There is a relation between the groups of letters *ext, ks, phys*. The *i*'s in *defiant edifice* are related. As these relations change, not only the sounds change, but the colors, the texture, the effects also change.

The poem with which the book opens, "The Steeple-Jack," is highly characteristic. The lines and stanzas flow innocently. Nevertheless, throughout the dozen stanzas the lines repeat themselves, syllable by syllable, without variation. The stanzas are mechanisms. Yet instead of producing a mechanical effect, they produce an effect of ease. In one of her poems Miss Moore writes of

> . . . intermingled echoes
> struck from thin glasses successively at random—.

In "The Steeple-Jack" she writes of

> a sea the purple of the peacock's neck is
> paled to greenish azure as Dürer changed
> the pine green of the Tyrol to peacock blue.

The strong sounds of *the purple of the peacock's neck* contrast and intermingle with the lighter sounds of *paled to greenish azure* and return again to the strong sounds of the last line. The colors of the first and second lines acquire a quality from their association with the word *Dürer* and the image of Dürer and the *pine green* and *peacock blue* of the last line owe something to the word *Tyrol* and the image of the Tyrol. This is not at all going too finely into minutiae. For with Miss Moore these things lie on the surface.

"The Steeple-Jack" serves, too, to illustrate what interests Miss Moore. The point of the poem is a view of the common-place. The view is that of Dürer or of Miss Moore in the mask or mood of Dürer, or, more definitely, perhaps, under the stimulus of Dürer. The common-place is, say, a New England fishing-village. Whatever the poem may do for Dürer or for the village, it does many happy things for Miss Moore and for those who delight in her. Obviously, having in mind the subject-matter of the poem, Miss Moore *donne dans le romanesque*. Consciously, the point of the poem may have been something wholly casual. It may lie in the words

> it is a privilege to see so
> much confusion.

Consciously, it may have had no more point than the wish to make note of observations made while in the cloud of a mood. That is Miss Moore's method. Subject, with her, is often incidental. There are in "The Steeple-Jack" the following creatures: eight stranded whales, a fish, sea-gulls, the peacock of the peacock's neck referred to a moment ago, a guinea, a twenty-five pound lobster, an exotic serpent (by allusion), a ring-lizard, a snake (also by allusion), a crocodile, cats, cobras, rats, the diffident little newt and a spider. This is a modest collection. Miss Moore makes the most lavish snake-charmer look like a visitor. The people in the poem are Dürer;

> The college student
> named Ambrose sits on the hill-side
> with his not-native books and hat
> and sees boats
>
> at sea progress white and rigid as if in
> a groove;

and C. J. Poole, Steeple-Jack, with one or two references to others. Poole is merely a sign on the sidewalk with his name on it. The last stanza is:—

> It could not be dangerous to be living
> in a town like this, of simple people,
> who have a steeple-jack placing danger signs by the church
> while he is gilding the solid-
> pointed star, which on a steeple
> stands for hope.

Stendhal in his *Pensées* said:

Le bel esprit comme on sait fut de tout temps l'ennemi le plus perfide du génie.

Miss Moore's wit, however, does not in the least imperil what she is about. Out of her whales and the college student and Poole and the danger signs she composes a poem simple, radiant with imagination, contemporaneous, displaying everywhere her sensitive handling. The poem leaves one indubitably convinced that she leans to the romantic.

And so she should, with a difference. In "The Steeple-Jack" she observes the fog on the sea-side flowers and trees

> so that you have
> the tropics at first hand: the trumpet vine . . .
> or moon vines trained on fishing-twine.

She then writes

> . . . There are no banyans, frangipani nor
> jack-fruit trees; nor an exotic serpent
> life.

If she had said in so many words that there were banyans, frangipani, and so on, she would have been romantic in the sense in which the romantic is a relic of the imagination. She hybridizes the thing by a negative. That is one way. Equally she hybridizes it by association. Moon-vines are moon-vines and tedious. But moon-vines trained on fishing-twine are something else and they are as perfectly as it is possible for anything to be what interests Miss Moore. They are an intermingling. The imagination grasps at such things and sates itself, instantaneously, in them. Yet clearly they are romantic. At this point one very well might stop for definitions. It is clear enough, without all that, to say that the romantic in the pejorative sense merely connotes obsolescence, but that the word has, or should have, another sense. Thus, when A. E. Powell in *The Romantic Theory of Poetry* writes of the romantic poet,

> He seeks to reproduce for us the feeling as it lives within himself; and for the sake of a feeling which he thinks interesting or important he will insert passages which contribute nothing to the effect of the work as a whole,

she is surely not thinking of the romantic in a derogatory sense. True, when Professor Babbitt speaks of the romantic, he means the romantic. Romantic objects are things, like garden furniture or colonial lingerie or, not to burden the imagination, country millinery.

Yes, but the romantic in its other sense, meaning always the living and at the same time the imaginative, the youthful, the delicate and a variety of things which it is not necessary to try to particularize at the moment, constitutes the vital element in poetry. It is absurd to wince at being called a romantic poet. Unless one is that, one is not a poet at all. That, of course, does not mean banyans and frangipani; and it cannot for long mean no banyans and no frangipani. Just what it means, Miss Moore's book discloses. It means, now-a-days, an uncommon intelligence. It means in a time like our own of violent feelings, equally violent feelings and the most skilful expression of the genuine. Miss Moore's lines,

> the shadows of the Alps
> imprisoning in their folds like flies in amber, the rhythms
> of the skating rink

might so easily have been pottered over and nullified; and how hilarious, how skilful they are! Only the other day there was a comment on "Samuel Prout's romantic renderings of mediaeval fountains." The commentator was far from meaning mediaeval renderings of romantic fountains. For him Prout's renderings were romantic because they delighted him and since the imagination does not often delight in the same thing twice, it may be assumed that by romantic he meant something that was, for his particular imagination, an indulgence and a satisfaction.

Professor Babbitt says that

a thing is romantic when, as Aristotle would say, it is wonderful rather than probable. . . . A thing is romantic when it is strange, unexpected, intense, superlative, extreme, unique, etc.

It must also be living. It must always be living. It is in the sense of living intensity, living singularity that it is the vital element in poetry. The most brilliant instance of the romantic in this sense is Mr. Eliot, who incessantly revives the past and creates the future. It is a process of cross-fertilization, an immense process, all arts considered, of hybridization. Mr. Eliot's "Prelude" with the smell of steaks in passageways, is an instance, in the sense that the smell of steaks in the Parnassian air is a thing perfectly fulfilling Professor Babbitt's specifications. Hamlet in modern dress is another instance of hybridization. Any playing of a well-known concerto by an unknown artist is another. Miss Moore's book is a collection of just that. It is not a matter of phrases, nor of odd-looking lines, nor of poems from which one must wholly take, giving anything whatsoever at one's peril. Poetry for her is "a place for the genuine." If the conception of the poet as a creature ferocious with ornamental fury survives anywhere except in the school books, it badly needs a few pungent footnotes. We do not want "high-sounding interpretation." We want to understand. We want, as she says,

imaginary gardens with real toads in them.

The very conjunction of imaginary gardens and real toads is one more specimen of the romantic of Miss Moore. Above all things she demands

the raw material of poetry in
all its rawness.

She demands the romantic that is genuine, that is living, the enriching poetic reality.

Miss Moore's form is not the quirk of a self-conscious writer. She is not a writer. She is a woman who has profound needs. In any project for poetry (and one wishes that the world of tailors, plasterers, barkeepers could bring itself to accept poets in a matter-of-fact way) the first effort should be devoted to establishing that poets are men and women, not writers. Miss

Moore may have had more than one reason for adding in the *Notes* appended to her book that in "Peter," the hero "built for the midnight grass-party," was a

Cat owned by Miss Magdalen Heuber and
Miss Maria Weniger.

But this amusing stroke is, after all, a bit of probity, whatever else it may be. That Miss Moore uses her wit is a bit of probity. The romantic that falsifies is rot and that is true even though the romantic inevitably falsifies: it falsifies but it does not vitiate. It is an association of the true and the false. It is not the true. It is not the false. It is both. The school of poetry that believes in sticking to the facts would be stoned if it was not sticking to the facts in a world in which there are no facts: or some such thing.

This brings one round to a final word. Miss Moore's *emportements* are few. Instead of being intentionally one of the most original of contemporary or modern poets, she is merely one of the most truthful. People with a passion for the truth are always original. She says:

Truth is no Apollo.

She has thought much about people and about poetry, and the truth, and she has done this with all the energy of an intense mind and imagination and this book is the significant result. It contains the veritable thing.

✿◇✿◇✿◇✿◇✿◇✿◇✿◇✿◇✿◇✿◇✿◇✿◇✿◇✿◇✿◇✿◇✿◇✿◇✿◇✿◇✿◇✿◇✿◇✿◇✿◇✿◇✿◇✿◇

# JACKET STATEMENT FROM
## *IDEAS OF ORDER*

We think of changes occurring today as economic changes, involving political and social changes. Such changes raise questions of political and social order.

While it is inevitable that a poet should be concerned with such questions, this book, although it reflects them, is primarily concerned with ideas of order of a different nature, as, for example, the dependence of the individual, confronting the elimination of established ideas, on the general sense of order; the idea of order created by individual concepts, as of the poet, in

"The Idea of Order at Key West"; the idea of order arising from the practice of any art, as of poetry in "Sailing after Lunch."

The book is essentially a book of pure poetry. I believe that, in any society, the poet should be the exponent of the imagination of that society. *Ideas of Order* attempts to illustrate the role of the imagination in life, and particularly in life at present. The more realistic life may be, the more it needs the stimulus of the imagination.

◇◇◇◇◇◇◇◇◇◇◇◇◇◇◇◇◇◇◇◇◇◇◇◇◇◇◇◇◇◇◇◇◇◇◇◇◇◇◇◇◇◇◇◇◇◇◇◇◇◇◇◇◇

## IN MEMORY OF HARRIET MONROE

Her job brought Miss Monroe into contact with the most ferocious egoists. I mean poets in general. You could see her shrewd understanding adapt itself to her visitors. When they had left her office she remained just as amiable. There must be many of her contributors to whom she gave the feeling not only that she liked their poems, but that she liked them personally, as she usually did.

No one could have been more agreeable, yet she had not a trace of the busy welcomer. She wanted more time so that she might know you better. She would go along to lunch and then invite you to her house for dinner. She did the most she could for you and gave you the best she had. To cite not too exalted an instance, I remember that on one occasion she produced after dinner as a liqueur a small bottle of whiskey which she said was something like ninety years old, almost colonial, as if stored up for that particular winter's night.

We had the pleasure of seeing her on several occasions in Hartford, where again she impressed us with her sincerity and good will.

All this reflected itself in *Poetry*, which might so easily have become something less than it was: something less in the sense of being the organ of a group or mode, or of having a rigid any-other standard. It was notably a magazine of many people; it was the widest possible. She made it so. She liked to be among people; in a group she was always most eager. It was not merely courtesy that made her think well and speak well of others; she did it because she enjoyed doing it.

223

# THE IRRATIONAL ELEMENT IN POETRY

## I

To begin with, the expression: the irrational element in poetry, is much too general to be serviceable. After one has thought about it a bit it spreads out. Then too we are at the moment so beset by the din made by the surrealists and surrationalists, and so preoccupied in reading about them that we may become confused by these romantic scholars and think of them as the sole exemplars of the irrational today. Certainly, they exemplify one aspect of it. Primarily, however, what I have in mind when I speak of the irrational element in poetry is the transaction between reality and the sensibility of the poet from which poetry springs.

## II

I am not competent to discuss reality as a philosopher. All of us understand what is meant by the transposition of an objective reality to a subjective reality. The transaction between reality and the sensibility of the poet is precisely that. A day or two before Thanksgiving we had a light fall of snow in Hartford. It melted a little by day and then froze again at night, forming a thin, bright crust over the grass. At the same time, the moon was almost full. I awoke once several hours before daylight and as I lay in bed I heard the steps of a cat running over the snow under my window almost inaudibly. The faintness and strangeness of the sound made on me one of those impressions which one so often seizes as pretexts for poetry. I suppose that in such a case one is merely expressing one's sensibility and that the reason why this expression takes the form of poetry is that it takes whatever form one is able to give it. The poet is able to give it the form of poetry because poetry is the medium of his personal sensibility. This is not the same thing as saying that a poet writes poetry because he writes poetry, although it sounds much like it. A poet writes poetry because he is a poet; and he is not a poet because he is a poet but because of his personal sensibility. What gives a man his personal sensibility I don't know and it does not matter because no one knows. Poets continue to be born not made and cannot, I am afraid, be predetermined. While, on the one hand, if they could be predetermined, they might long since have become extinct, they might, on the other hand, have changed life from what it is today into one

224

of those transformations in which they delight, and they might have seen
to it that they greatly multiplied themselves there.

### III

There is, of course, a history of the irrational element in poetry, which is,
after all, merely a chapter of the history of the irrational in the arts generally. With the irrational in a pathological sense we are not concerned.
Fuseli used to eat raw beef at night before going to bed in order that his
dreams might attain a beefy violence otherwise lacking. Nor are we concerned with that sort of thing; nor with any irrationality provoked by prayer,
whiskey, fasting, opium, or the hope of publicity. The Gothic novels of
eighteenth-century England are no longer irrational. They are merely boring. What interests us is a particular process in the rational mind which we
recognize as irrational in the sense that it takes place unaccountably. Or,
rather, I should say that what interests us is not so much the Hegelian
process as what comes of it. We should probably be much more intelligently interested if from the history of the irrational there had developed
a tradition. It is easy to brush aside the irrational with the statement that
we are rational beings, Aristotelians and not brutes. But it is becoming easier
every day to say that we are irrational beings; that all irrationality is not
of a piece and that the only reason why it does not yet have a tradition is
that its tradition is in progress. When I was here at Harvard, a long time
ago, it was a commonplace to say that all the poetry had been written and
all the paintings painted. It may be something of that sort that first interested us in the irrational. One of the great figures in the world since then
has been Freud. While he is responsible for very little in poetry, as compared,
for example, with his effect elsewhere, he has given the irrational a legitimacy
that it never had before. More portentous influences have been Mallarmé
and Rimbaud.

### IV

It may be that my subject expressed with greater nicety is irrational manifestations of the irrational element in poetry; for if the irrational element
is merely poetic energy, it is to be found wherever poetry is to be found.
One such manifestation is the disclosure of the individuality of the poet.
It is unlikely that this disclosure is ever visible as plainly to anyone as to
the poet himself. In the first of the poems that I shall read to you in a
moment or two the subject that I had in mind was the effect of the depression on the interest in art. I wanted a confronting of the world as it had

225

been imagined in art and as it was then in fact. If I dropped into a gallery I found that I had no interest in what I saw. The air was charged with anxieties and tensions. To look at pictures there was the same thing as to play the piano in Madrid this afternoon. I was as capable of making observations and of jotting them down as anyone else; and if that is what I had wished to do, I could have done it. I wanted to deal with exactly such a subject and I chose that as a bit of reality, actuality, the contemporaneous. But I wanted the result to be poetry so far as I was able to write poetry. To be specific, I wanted to apply my own sensibility to something perfectly matter-of-fact. The result would be a disclosure of my own sensibility or individuality, as I called it a moment ago, certainly to myself. The poem is called "The Old Woman and the Statue." The old woman is a symbol of those who suffered during the depression and the statue is a symbol of art, although in several poems of which *Owl's Clover*, the book from which I shall read, consists, the statue is a variable symbol. While there is nothing automatic about the poem, nevertheless it has an automatic aspect in the sense that it is what I wanted it to be without knowing before it was written what I wanted it to be, even though I knew before it was written what I wanted to do. If each of us is a biological mechanism, each poet is a poetic mechanism. To the extent that what he produces is mechanical: that is to say, beyond his power to change, it is irrational. Perhaps I do not mean wholly beyond his power to change, for he might, by an effort of the will, change it. With that in mind, I mean beyond likelihood of change so long as he is being himself. This happens in the case of every poet.

v

I think, too, that the choice of subject-matter is a completely irrational thing, provided a poet leaves himself any freedom of choice. If you are an imagist, you make a choice of subjects that is obviously limited. The same thing is true if you are anything else in particular and profess rigidly. But if you elect to remain free and to go about in the world experiencing whatever you happen to experience, as most people do, even when they insist that they do not, either your choice of subjects is fortuitous or the identity of the circumstances under which the choice is made is imperceptible. Lyric poets are bothered by spring and romantic poets by autumn. As a man becomes familiar with his own poetry, it becomes as obsolete for himself as for anyone else. From this it follows that one of the motives in writing is renewal. This undoubtedly affects the choice of subjects as definitely as it affects changes in rhythm, diction and manner. It is elementary that we vary rhythms instinctively. We say that we perfect diction. We simply grow tired. Manner is something that has not yet been disengaged adequately. It does not mean style; it means the attitude of the writer, his bearing rather than his point of view. His bearing toward what? Not toward anything in particular, simply his pose. He hears the cat on the snow. The running feet set the rhythm. There is no subject beyond the cat running on the snow in the moonlight. He grows completely tired of the thing, wants a subject, thought, feeling, his whole manner changes. All these things enter into the choice of subject. The man who has been brought up in an artificial school becomes intemperately real. The Mallarmiste becomes the proletarian novelist. All this is irrational. If the choice of subject was predictable it would be rational. Now, just as the choice of subject is unpredictable at the outset, so its development, after it has been chosen, is unpredictable. One is always writing about two things at the same time in poetry and it is this that produces the tension characteristic of poetry. One is the true subject and the other is the poetry of the subject. The difficulty of sticking to the true subject, when it is the poetry of the subject that is paramount in one's mind, need only be mentioned to be understood. In a poet who makes the true subject paramount and who merely embellishes it, the subject is constant and the development orderly. If the poetry of the subject is paramount, the true subject is not constant nor its development orderly. This is true in the case of Proust and Joyce, for example, in modern prose.

### VI

Why does one write poetry? I have already stated a number of reasons, among them these: because one is impelled to do so by personal sensibility and also because one grows tired of the monotony of one's imagination, say, and sets out to find variety. In his discourse before the Academy, ten years or more ago, M. Brémond elucidated a mystical motive and made it clear that, in his opinion, one writes poetry to find God. I should like to consider this in conjunction with what might better be considered separately, and that is the question of meaning in poetry. M. Brémond proposed the identity of poetry and prayer, and followed Bergson in relying, in the last analysis, on faith. M. Brémond eliminated reason as the essential element in poetry. Poetry in which the irrational element dominated was pure poetry. M. Brémond himself does not permit any looseness in the expression pure poetry, which he confines to a very small body of poetry, as he should, if the lines in which he recognizes it are as precious to his spirit as they appear to be. In spite of M. Brémond, pure poetry is a term that has grown to be descriptive of poetry in which not the true subject but the poetry of the subject is paramount. All mystics approach God through the irrational. Pure poetry is both mystical and irrational. If we descend a little from this height and apply the looser and broader definition of pure poetry, it is possible to say that, while it can lie in the temperament of very few of us to write poetry in order to find God, it is probably the purpose of each of us to write poetry to find the good which, in the Platonic sense, is synonymous with God. One writes poetry, then, in order to approach the good in what is harmonious and orderly. Or, simply, one writes poetry out of a delight in the harmonious and orderly. If it is true that the most abstract painters paint herrings and apples, it is no less true that the poets who most urgently search the world for the sanctions of life, for that which makes life so prodigiously worth living, may find their solutions in a duck in a pond or in the wind on a winter night. It is conceivable that a poet may arise of such scope that he can set the abstraction on which so much depends to music. In the meantime we have to live by the literature we have or are able to produce. I say live by literature, because literature is the better part of life, provided it is based on life itself. From this point of view, the meaning of poetry involves us profoundly. It does not follow that poetry that is irrational in origin is not communicable poetry. The pure poetry of M. Brémond is irrational in origin. Yet it communicates so much that M. Brémond regards it as supreme. Because most of us are incapable of sharing the experiences of M. Brémond, we have to be content with less. When we find in poetry that which gives us a momentary existence on an exquisite plane, is it necessary to ask the meaning of the poem? If the poem had a meaning and if its explanation destroyed the illusion, should we have gained or lost? Take, for instance, the poem of Rimbaud, one of *Les Illuminations*, entitled "Beaten Tracks." I quote Miss Rootham's translation:

On the right the summer dawn wakes the leaves, the mists and the sounds in this corner of the park. The slopes on the left clasp in their purple shade the myriad deep-cut tracks of the damp highway. A procession from fairyland passes by. There are chariots loaded with animals of gilded wood, with masts and canvas painted in many colors, drawn by twenty galloping piebald circus-ponies; and children and men on most astonishing beasts; there are twenty vehicles, embossed, and decked with flags and flowers like coaches of by-gone days, as coaches out of a fairytale; they are full of children dressed up for a suburban pastoral. There are even coffins under their night-dark canopies and sable plumes, drawn by trotting mares, blue and black.

I do not know what images the poem has created. M. Delahaye says that the poem was prompted by an American circus which visited Charleville, where Rimbaud lived as a boy, in 1868 or 1869. What is the effect of this explanation? I need not answer that. Miss Sitwell wrote the introduction to the collection of Miss Rootham's translations of the poems of Rimbaud.

Something that she said in the course of that introduction illustrates the way the true subject supersedes the nominal subject. She said:

How different was this life [of the slum] from that sheltered and even rather stuffy life of perpetual Sundays that he had led when he was a little boy in Charleville, and on these ever-recurring days of tight clothing and prayer, when Madame Rimbaud had escorted him, his brother and two sisters, to the eleven o'clock Mass, along the bright light dust-powdery roads, under trees whose great glossy brilliant leaves and huge pink flowers that seemed like heavenly trans-figurations of society ladies, appeared to be shaking with laughter at the sober procession.

Miss Sitwell herself could not say whether the eleven o'clock Mass suggested the bright light flowers or whether the society ladies came into her mind with the great glossy brilliant leaves and were merely trapped there by the huge pink flowers, or whether they came with the huge pink flowers. It might depend upon whether, in Miss Sitwell's mind, society ladies are, on the one hand, great glossy and brilliant, or, on the other hand, huge and pink. Here the true subject was the brilliance and color of an impression.

VII

The pressure of the contemporaneous from the time of the beginning of the World War to the present time has been constant and extreme. No one can have lived apart in a happy oblivion. For a long time before the war nothing was more common. In those days the sea was full of yachts and the yachts were full of millionaires. It was a time when only maniacs had disturbing things to say. The period was like a stage-setting that since then has been taken down and trucked away. It had been taken down by the end of the war, even though it took ten years of struggle with the consequences of the peace to bring about a realization of that fact. People said that if the war continued it would end civilization, just as they say now that another such war will end civilization. It is one thing to talk about the end of civiliza-tion and another to feel that the thing is not merely possible but measurably probable. If you are not a communist, has not civilization ended in Russia? If you are not a Nazi, has it not ended in Germany? We no sooner say that it never can happen here than we recognize that we say it without any illu-sions. We are preoccupied with events, even when we do not observe them closely. We have a sense of upheaval. We feel threatened. We look from an uncertain present toward a more uncertain future. One feels the desire to collect oneself against all this in poetry as well as in politics. If politics is nearer to each of us because of the pressure of the contemporaneous, poetry, in its way, is no less so and for the same reason. Does anyone suppose that

229

the vast mass of people in this country was moved at the last election by rational considerations? Giving reason as much credit as the radio, there still remains the certainty that so great a movement was emotional and, if emotional, irrational. The trouble is that the greater the pressure of the contemporaneous, the greater the resistance. Resistance is the opposite of escape. The poet who wishes to contemplate the good in the midst of confusion is like the mystic who wishes to contemplate God in the midst of evil. There can be no thought of escape. Both the poet and the mystic may establish themselves on herrings and apples. The painter may establish himself on a guitar, a copy of *Figaro* and a dish of melons. These are fortifyings, although irrational ones. The only possible resistance to the pressure of the contemporaneous is a matter of herrings and apples or, to be less definite, the contemporaneous itself. In poetry, to that extent, the subject is not the contemporaneous, because that is only the nominal subject, but the poetry of the contemporaneous. Resistance to the pressure of ominous and destructive circumstance consists of its conversion, so far as possible, into a different, an explicable, an amenable circumstance.

### VIII

M. Charles Mauron says that a man may be characterized by his obsessions. We are obsessed by the irrational. This is because we expect the irrational to liberate us from the rational. In a note on Picasso with the tell-tale title of "Social Fact and Cosmic Vision," Christian Zervos says:

The explosion of his spirit has destroyed the barriers which art . . . impressed on the imagination. Poetry has come forward with all that it has of the acute, the enigmatical, the strange sense which sees in life not only an image of reality but which conceives of life as a mystery that wraps us round everywhere.

To take Picasso as the modern one happens to think of, it may be said of him that his spirit is the spirit of any artist that seeks to be free. A superior obsession of all such spirits is the obsession of freedom. There is, however, no longer much excuse for explosions for, as in painting, so in poetry, you can do as you please. You can compose poetry in whatever form you like. If it seems a seventeenth-century habit to begin lines with capital letters, you can go in for the liquid transitions of greater simplicity; and so on. It is not that nobody cares. It matters immensely. The slightest sound matters. The most momentary rhythm matters. You can do as you please, yet everything matters. You are free, but your freedom must be consonant with the freedom of others. To insist for a moment on the point of sound. We no longer like Poe's tintinnabulations. You are free to tintinnabulate if you like. But others are equally free to put their hands over their ears. Life may not be a cosmic mystery that wraps us round everywhere. You have somehow to know the sound that is the exact sound; and you do in fact know, without knowing how. Your knowledge is irrational. In that sense life is mysterious; and if it is mysterious at all, I suppose that it is cosmically mysterious. I hope that we agree that it is at least mysterious. What is true of sounds is true of everything: the feeling for words, without regard to their sound, for example. There is, in short, an unwritten rhetoric that is always changing and to which the poet must always be turning. That is the book in which he learns that the desire for literature is the desire for life. The incessant desire for freedom in literature or in any of the arts is a desire for freedom in life. The desire is irrational. The result is the irrational searching the irrational, a conspicuously happy state of affairs, if you are so inclined.

Those who are so inclined and without reserve say: The least fastidiousness in the pursuit of the irrational is to be repudiated as an abomination. Rational beings are canaille. Instead of seeing, we should make excavations in the eye; instead of hearing, we should juxtapose sounds in an emotional clitter-clatter.

This seems to be freedom for freedom's sake. If we say that we desire freedom when we are already free, it seems clear that we have in mind a freedom not previously experienced. Yet is not this an attitude toward life resembling the poet's attitude toward reality? In spite of the cynicisms that occur to us as we hear of such things, a freedom not previously experienced, a poetry not previously conceived of, may occur with the suddenness inherent in poetic metamorphosis. For poets, that possibility is the ultimate obsession. They purge themselves before reality, in the meantime, in what they intend to be saintly exercises.

You will remember the letter written by Rimbaud to M. Delahaye, in which he said:

It is necessary to be a seer, to make oneself a seer. The poet makes himself a seer by a long, immense and reasoned unruliness of the senses. . . . He attains the unknown.

## IX

Let me say a final word about the irrational as part of the dynamics of poetry. The irrational bears the same relation to the rational that the unknown bears to the known. In an age as harsh as it is intelligent, phrases about the unknown are quickly dismissed. I do not for a moment mean to indulge in mystical rhetoric, since for my part, I have no patience with that sort of thing. That the unknown as the source of knowledge, as the object

231

of thought, is part of the dynamics of the known does not permit of denial. It is the unknown that excites the ardor of scholars, who, in the known alone, would shrivel up with boredom. We accept the unknown even when we are most skeptical. We may resent the consideration of it by any except the most lucid minds; but when so considered, it has seductions more powerful and more profound than those of the known.

Just so, there are those who, having never yet been convinced that the rational has quite made us divine, are willing to assume the efficacy of the irrational in that respect. The rational mind, dealing with the known, expects to find it glistening in a familiar ether. What it really finds is the unknown always behind and beyond the known, giving it the appearance, at best, of chiaroscuro. There are, naturally, charlatans of the irrational. That, however, does not require us to identify the irrational with the charlatans. I should not want to be misunderstood as having the poets of surrealism in mind. They concentrate their prowess in a technique which seems singularly limited but which, for all that, exhibits the dynamic influence of the irrational. They are extraordinarily alive and that they make it possible for us to read poetry that seems filled with gaiety and youth, just when we were beginning to despair of gaiety and youth, is immensely to the good. One test of their dynamic quality and, therefore, of their dynamic effect, is that they make other forms seem obsolete. They, in time, will be absorbed, with the result that what is now so concentrated, so inconsequential in the restrictions of a technique, so provincial, will give and take and become part of the process of give and take of which the growth of poetry consists.

Those who seek for the freshness and strangeness of poetry in fresh and strange places do so because of an intense need. The need of the poet for poetry is a dynamic cause of the poetry that he writes. By the aid of the irrational he finds joy in the irrational. When we speak of fluctuations of taste, we are speaking of evidences of the operation of the irrational. Such changes are irrational. They reflect the effects of poetic energy; for where there are no fluctuations, poetic energy is absent. Clearly, I use the word irrational more or less indifferently, as between its several senses. It will be time enough to adopt a more systematic usage, when the critique of the irrational comes to be written, by whomever it may be that this potent subject ultimately engages. We must expect in the future incessant activity by the irrational and in the field of the irrational. The advances thus to be made would be all the greater if the character of the poet was not so casual and intermittent a character. The poet cannot profess the irrational as the priest professes the unknown. The poet's role is broader, because he must be possessed, along with everything else, by the earth and by men in their earthy implications. For the poet, the irrational is elemental; but neither poetry nor life is commonly at its dynamic utmost. We know Sweeney as he is and, for the most part, prefer him that way and without too much effulgence and, no doubt, always shall.

◇◇◇◇◇◇◇◇◇◇◇◇◇◇◇◇◇◇◇◇◇◇◇◇◇◇◇◇◇◇◇◇◇◇◇◇◇◇◇◇◇◇◇◇◇◇◇◇◇◇◇

# JACKET STATEMENT FROM
## *THE MAN WITH THE BLUE GUITAR AND OTHER POEMS*

In one group, *Owl's Clover,* while the poems reflect what was then going on in the world, that reflection is merely for the purpose of seizing and stating what makes life intelligible and desirable in the midst of great change and great confusion. The effect of *Owl's Clover* is to emphasize the opposition between things as they are and things imagined; in short, to isolate poetry.

Since this is of significance, if we are entering a period in which poetry may be of first importance to the spirit, I have been making notes on the subject in the form of short poems during the past winter. These short poems, some thirty of them, form the other group, *The Man with the Blue Guitar,* from which the book takes its title. This group deals with the incessant conjunctions between things as they are and things imagined. Although the blue guitar is a symbol of the imagination, it is used most often simply as a reference to the individuality of the poet, meaning by the poet any man of imagination.

✿◆✿◆✿◆✿◆✿◆✿◆✿◆✿◆✿◆✿◆✿◆✿◆✿◆✿◆✿◆✿◆✿◆✿◆✿◆✿◆✿◆✿◆✿◆✿◆✿◆✿◆✿◆✿◆✿◆

# INSURANCE AND SOCIAL CHANGE

If each of us could put his hand on money whenever money was necessary: to repair any damage, to meet any emergency, we should all be willing to stop so far as money goes. To be certain of a regular income, as in the case of social security, is not the same thing as to be able to repair any damage, or to meet any emergency. Obviously, in a world in which insurance had become perfect, the case of social security would be a minor case. In short, universal insurance or insurance for all is not the same thing as ubiquitous insurance or insurance for everything.

The significance of a business is not wholly an affair of its statistics. This note is written lightly and is intended to touch the imagination, because that seems to be the best way to come quickly to the point. The objective of all of us is to live in a world in which nothing unpleasant can happen. Our prime instinct is to go on indefinitely like the wax flowers on the mantelpiece. Insurance is the most easily understood geometry for calculating how to bring the thing about.

The truth is that we may well be entering an insurance era. Compare the man who, as an individual, insures his dwelling against fire with that personality of the first plane who, at a stroke, insures all dwellings against fire; and who, without stopping to think about it, insures not only the lives of all those that live in the dwellings, but insures all people against all happenings of everyday life, even the worm in the apple or the piano out of tune. These are instances of insurance as it exists; and if they were not, there would be Lloyds or the future. There is no difference between the worm in the apple and the tack in the can of sardines, and not the slightest difference between the piano out of tune and a person disabled.

It helps us to see the actual world to visualize a fantastic world. Thus, when Mr. Wells creates a world of machines, a matter-of-fact truth about the world in which we live becomes clear for all the fiction. When he passes from the international to the interstellar, we hug the purely local. In the same way it helps us to see insurance in the midst of social change to imagine a world in which insurance had been made perfect. In such a world we should be certain of an income. Out of the income we should be able, by the payment of a trivial premium, to protect ourselves, our families and our property against everything. The procedure would necessarily be simple: Probably the dropping of a penny each morning in a box at the corner nearest one's place of residence on the way to one's place of employment. Each of us would have a personal or peculiar penny. What is the difference between a personal penny and a social security number? The circle just stated: income, insurance, the thing that happens and income again, would widen and soon become income, insurance, the thing that fails to happen and income again. In other words, not only would all our losses be made good, but all our wishes would come true.

If Mr. Wells has preferred the machine to insurance as his field, he has only left insurance to others. How far have others gone? The Italians have a quasi-governmental insurance organization, known as the National Insurance Institute, which came into being as the result of a national law passed in 1912. A consular report says . . .

The law was passed in pursuance of a proposal of a state monopoly of life insurance made the same year by Premier Giolitti. The avowed purposes of this proposal were to make monopoly profits available for social welfare expenditure and to enable the employment of state guarantees to stimulate increase of life insurance in Italy.

This does not mean, however, that private companies have been required to cease operations. In 1923 the Fascist government issued a decree permitting private companies to operate under conditions; and the fact is that private companies, both domestic and foreign, are in operation at the present time, although it is said that they operate under severe competitive handicaps. It is not surprising to hear it reported that approximately half of the life insurance in the Kingdom is in the Institute. Private companies must cede or reinsure substantial parts of their business to the Institute. Note, too, that in Italy postal officials are among those that sell life insurance.

Liability insurance, or civil responsibility business, as they call it, is not so attractive a subject for the monopolistically-minded politician, and this field remains in Italy a field for private enterprise. There is little to be said about fire insurance in Italy, where virtually all buildings are constructed chiefly of non-combustible materials. The government has a monopoly of obligatory social insurance (Cassa Nazionale per le Assicurazioni Sociali, of Rome). Social insurance relates to disability, tuberculosis, old age and unemployment. The funds of Cassa Nazionale are invested largely in public works.

In Germany private companies survive, but under a supervision described as "a continuous supervision of the whole business management whereby the Supervision Board may to a great extent act at its own decision." There are compulsory standard rules relating, for example, even to bookkeeping. As the field of insurance expands, and as the interest of the government in it becomes intensified to a point approaching identity, supervision justifiably becomes increasingly more severe. If this would be true in normal circumstances, it is all the more true in a period in which exhaustion has been an aggressive force.

In England, a Parliamentary committee on obligatory insurance has only recently reported in favor of a licensing system in which the approval of companies will be vested in other companies which will contribute to a central fund. Losses from the insolvency of any company will be payable from the central fund. Third party losses, uncollectible because of the operation of conditions, will also be payable from the central fund.

In the vast monopoly of Communism, insurance is itself a monopoly. The organization, Gosstrakh, is a state department and, by government decree, no other organization has the right to do an insurance business in the territory of the Soviets. This would put insurance agents on a footing with letter carriers or government employees generally, if it were not for the fact that, in Russia, everybody is on the same footing. Gosstrakh issues policies in several foreign companies which are its correspondents.

These very inadequate glimpses of the situation in those European countries where social pressure has been most acute and social and political change most marked indicate that, as the social mass seeks to maintain itself, it relies more and more on insurance and treats it as of such significance that the preservation of the insurers becomes a governmental function or a highly important object of governmental solicitude. Moreover, the government, in turn, avails itself of insurance not only in its social and political aspects but, in some directions, itself becomes an insurer and opens to its requirements the huge accumulation of funds from that source, which it applies, sometimes to social purposes, sometimes to general purposes, its own credit taking the place of reserves.

We shall never live in a world quite so mechanical as the one that Mr. Wells has imagined, nor in a world in which insurance has been made perfect, and where we can buy peace and prosperity as readily and as cheaply as we can buy the morning newspaper. All the same, we have advanced remarkably; and future advances seem to be not fantastic but certain. It is all a question of remaining solvent, a question of making a reasonable profit. Agents have as much at stake as any group in the making of a reasonable profit. Even if the point is considered from the view of the nationalization of the business, it is not to be supposed that any government can maintain an entire population indefinitely at a loss. If private companies can continue to expand with profit, no question of nationalization, except in regulatory and certain social aspects, is likely to arise under our system.

Under other systems, that is to say, under both Fascist and Communist systems, the finely-tailored agent, wearing a boutonniere, gives way to the letter carrier. In a late number of the Accident Company's Confidential Bulletin, it was said that . . .

Cemeteries have been found by a number of offices to be a very definite market for the Hartford's All Risk Securities Policy.

This observation would apply to the Hartford's policies generally under Communism and, to some extent, under Fascism. In short, then, the activities of the insurance business are likely, the greater and more significant they are, to make one reflect on the possibilities of nationalization, particularly in a period of unrest and the changes incident to unrest, a period so easily to be regarded as a period of transition. Yet the greater these activities are: that is to say, the more they are adapted to the changing needs of changing times (provided they are conducted at a profit) the more certain they are to endure on the existing basis. But this exacts of each of us all that each of us, in his own job, has to give.

## SURETY AND FIDELITY CLAIMS

People suppose, since there is so much human interest in selling Fuller brushes or sorting postcards in a post office, that the same thing must be true of handling fidelity and surety claims. After all, over a period of time, you spend an immense amount of money, millions.

But, actually, you never see a dollar. You sign a lot of drafts. You see surprisingly few people. You do the greater part of your work either in your own office or in lawyers' offices. You don't even see the country; you see law offices and hotel rooms. You try to do your traveling at night and often do it night after night. You wind up by knowing every county court house in the United States.

In particular, people suppose that there must be an immense amount of dishonesty in the way claims are made. Yet every man knows that he will have to establish his claim. Besides, to make a dishonest claim requires an intention to defraud the company. The danger from ignorance is far greater. A claim man is constantly separating the good from the bad. Some of the bad is due to a disposition to claim everything and let the company look after itself; some of it is due to improper constructions placed on language used by the company; some of it is due to a willingness to make a nuisance of yourself unless you are bought off. But most of it is due to ignorance. "Read your policy" relates to ignorance.

The major activity of a fidelity and surety claim department lies, of course, in paying claims. This involves much more than merely drawing drafts. It involves making sure that there has been a loss; that the company is liable for it; that you are discharging the liability by the payment, and that you are protecting whatever is available by way of salvage. There is

237

nothing cut and dried about any of these things; you adapt yourself to each case.

A bookkeeper makes false entries in his books and keeps a memorandum of them and of the amounts embezzled by him. You make sure of the loss by checking. It may seem morbid of an embezzler to keep a memorandum, yet many of them do. It may be mere neatness. Public officials seem to be a little less fastidious. They collect taxes without making records. In such a case we look for people with receipts. Tellers in savings banks take money from their cash and make charges against inactive accounts. In such a case the bank tries to persuade depositors to bring in their books. A filling station man asks you to pay him a large sum of money under a bond for a contractor conditioned for the payment of labor and materials. You find that part of the bill covers gasoline supplied to the contractor's wife for her personal car, that part of it is for repairs ordered by a man who rented a truck to a sub-contractor, and you pay the balance. These are instances of determining that there has been a loss.

You find that, while a sheriff failed to make a levy on property belonging to a judgment debtor and specifically called to his attention, this occurred in October in one term of office, while you did not become liable until January in another term of office. One of the next of kin sues you on the bond of an administrator. The administrator has been in office for a few months only and neither he nor you are subject to suit. A boy sues you on a bond for his mother as his guardian; you find that he has released his mother. A manufacturer of cement sues you for $80,000 on a bond which ordinarily would protect him. His right to sue you is based on a statute which limits the time for suit. It is too late and besides the manufacturer has taken $65,000 from payments made to him by the contractor out of the proceeds of the job covered by your bond and has applied the money (as he is free to do) to a balance due on a job not bonded by you. You contest the suit and defeat the claim. These are instances in which the company is not liable.

You have a bond guaranteeing that an electrician will pay his bills. The bond is for $1,000. His books show that he owes $3,000 and, if his books are incorrect, he may owe twice as much. You are threatened by suits; how are you to proceed? A family is killed by fumes from a gas stove in a cabin in a tourist camp. If the husband died first, his estate goes to A, B and C; if the wife died first, the husband's estate goes to X, Y and Z. The estate amounts to $50,000. You are on the bond of the administrator of the husband's estate. The $50,000 consisted of cash on deposit in a bank which failed several years after you gave your bond. A, B and C will settle for

$10,000, but X, Y and Z want $50,000. What had you better do? You are on a very large bond for a woman as executrix of her husband's estate. She has not accounted and you are unable to form any idea respecting her ability to account. What is more, she does not reside in the jurisdiction of the court, and you are not at all sure even that she exists. She was represented by lawyers who are willing to tell you what they know if you will first pay them the fee which she has failed to pay. They want, say, $25,000. You do not know whether what they will tell you will clear you or will disclose a liability for some hundreds of thousands of dollars. Shall you pay the $25,000? A contractor asks you to lend him a week's payroll for a few days or to pay off an accumulation of bills until he collects the amount of an estimate, within a week or two. To do so will not cut down the amount of your liability; shall you do it? These are instances of questions relating to payments as discharging or not discharging the company's liability.

Then there is salvage: People would not so commonly be required to give bonds if they had money. This means that people are required to give bonds because they don't have money. From this point of view, the saying among claim men that often the only salvage recoverable lies in an advantageous settlement, is true. In any case, the recovering of salvage is closely involved with the treatment of claims. A man investigating a claim investigates at the same time the chance of getting the money back. The possibility of recovering salvage frequently dictates the kind of papers to take when settling. It is an essential part of the claim man's job to lay the foundation for the recovery of salvage, if that is at all possible, in every case handled by him.

A man in the home office tends to conduct his business on the basis of the papers that come before him. After twenty-five years or more of that sort of thing, he finds it difficult sometimes to distinguish himself from the papers he handles and comes almost to believe that he and his papers constitute a single creature, consisting principally of hands and eyes: lots of hands and lots of eyes. Fortunately, this singular creature yields to more mature types: fortunately, because a business alive and expanding in other respects must be alive and expanding equally in respect to claims. The truth is that the most conspicuous element from the point of view of human interest in the handling of claims is the claim man himself.

# A NOTE ON POETRY

My intention in poetry is to write poetry: to reach and express that which, without any particular definition, everyone recognizes to be poetry, and to do this because I feel the need of doing it.

There is such a complete freedom now-a-days in respect to technique that I am rather inclined to disregard form so long as I am free and can express myself freely. I don't know of anything, respecting form, that makes much difference. The essential thing in form is to be free in whatever form is used. A free form does not assure freedom. As a form, it is just one more form. So that it comes to this, I suppose, that I believe in freedom regardless of form.

# TRIBUTE TO T. S. ELIOT

I don't know what there is (any longer) to say about Eliot. His prodigious reputation is a great difficulty.

While that sort of thing: more or less complete acceptance of it, helps to create the poetry of any poet, it also helps to destroy it.

Occasionally I pick up Eliot's poems and read them, eliminating from my mind all thought of his standing. It is like having an opportunity to see, in an out of the way place, a painting that has made a great stir: for example, it is like having a Giotto in what is called a breakfast nook.

Reading Eliot out of the pew, so to speak, goes on keeping one young. He remains an upright ascetic in a world that has grown exceedingly floppy and is growing floppier.

# NOTES ON JEAN LABASQUE

## I

It seems that painting based on the man and having a moral axis would be likely to possess a strong literary element. Mr. Labasque agrees. It would

240

also be likely to be allegorical in nature. Since allegory is so conspicuous in moral or architectural painting, it may be that Mr. Labasque is preoccupied with "civic" painting, "civic" art. Thus, his moral and social interests would lead to a role for him, as a "civic" artist. *Préface à une peinture* read in the light of this comment contains many accents justifying the comment.

## II

Mr. Labasque shows a passionate admiration for the work of Rousseau and, by inference, for the work of any primitive deriving from popular art. He works for the people or, at least, finds those that do so congenial. He is interested in communal synthesis. He is hostile to the egocentric. He believes in the human, the simple in art that springs from despair, hope, joy, emotion specified by him.

## III

What he does not appear to concede is the interest in painting (from the point of view of Cézanne) on the part of the public, and in poetry. Even though the amateur is ignorant of the technique of painting (for example, the manner in which Cézanne composes), the fact remains that there is a vast amount of art criticism, art history, etc., in circulation and that this has created (or that it fosters) a class of people who "live" in this sort of thing, whether from snobbism or otherwise; and certainly there are many much better reasons than snobbism, and perfectly legitimate ones. Impressionism, in so far as the public was concerned, was a poetic movement. The parasitic developments following it were different. But if the only really great thing in modern art: impressionism, was poetic, the poetic is not to be flipped away because that particular poetic expression is *vieux jeu*.

◇◇◇◇◇◇◇◇◇◇◇◇◇◇◇◇◇◇◇◇◇◇◇◇◇◇◇◇◇◇◇◇◇◇◇◇◇◇◇◇◇◇◇◇◇◇◇◇◇◇◇◇◇◇◇

# POETRY AND WAR

The immense poetry of war and the poetry of a work of the imagination are two different things. In the presence of the violent reality of war, consciousness takes the place of the imagination. And consciousness of an immense war is a consciousness of fact. If that is true, it follows that the poetry of war as a consciousness of the victories and defeats of nations, is a consciousness of fact, but of heroic fact, of fact on such a scale that the mere consciousness of it affects the scale of one's thinking and constitutes a participating in the heroic.

It has been easy to say in recent times that everything tends to become real, or, rather, that everything moves in the direction of reality, that is to say, in the direction of fact. We leave fact and come back to it, come back to what we wanted fact to be, not to what it was, not to what it has too often remained. The poetry of a work of the imagination constantly illustrates the fundamental and endless struggle with fact. It goes on everywhere, even in the periods that we call peace. But in war, the desire to move in the direction of fact as we want it to be and to move quickly is overwhelming.

Nothing will ever appease this desire except a consciousness of fact as everyone is at least satisfied to have it be.

❀◇❀◇❀◇❀◇❀◇❀◇❀◇❀◇❀◇❀◇❀◇❀◇❀◇❀◇❀◇❀◇❀◇❀◇❀◇❀◇❀◇❀◇❀◇❀◇❀◇❀◇❀◇❀◇❀◇❀◇

## NOTE ON A PERSONAL CHOICE OF POEMS

Poems may have, for their author, values not apparent to one who reads them. In the following group the poem, "Domination of Black," was only one of a projected series and it has, therefore, for its author, a value as referring to many poems never actually written, which it cannot possibly have for anyone else. Other poems, "In the Carolinas" and "The Load of Sugar Cane," for example, revive times and places on which the poems are the slightest possible notes. Thus, a personal choice of poems is obscure. This group is a personal choice and not a critical choice. It contains a good many more poems from my first book than from my last, although the poems in my last book are no doubt more important than those in my first book, more important because, as one grows older, one's objectives become clearer.

The themes of life are the themes of poetry. It seems to be, so clearly, that what is the end of life for the politician or the philosopher, say, ought to be the end of life for the poet, and that his important poems ought to be the poems of the achievement of that end. But poetry is neither politics nor philosophy. Poetry is poetry, and one's objective as a poet is to achieve poetry, precisely as one's objective in music is to achieve music. There are poets who would regard that as a scandal and who would say that a poem that had no importance except its importance as poetry had no importance

242

at all, and that a poet who had no objective except to achieve poetry was a fribble and something less than a man of reason. We have a curious way, however, of being dependent on unexpected things, and among these are the unexpected transformations of poetry. Perhaps the poems gathered together here will illustrate these remarks. The period during which they were written, the last twenty years, has been terribly alive, and these poems have been at least related to that life.

◇◇◇◇◇◇◇◇◇◇◇◇◇◇◇◇◇◇◇◇◇◇◇◇◇◇◇◇◇◇◇◇◇◇◇◇◇◇◇◇◇◇◇◇◇◇◇◇◇◇

## A NOTE ON SAMUEL FRENCH MORSE

What is there about a book of first poems that immediately interests us? For one thing, it is possible that we are going to have a fresh opportunity to become aware that the people in the world, and the objects in it, and the world as a whole, are not absolute things, but, on the contrary, are the phenomena of perception. In short, it is possible that a new poet is that special person at our elbow with his special, possibly even extraordinary, perception, to whom Thoreau refers at the end of the passage from "Autumnal Tints," with which Mr. Morse introduces his collection. Since the perception of life is life itself, a book containing the first poems of a poet new to us has a natural and intense attraction.

This is true even if, as we turn the pages, we find them a little obstinate. But they could hardly be anything else. If we were all alike; if we were millions of people saying do, re, mi in unison, one poet would be enough and Hesiod himself would do very well. Everything he said would be in no need of expounding or would have been expounded long ago. But we are not all alike and everything needs expounding all the time because, as people live and die, each one perceiving life and death for himself, and mostly by and in himself, there develops a curiosity about the perceptions of others. This is what makes it possible to go on saying new things about old things. The fact is that the saying of new things in new ways is grateful to us. If a bootblack says that he was so tired that he lay down like a dog under a tree, he is saying a new thing about an old thing, in a new way. His new way is not a literary novelty; it is an unaffected statement of his perception of the thing.

Poems written with this in mind will often not possess, nor be intended to possess, either emotion or the music of emotion. Instead, they will possess, and be intended to possess, the "moral beauty" that Mr. Venturi spoke of recently as being present in the painting of Cézanne. As the writer of such poems becomes more and more the master of his own poetry: that is to say, as he becomes better able to realize his individual perceptions, and as he acquires faith in his function as poet, he is likely to project the rigors of his early work into what he does later. So that his early work really discloses his identity.

What, then, is the identity of Mr. Morse? It is something that he is serious about poetry. The passage from Thoreau demonstrates that, and so do the three or four words from Job which, in the Bible, follow the verse in which Job cries

Or seest thou as man seeth?

But what is his exact character as a poet? One of his poems, "The Track into the Swamp," relates to one of the abandoned roads, the lost roads, of which New England is so full. We have been accustomed to think that at the far end of such roads the ghosts of the Transcendentalists still live. Obviously they do not live at this end. Mr. Morse is not the ghost of a Transcendentalist. If he has any use at all for Kant, it is to keep up the window in which the cord is broken. He is anti-transcendental. His subject is the particulars of experience. He is a realist; he tries to get at New England experience, at New England past and present, at New England foxes and snow and thunderheads. When he generalizes, as in "End of a Year," his synthesis is essentially a New England synthesis. He writes about his own people and his own objects as closely as possible according to his own perception. This rectitude characterizes everything that he does.

❀◇❀◇❀◇❀◇❀◇❀◇❀◇❀◇❀◇❀◇❀◇❀◇❀◇❀◇❀◇❀◇❀◇❀◇❀◇❀◇❀◇❀◇❀◇❀◇❀◇❀◇❀◇❀◇❀◇

## RUBBINGS OF REALITY

If a man writes a little every day, as Williams does, or used to do, it may be that he is merely practicing in order to make perfect. On the other hand he may be practicing in order to get at his subject. If his subject is, say, a sense, a mood, an integration, and if his representation is faint or obscure, and if he practices in order to overcome his faintness or obscurity, what he really does is to bring, or try to bring, his subject into that degree of focus at which he sees it, for a moment, as it is and at which he is able to represent it in exact definition.

A man does not spend his life doing this sort of thing unless doing it is something he needs to do. One of the sanctions of the writer is that he is doing something that he needs to do. The need is not the desire to accomplish through writing something not incidental to the writing itself. Thus a political or a religious writer writes for political or religious reasons. Williams writes, I think, in order to write. He needs to write.

What is the nature of this need? What does a man do when he delineates the images of reality? Obviously, the need is a general need and the activity a general activity. It is of our nature that we proceed from the chromatic to the clear, from the unknown to the known. Accordingly the writer who practices in order to make perfect is really practicing to get at his subject and, in that exercise, is participating in a universal activity. He is obeying his nature. Imagism (as one of Williams' many involvements, however long ago) is not something superficial. It obeys an instinct. Moreover, imagism is an ancient phase of poetry. It is something permanent. Williams is a writer to whom writing is the grinding of a glass, the polishing of a lens by means of which he hopes to be able to see clearly. His delineations are trials. They are rubbings of reality.

The modern world is the result of such activity on a grand scale, not particularly in writing but in everything. It may be said, for instance, that communism is an effort to improve the human focus. The work of Picasso is an attempt to get at his subject, an attempt to achieve a reality of the intelligence. But the world of the past was equally the result of such activity. Thus the German pietists of the early 1700's who came to Pennsylvania to live in the caves of the Wissahickon and to dwell in solitude and meditation were proceeding, in their way, from the chromatic to the clear. Is not Williams in a sense a literary pietist, chastening himself, incessantly, along the Passaic?

This is an intellectual *tenue*. It is easy to see how underneath the chaos of life today and at the bottom of all the disintegrations there is the need to see, to understand: and, in so far as one is not completely baffled, to re-create. This is not emotional. It springs from the belief that we have only our own intelligence on which to rely. This manifests itself in many ways, in every living art as in every living phase of politics or science. If we could suddenly re-make the world on the basis of our own intelligence, see it clearly and represent it without faintness or obscurity, Williams' poems would have a place there.

245

# THE SHAPER

Paul Rosenfeld was a shaper who lived a life of shaping, that is to say, a *Schöpfer*, who lived for the sake of *Schöpfung*. Perhaps there existed for him an ideal *Schöpfung*, a world composed of music, but which did not whirl round in music alone; or of painting, but which did not expand in color and form alone; or of poetry, but which did not limit itself to the *explication orphique* of the poet. But whether or not there was an ideal *Schöpfung*, in which everything coalesced, toward which everything converged, the truth about him seems to be that he was incessantly engaged or involved or attracted by the activity of shaping.

This is the life of the artist, whether the artist be the young sculptor or the old politician, or, say, sociologist; whether the artist be the young Spanish painter or the barbarian statesman. Thus, if the uncertainty in the case of Rosenfeld suggested by the words "engaged or involved or attracted" had been a certainty, if the shaping had been the obsession of a single shape, if the fascinated interest had become a determination of the will to be executed with all the *Schöpferkraft* of which he was capable, we should have said, afterward, that this urbane and somewhat placid figure had not really surprised us. The uninterrupted activity of shaping dissipated the possibility of an ultimate shape.

This constant shaping, as distinguished from constancy of shape, is characteristic of the poet. Rosenfeld appears to have been too eagerly sensitive to the figures about him to be able to isolate himself or to permit himself to be isolated, in any single shaping of his own. He was the young man (for a long time) of eager intelligence, conscious of the creative forces of his generation and delighting in them. In a way, he lived and spoke in constant praise of his generation. It may be that his generation as a whole was the ideal *Schöpfung* to which Rosenfeld has been related. He was conscious of his generation as a whole and while he may have praised it without thinking that that was what he was doing, he would have done it just the same had it occurred to him because, although he itemized, the sum of the items was his generation. In short, he saw the world in his character as poet. To be explicit, he delighted in and praised the poetry in the activity of the young sculptor, the young painter, and so on.

To be still more explicit, his character as poet made it easy and natural

246

for him to give character to the young poet, the most inchoate of human beings and yet potentially the most choate. If it should not be quite true that poets are born, not made, it seems certain that if made they must be made shortly after being born. Even then they lose character quickly. The existence of certain figures checks this loss of character. The figure most likely to do this seems to be that of the perfectly normal creature who is touched by poetry, the man of intelligence who discloses by his interest and sympathy that poetry is something significant to him. Rosenfeld was such a character.

He was not the critic angered by the idea that poetry is so much twaddle fit for fools. He was a poet himself; and he would as soon have thought that philosophy is the nonsense of apt comedians. As a member of a group, as a familiar figure, without eccentricity, saying and writing things of understanding, he communicated confidence and discipline, and a sense of the necessity of both; and in that, too, he was shaping, helping to give shape, to those to whom that meant becoming choate.

✿◈✿◈✿◈✿◈✿◈✿◈✿◈✿◈✿◈✿◈✿◈✿◈✿◈✿◈✿◈✿◈✿◈✿◈✿◈✿◈✿◈✿◈✿◈✿◈✿◈✿◈✿◈✿◈✿◈✿◈✿◈◈✿◈

## JOHN CROWE RANSOM: TENNESSEAN

What John Crowe Ransom does is to make a legend of reality. One picks up a sense of his personality in its native condition without any of the trophies of his experience as an outsider. It might be clearer to say before any of the trophies, etc., instead of without, because the reality of which he makes a legend is the reality of Tennessee. They say that there are even more Ransoms in Tennessee than Tates in Kentucky. However that may be, the more there are of you, the more you possess and the more you are possessed. To be a Ransom in Tennessee is something more precious than it is easy to say.

There are scholars who have never been anybody anywhere and never will be. Mr. Ransom is not one of them. It is hard in speaking of this sort of thing to keep on the right side. When one speaks of the personality of the Tennessean, the exact sense one has of the words cannot be conveyed hastily. The Tennessean is not the New Englander. He is not the Westerner. He is not even the Southerner. He lives in a land of his own as endeared and as beloved as any in the world, and among a people, whose chief

247

characteristic is its raciness. He would say that he lives in Tennessee and among the Tennesseans and it would be the same thing. I don't in the least mean anything romantic. On the contrary, I mean a real land and a real people and I mean Mr. Ransom as the instinct and expression of them.

One turns with something like ferocity toward a land that one loves, to which one is really and essentially native, to demand that it surrender, reveal, that in itself which one loves. This is a vital affair, not an affair of the heart (as it may be in one's first poems), but an affair of the whole being (as in one's last poems), a fundamental affair of life, or, rather, an affair of fundamental life; so that one's cry of O Jerusalem becomes little by little a cry to something a little nearer and nearer until at last one cries out to a living name, a living place, a living thing, and in crying out confesses openly all the bitter secretions of experience. This is why trivial things often touch us intensely. It is why the sight of an old berry patch, a new growth in the woods in the spring, the particular things on display at a farmers' market, as, for example, the trays of poor apples, the few boxes of black-eyed peas, the bags of dried corn, have an emotional power over us that for a moment is more than we can control.

There are men who are not content merely to acknowledge these emotions. There are men who must understand them, who isolate them in order to understand them. Once they understand them it may be said that they cease to be natives. They become outsiders. Yet it is certain that, at will, they become insiders again. In ceasing to be natives they have become insiders and outsiders at once. And where this happens to a man whose life is that of the thinker, the poet, the philosopher, the teacher, and in a broad generalized sense, the artist, while his activity may appear to be that of the outsider, the insider remains as the base of his character, the essential person, something fixed, the play of his thoughts, that on which he lavishes his sense of the prodigious and the legendary, the material of his imagination.

Mr. Ransom's poems are composed of Tennessee. It would not necessarily be the case that the poems of a native of another land would be composed of that land. But a Tennessean has no choice. O Jerusalem. O Appalachia. Above everything else Mr. Ransom's poems are not composed of the books he has read, of the academies he has seen, of the halls and columns and carvings on the columns, the stairs and towers and doorways and tombs, the wise old men and the weak young men of nowhere in particular, going nowhere at all. He himself comes out of a region dense with a life of its own, so individualized that he can tell a fellow countryman by a thousand things and not know how he does it. It is not a question of his being bold enough to be himself. He is of that hard stuff on which a mountain has been bearing down for a long time with such a weight that its impress on him has passed into everything he does and passes, through him, outward, a long distance.

But it is as a legend. As he grew into an outsider without ceasing to be an insider, it was as if everything to which he was native took on a special quality, an exact identity, a microscopic reality, which, only for what it was, had a value because it was wholly free from his outsidedness. This is what happens to things we love. He picked it up and took it with him. He drew a picture of it, many pictures of it, in his books. The greater the value he set on it, the dearer it became, the more closely he sought out its precise line and look, the more it became a legend, the peculiar legend of things as they are when they are as we want them to be, without any of the pastiche of which the presence vulgarizes so many legends and possibly everything legendary in things, not as they are, but as we should like them to be.

◇◇◇◇◇◇◇◇◇◇◇◇◇◇◇◇◇◇◇◇◇◇◇◇◇◇◇◇◇◇◇◇◇◇◇◇◇◇◇◇◇◇◇◇◇◇◇◇◇◇◇◇

## POETRY AND MEANING

Things that have their origin in the imagination or in the emotions (poems) very often have meanings that differ in nature from the meanings of things that have their origin in reason. They have imaginative or emotional meanings, not rational meanings, and they communicate these meanings to people who are susceptible to imaginative or emotional meanings. They may communicate nothing at all to people who are open only to rational meanings. In short, things that have their origin in the imagination or in the emotions very often take on a form that is ambiguous or uncertain. It is not possible to attach a single, rational meaning to such things without destroying the imaginative or emotional ambiguity or uncertainty that is inherent in them and that is why poets do not like to explain. That the meanings given by others are sometimes meanings not intended by the poet or that were never present in his mind does not impair them as meanings. On the inside cover of the album of Mahler's Fifth Symphony recently issued by Columbia there is a note on the meanings of that work. Bruno Walter, however, says that he never heard Mahler intimate that the symphony had any meanings except the meanings of the music. Does this impair the meanings of the commentators as meanings? Certainly this

249

music had no single meaning which alone was the meaning intended and to which one is bound to penetrate. If it had, what justification could the composer have had for concealing it? The score with its markings contains any meaning that imaginative and sensitive listeners find in it. It takes very little to experience the variety in everything. The poet, the musician, both have explicit meanings but they express them in the forms these take and not in explanation.

## MARCEL GROMAIRE

Catalogues for exhibitions of pictures are the natural habitat of the prose-poem. But in the case of Marcel Gromaire one feels that the need for definition comes first.

Gromaire was born in 1892 in the Département du Nord. This is the Département farthest North East in France beginning at the edge of the North Sea and running, in a narrow strip of farms and factories, half of the whole length of the Belgian border. It is a region in which the relationship with the Belgian of the present and, more particularly, the kinship with the Fleming of the past are strong, so strong, in the case of Gromaire that one's immediate impression of his work is that it is work typical of the mystical realism of a Northerner. One does not usually think of Frenchmen as mystical realists or Northerners.

Yet, for all that, Gromaire is very much of a Frenchman. He lives in Paris and has his atelier there. The paintings shown in the present exhibition are paintings of his maturity. He is now fifty-seven. Some critics have spoken of elements in his work derived from Matisse and Soutine and others have denied these derivations. Certainly, Gromaire is in no way derivative. His principal characteristic is that he is just the opposite. These oddly hallucinatory tableaux (in the English sense) are the pictures of a determined man, somewhat possessed, predestined and, because of these characteristics, also rebellious. Being rebellious is being oneself and being oneself is not being one of the automata of one's time. In consequence of being himself, Gromaire's appearances come to us, one by one, as he experiences them and not as part of the day's great, common flocks and herds and shoals of things alike.

One thing that he is determined about is substance. This is one of the truths about Gromaire. He himself speaks of "la recherche de la substance": the pursuit of substance. By substance he means the spiritual fund of the picture, the fund originating in the thought and feeling of the artist and perceptible in the painting. He does not mean the picture as itself a spiritual fund, except in that objective way. He speaks of "la qualité des œuvres, qui est leur vie même et leur pensée profonde": the property of works which is their very life and profound meaning. He speaks of the human spirit seeking its own architecture, its own "mesure" that will enable it to be in harmony with the world. It is from the intensity, the passion, of this search that the quality of works is derived, not from the codes and manuals of painting compiled by doctrinaires and conformist pedagogues. And this is the quality sought after by the clairvoyant spectator. These remarks illustrate Gromaire's mystical side.

At the same time he postulates an "art directement social" which transmits itself to the spectator without mediation or explanation, as much by reason of its "chimie intérieure": sublimation, say, as by the idea which it materializes; social in the sense of something that affects the march of events, fixes the ephemeral sensation and makes it possible for this sensation "grâce à cette pérennité conquise, d'agir sur le futur et sur le comportement humain," makes it possible for the ephemeral sensation, thanks to this acquired characteristic of being perennial, to act on the future and on human behavior. This is not the language of the individual escapist. On the contrary it is that of a painter who visualizes a great epoch for his art, in which painting instead of being "un jeu désespéré": a spiritless game, will be as he says "un don continu et fraternel, la présence de l'homme et du rythme universel qui nous régit" or, paraphrased, a brother's constant giving, a human association and the activity of the universal rhythm that dominates us.

These statements of theory define Gromaire in his own words. They help us to look at his pictures as they are: heterodox, slightly grim (an orthodox element in anything intended to be social comment), dense in color, as becomes a Goth, rugged with realism (what one expects of pictures much thought over and not exclusively sensory or abstract), uncompromising, in the idiom of Verhaeren, endowed with the strength that comes from participation in life's struggle, full of the mesmeric presence of meanings below the surface, things not of the school of Paris, but of some harsher, more fundamental zone—and one need only have in mind, say, much of Europe, much of everywhere, always.

## ON RECEIVING THE GOLD MEDAL FROM
## THE POETRY SOCIETY OF AMERICA

I am happy to receive this evening's medal and grateful that a society occupying the position of the Poetry Society of America should think me worthy of this award. Thank you. That the medal should be presented in the name of a young poet makes it all the more precious, since, among all the images of the poet, the purest is that of the young poet.

We are, here, a group of people who regard poetry as one of the sanctions of life. We believe it to be a vital engagement between the imagination and reality. The outcome of that engagement, if successful, is fulfillment. We say, also, that poetry is an instrument of the will to perceive the innumerable accords, whether of the imagination or of reality, that make life a thing different from what it would be without such insights. If we are right, then, from this serious point of view, the act of bestowing an honor on a poet is equal to the honor of receiving it.

The other day, in the middle of January, as I was taking a walk in Elizabeth Park, in Hartford, I saw at a little distance across the snow a group of automobiles that had pulled up on one side of the road. A dozen people or more got out of them. They took off their coats and threw them together in a pile on the asphalt. It was then possible to see that this was a wedding party. Often in the summer, particularly on Saturday mornings, one sees such parties there. They come to have photographs taken in the gardens. But these people had come in January. The bride stood up in white satin covered with a veil. An ornament in her hair caught the sunlight and sparkled brightly in the cold wind. The bridesmaids were dressed in dark crimson gowns with low necks. They carried armfuls of chrysanthemums. One of the men stood in the snow taking pictures of the bride, then of the bride surrounded by the bridesmaids, and so on, until nothing more was possible. Now, this bride with her gauze and glitter was the genius of poetry. The only thing wrong with her was that she was out of place.

What is the apt locale of the genius of poetry? As it happens, she creates her own locale as she goes along. Unlike the bride, she recognizes that she cannot impose herself on the scene. She is the spirit of visible and invisible change. She knows that if poetry is one of the sanctions of life, if it is truly a vital engagement between man and his environment of the world, if it is genuinely a means by which to achieve balance and measure in our circum-

252

stances, it is something major and not minor; and that if it is something major it must have its place with other major things. And knowing this and in consequence of it, she has herself chosen as her only apt locale in a final sense the love and thought of the poet, where everything she does is right and reasonable. Her power to change is so great that out of the love and thought of individual poets she makes the love and thought of the poet, the single image. Out of that which is often untutored and seemingly incapable of being tutored, insensible to custom and law, marginal, grotesque, without a past, the creation of unfortunate chance, she evolves a power that dominates life, a central force so subtle and so familiar that its presence is most often unrealized. Individual poets, whatever their imperfections may be, are driven all their lives by that inner companion of the conscience which is, after all, the genius of poetry in their hearts and minds. I speak of a companion of the conscience because to every faithful poet the faithful poem is an act of conscience.

The answer I have given to the question as to the apt locale of the genius of poetry is also the answer to the question as to the position of poetry in the world today. There is no doubt that poetry does in fact exist for the thoughtful young man in Basel or the votary in Naples. The Marxians, and for that matter a good many other people, think of it in terms of its social impact. In one direction it moves toward the ultimate things of pure poetry; in the other it speaks to great numbers of people of themselves, making extraordinary texts and memorable music out of what they feel and know. In both cases it makes itself manifest in a kind of speech that comes from secrecy. Its position is always an inner position, never certain, never fixed. It is to be found beneath the poet's word and deep within the reader's eye in those chambers in which the genius of poetry sits alone with her candle in a moving solitude.

❀◇❀◇❀◇❀◇❀◇❀◇❀◇❀◇❀◇❀◇❀◇❀◇❀◇❀◇❀◇❀◇❀◇❀◇❀◇❀◇❀◇❀◇❀◇❀◇❀◇❀◇❀◇❀◇

## ON RECEIVING THE NATIONAL
## BOOK AWARD FOR POETRY (1951)

Not long ago I was listening to a conversation between two men about modern poetry. One said to the other, "Do you really think that any of these fellows are as good, say, as Sir Walter Scott?" Now, how many of you when you go home tonight are likely to sit down and read *The Lady of the Lake?* Sir Walter Scott's poetry is like the scenery of a play that has come to an end. It is scenery that has been trucked away and stored somewhere on the horizon or just a little below. In short, the world of Sir Walter Scott no longer exists. It means nothing to compare a modern poet with the poet of a century or more ago. It is not a question of comparative goodness. It is like comparing a modern soldier, say, with an ancient one, like comparing Eisenhower with Agamemnon.

I have just used the words "a modern poet." These words are intended to mean nothing more than a poet of the present time. The word "modern" to whatever it may be attached, as, for example, a modern publisher or a bookseller with a modern shop, usually implies a sense of modishness. A modern painter is more than likely to be the product of a movement. A modern musician sounds like one the moment you hear him. However that may be, what a modern poet desires, above everything else, is to be nothing more than a poet of the present time. I think it may be said that he considers his function to be this: to find, by means of his own thought and feeling, what seems to him to be the poetry of his time as differentiated from the poetry of the time of Sir Walter Scott, or the poetry of any other time, and to state it in a manner that effectively discloses it to his readers.

I say that he is to find it by his own thought and feeling; and the reason for this is that the only place for him to find it is in the thought and feeling of other people of which he becomes aware through his own thought and feeling. Becoming aware does not always mean becoming consciously aware. His awareness may be limited to instinct. There is about every poet a vast world of other people from which he derives himself and through himself his poetry. What he derives from his generation he returns to his generation, as best he can. His poetry is theirs and theirs is his, because of the interaction between the poet and his time, which publishers, booksellers and printers do more than any others in the world to broaden and deepen.

I am happy to receive this afternoon's award and appreciate the honor that has been done me. I should like to thank the book industry for its great generosity. At the same time, I should like to thank the panel of judges of the poetry division for the pleasure they have given me and for their good will which is itself a distinction.

◇◇◇◇◇◇◇◇◇◇◇◇◇◇◇◇◇◇◇◇◇◇◇◇◇◇◇◇◇◇◇◇◇◇◇◇◇◇◇◇◇◇◇◇◇◇◇◇◇◇◇◇◇◇◇◇

# ON RECEIVING AN HONORARY DEGREE
# FROM BARD COLLEGE

The act of conferring an honor on a poet is a poetic act. By a poetic act
I mean an act that is a projection of poetry into reality. The act of conferring an academic honor on a poet is a poetic act specifically because it
engages all those that participate in it with at least the idea of poetry, for
at least a moment, that is to say it engages them with something that is
unreal, as if they had opened a door and stepped into another dimension
full of the potentialities of any dimension not immediately calculable. What
is unreal here is the idea of poetry and the projection of that idea into this
present place. To choose this immediate act as an illustration of the poetic
act is a choice of expediency only.

The act should be observed for a moment. When we go to the corner to
catch a bus or walk down the block to post a letter, our acts in doing these
things are direct. But when we gather together and become engaged with
something unreal our act is not so much the act of gathering together as it
is the act of becoming engaged with something unreal. We do this sort of
thing on a large scale when we go to church on Sunday, when we celebrate
days like Christmas or the much more impressive days of the end of Lent.
On Easter the great ghost of what we call the next world invades and vivifies
this present world, so that Easter seems like a day of two lights, one the sunlight of the bare and physical end of winter, the other the double light.
However, we find the poetic act in lesser and everyday things, as for example, in the mere act of looking at a photograph of someone who is absent
or in writing a letter to a person at a distance, or even in thinking of a remote
figure, as when Virgil, in the last lines of the last of the *Georgics*, thinks of
Cæsar and of the fact that while the poet was writing his poem

> . . . great Cæsar fired his lightnings and conquered
> By deep Euphrates.

As to this last example, it is an instance of one of the commonplaces of the
romantic. Just as in space the air envelops objects far away with an ever-
deepening blue, so in the dimension of the poetic act the unreal increasingly
subtilizes experience and varies appearance. The real is constantly being
engulfed in the unreal. But I want to be quite sure that you recognize that
I am talking about something existing, not about something purely poetic;

255

and for that reason I add one or two more examples from actuality. The act of thinking of the life of the rich is a poetic act and this seems to be true whether one thinks of it with liking or with dislike. The same thing may be said of the act of thinking of the life of the poor. Most of us do not share the life of either the one or the other and for that reason both are unreal. It is possible, too, to think of the national economy as a poetico-economy; and surely for millions of men and women the act of joining the armed forces is measurably a poetic act, since for all of them it is a deviation from the normal, impelled by senses and necessities inoperative on the ordinary level of life. The activity of the unreal in reality, that is to say, the activities of poetry in everyday life, would be like the activity of an hallucination in the mind, except for this, that the examples cited have been cited as poetic acts in the course of the visible life about us. An awareness of poetic acts may change our sense of the texture of life, but it does not falsify the texture of life. When Joan of Arc said:

> Have no fear: what I do, I do by command.
> My brothers of Paradise tell me what I have to do.

those words were the words of an hallucination. No matter what her brothers of Paradise drove her to do, what she did was never a poetic act of faith in reality because it could not be.

The important question is: what is the significance of the poetic act or, in short, what is the philosophy of what we are talking about? I am thinking of it in terms of meaning and value for the poet. Ordinarily the poet is associated with the word, not with the act; and ordinarily the word collects its strength from the imagination or, with its aid, from reality. The poet finds that as between these two sources: the imagination and reality, the imagination is false, whatever else may be said of it, and reality is true; and being concerned that poetry should be a thing of vital and virile importance, he commits himself to reality, which then becomes his inescapable and ever-present difficulty and inamorata. In any event, he has lost nothing; for the imagination, while it might have led him to purities beyond definition, never yet progressed except by particulars. Having gained the world, the imaginative remains available to him in respect to all the particulars of the world. Instead of having lost anything, he has gained a sense of direction and a certainty of understanding. He has strengthened himself to resist the bogus. He has become like a man who can see what he wants to see and touch what he wants to touch. In all his poems with all their enchantments for the poet himself, there is the final enchantment that they are true. The significance of the poetic act then is that it is evidence. It is instance and illustration. It is an illumination of a surface, the movement of a self in the rock. Above all it is a new engagement with life. It is that miracle to which the true faith of the poet attaches itself.

Mr. President, I have tried to portray, in a few words, the way of the poet as the way of the truth and I have tried to say that the need to follow this way is a need of his nature and that, at least for this generation, it is a way through reality. That sums it up. I am happy to receive the degree that you have been generous enough to confer on me. I appreciate the honor and thank you for it and for your courtesy and for the courtesy and hospitality of Bard College.

❁❖❀❖❀❖❀❖❀❖❀❖❀❖❀❖❀❖❀❖❀❖❀❖❀❖❀❖❀❖❀❖❀❖❀❖❀❖❀❖❀❖❀❖❀❖❀❖❀❖

## TWO OR THREE IDEAS

My first proposition is that the style of a poem and the poem itself are one. One of the better known poems in *Fleurs du Mal* is the one (XII) entitled "La Vie antérieure" or "Former Life." It begins with the line

J'ai longtemps habité sous de vastes portiques

or

A long time I lived beneath tremendous porches.

It continues:

Which the salt-sea suns tinged with a thousand fires
And which great columns, upright and majestic,
At evening, made resemble basalt grottoes.

The poem concerns the life among the images, sounds and colors of those calm, sensual presences

At the center of azure, of waves, of brilliances,

and so on. I have chosen this poem to illustrate my first proposition, because it happens to be a poem in which the poem itself is immediately recognizable without reference to the manner in which it is rendered. If the style and the poem are one, one ought to choose, for the purpose of illustration, a poem that illustrates this as, for example, Yeats's "Lake-Isle of Innisfree." To

257

choose a French poem which has to be translated is to choose an example in which the style is lost in the paraphrase of translation. On the other hand, Baudelaire's poem is useful because it identifies what is meant by the poem itself. The idea of an earlier life is, like the idea of a later life, or like the idea of a different life, part of the classic repertory of poetic ideas. It is part of one's inherited store of poetic subjects. Precisely, then, because it is traditional and because we understand its romantic nature and know what to expect from it, we are suddenly and profoundly touched when we hear it declaimed by a voice that says:

> I lived, for long, under huge porticoes.

It is as if we had stepped into a ruin and were startled by a flight of birds that rose as we entered. The familiar experience is made unfamiliar and from that time on, whenever we think of that particular scene, we remember how we held our breath and how the hungry doves of another world rose out of nothingness and whistled away. We stand looking at a remembered habitation. All old dwelling-places are subject to these transmogrifications and the experience of all of us includes a succession of old dwelling-places: abodes of the imagination, ancestral or memories of places that never existed. It is plain that when, in this world of weak feeling and blank thinking, in which we are face to face with the poem every moment of time, we encounter some integration of the poem that pierces and dazzles us, the effect is an effect of style and not of the poem itself or at least not of the poem alone. The effective integration is not a disengaging of the subject. It is a question of the style in which the subject is presented.

Although I have limited myself to an instance of the relation between style and the familiar, one gets the same result in considering the relation between style and its own creations, that is between style and the unfamiliar. What we are really considering here are the creations of modern art and modern literature. If one keeps in mind the fact that most poets who have something to say are content with what they say and that most poets who have little or nothing to say are concerned primarily with the way in which they say it, the importance of this discussion becomes clear. I do not mean to imply that the poets who have something to say are the poets that matter; for obviously if it is true that the style of a poem and the poem itself are one, it follows that, in considering style and its own creations, that is to say, the relation between style and the unfamiliar, it may be, or become, that the poets who have little or nothing to say are, or will be, the poets that matter. Today, painters who have something to say are less admired than painters who seem to have little or nothing to say but who do at least believe that style and the painting are one. The inclination toward arbitrary or schematic constructions in poetry is, from the point of view of style, very strong; and certainly if these constructions were effective it would be true that the style and the poem were one.

In the light of this first idea the prejudice in favor of plain English, for instance, comes to nothing. I have never been able to see why what is called Anglo-Saxon should have the right to higgle and haggle all over the page, contesting the right of other words. If a poem seems to require a hierophantic phrase, the phrase should pass. This is a way of saying that one of the consequences of the ordination of style is not to limit it, but to enlarge it, not to impoverish it, but to enrich and liberate it.

The second idea relates to poetry and the gods, both ancient and modern, both foreign and domestic. To simplify, I shall speak only of the ancient and the foreign gods. I do not mean to refer to them in their religious aspects but as creations of the imagination; and I suppose that as with all creations of the imagination I have been thinking of them from the point of view of style, that is to say of their style. When we think of Jove, while we take him for granted as the symbol of omnipotence, the ruler of mankind, we do not fear him. He does have a superhuman size, but at least not so superhuman as to amaze and intimidate us. He has a large head and a beard and is a relic, a relic that makes a kindly impression on us and reminds us of stories that we have heard about him. All of the noble images of all of the gods have been profound and most of them have been forgotten. To speak of the origin and end of gods is not a light matter. It is to speak of the origin and end of eras of human belief. And while it is easy to look back on those that have disappeared as if they were the playthings of cosmic make-believe, and on those that made petitions to them and honored them and received their benefits as legendary innocents, we are bound, nevertheless, to concede that the gods were personae of a peremptory elevation and glory. It would be wrong to look back to them as if they had existed in some indigence of the spirit. They were in fact, as we see them now, the clear giants of a vivid time, who in the style of their beings made the style of the gods and the gods themselves one.

This brings me to the third idea, which is this: In an age of disbelief, or, what is the same thing, in a time that is largely humanistic, in one sense or another, it is for the poet to supply the satisfactions of belief, in his measure and in his style. I say in his measure to indicate that the figures of the philosopher, the artist, the teacher, the moralist and other figures, including the poet, find themselves, in such a time, to be figures of an importance greatly enhanced by the requirements both of the individual and of society; and I say in his style by way of confining the poet to his role and thereby by intensifying that role. It is this that I want to talk about today. I want to try to formulate a conception of perfection in poetry with reference to the present time and the near future and to speculate on the activities possible to it as it deploys itself throughout the lives of men and women. I think of it as a role of the utmost seriousness. It is, for one thing, a spiritual role. One might stop to draw an ideal portrait of the poet. But that would be parenthetical. In any case, we do not say that the philosopher, the artist or the teacher is to take the place of the gods. Just so, we do not say that the poet is to take the place of the gods.

To see the gods dispelled in mid-air and dissolve like clouds is one of the great human experiences. It is not as if they had gone over the horizon to disappear for a time; nor as if they had been overcome by other gods of greater power and profounder knowledge. It is simply that they came to nothing. Since we have always shared all things with them and have always had a part of their strength and, certainly, all of their knowledge, we shared likewise this experience of annihilation. It was their annihilation, not ours, and yet it left us feeling that in a measure we, too, had been annihilated. It left us feeling dispossessed and alone in a solitude, like children without parents, in a home that seemed deserted, in which the amical rooms and halls had taken on a look of hardness and emptiness. What was most extraordinary is that they left no momentoes behind, no thrones, no mystic rings, no texts either of the soil or of the soul. It was as if they had never inhabited the earth. There was no crying out for their return. They were not forgotten because they had been a part of the glory of the earth. At the same time, no man ever muttered a petition in his heart for the restoration of those unreal shapes. There was always in every man the increasingly human self, which instead of remaining the observer, the non-participant, the delinquent, became constantly more and more all there was or so it seemed; and whether it was so or merely seemed so still left it for him to resolve life and the world in his own terms.

Thinking about the end of the gods creates singular attitudes in the mind of the thinker. One attitude is that the gods of classical mythology were merely aesthetic projections. They were not the objects of belief. They were expressions of delight. Perhaps delight is too active a word. It is true that they were engaged with the future world and the immortality of the soul. It is true, also, that they were the objects of veneration and therefore of religious dignity and sanctity. But in the blue air of the Mediterranean these white and a little colossal figures had a special propriety, a special felicity. Could they have been created for that propriety, that felicity? Notwithstanding their divinity, they were close to the people among whom they moved. Is it one of the normal activities of humanity, in the solitude of reality and in the unworthy treatment of solitude, to create companions, a little colossal as I have said, who, if not superficially explicative, are, at least, assumed to be full of the secret of things and who in any event bear in themselves, even if they do not always wear it, the peculiar majesty of mankind's sense of worth, neither too much nor too little? To a people of high intelligence, whose gods have benefited by having been accepted and addressed by the superior minds of a superior world, the symbolic paraphernalia of the very great becomes unnecessary and the very great become the very natural. However all that may be, the celestial atmosphere of these deities, their ultimate remote celestial residences are not matters of chance. Their fundamental glory is the fundamental glory of men and women, who being in need of it create it, elevate it, without too much searching of its identity.

The people, not the priests, made the gods. The personages of immortality were something more than the conceptions of priests, although they may have picked up many of the conceits of priests. Who were the priests? Who have always been the high priests of any of the gods? Certainly not those officials or generations of officials who administered rites and observed rituals. The great and true priest of Apollo was he that composed the most moving of Apollo's hymns. The really illustrious archimandrite of Zeus was the one that made the being of Zeus people the whole of Olympus and the Olympian land, just as the only marvelous bishops of heaven have always been those that made it seem like heaven. I said a moment ago that we had not forgotten the gods. What is it that we remember of them? In the case of those masculine do we remember their ethics or is it their port and mien, their size, their color, not to speak of their adventures, that we remember? In the case of those feminine do we remember, as in the case of Diana, their fabulous chastity or their beauty? Do we remember those masculine in any way differently from the way in which we remember Ulysses and other men of supreme interest and excellence? In the case of those feminine do we remember Venus in any way differently from the way in which we remember Penelope and other women of much mark and feeling? In short, while the priests helped to realize the gods, it was the people that spoke of them and to them and heard their replies.

Let us stop now and restate the ideas which we are considering in relation to one another. The first is that the style of a poem and the poem itself are one; the second is that the style of the gods and the gods themselves are one; the third is that in an age of disbelief, when the gods have come to an end, when we think of them as the aesthetic projections of a time that has passed, men turn to a fundamental glory of their own and from that create a style of bearing themselves in reality. They create a new style of a new bearing in a new reality. This third idea, then, may be made to conform to the way in which the other two have been expressed by saying that the style of men and men themselves are one. Now, if the style of a poem and the poem itself are one; if the style of the gods and the gods themselves are one; and if the style of men and men themselves are one; and if there is any true relation between these propositions, it might well be the case that the parts of these propositions are interchangeable. Thus, it might be true that the style of a poem and the gods themselves are one; or that the style of the gods and the style of men are one; or that the style of a poem and the style of men are one. As we hear these things said, without having time to think about them, it sounds as if they might be true, at least as if there might be something to them. Most of us are prepared to listen patiently to talk of the identity of the gods and men. But where does the poem come in? And if my answer to that is that I am concerned primarily with the poem and that my purpose this morning is to elevate the poem to the level of one of the major significances of life and to equate it, for the purpose of discussion, with gods and men, I hope it will be clear that it comes in as the central interest, the fresh and foremost object.

If in the minds of men creativeness was the same thing as creation in the natural world, if a spiritual planet matched the sun, or if without any question of a spiritual planet, the light and warmth of spring revitalized all our faculties, as in a measure they do, all the bearings one takes, all the propositions one formulates would be within the scope of that particular domination. The trouble is, however, that men in general do not create in light and warmth alone. They create in darkness and coldness. They create when they are hopeless, in the midst of antagonisms, when they are wrong, when their powers are no longer subject to their control. They create as the ministers of evil. Here in New England at this very moment nothing but good seems to be returning; and in that good, particularly if we ignore the difference between men and the natural world, how easy it is suddenly to believe in the poem as one has never believed in it before, suddenly to require of it a meaning beyond what its words can possibly say, a sound beyond any giving of the ear, a motion beyond our previous knowledge of feeling. And, of course, our three ideas have not only to be thought of as deriving what they have in common from the intricacies of human nature as distinguished from what the things of the natural world have in common, derived from strengths like light and warmth. They have to be thought of with reference to the meaning of style. Style is not something applied. It is something inherent, something that permeates. It is of the nature of that in which it is found, whether the poem, the manner of a god, the bearing of a man. It is not a dress. It may be said to be a voice that is inevitable. A man has no choice about his style. When he says I am my style the truth reminds him that it is his style that is himself. If he says, as my poem is, so are my gods and so am I, the truth remains quiet and broods on what he has said. He knows that the gods of China are always Chinese; that the gods of Greece are always Greeks and that all gods are created in the images of their creators; and he sees in these circumstances the operation of a style, a basic law. He observes the uniform enhancement of all things within the category of the imagination. He sees, in the struggle between the perfectible and the imperfectible, how the perfectible prevails, even though it falls short of perfection.

It is no doubt true that the creative faculties operate alike on poems, gods and men up to a point. They are always the same faculties. One might even say that the things created are always the same things. In case of a universal artist, all of his productions are his peculiar own. When we are dealing with racial units of the creative faculties all of the productions of one unit resemble one another. We say of a painting that it is Florentine. But we say the same thing and with equal certainty of a piece of sculpture. There is no difficulty in arguing about the poems, gods and men of Egypt or India that they look alike. But if the gods of India disappeared would not the poems of India and the men of India still remain alike. And if there were no poems, a new race of poets would produce poems that would take the place of the gods that had disappeared. What, then, is the nature of poetry in a time of disbelief? The truistic nature of some of the things that I have said shows how the free-will of the poet is limited. They demonstrate that the poetry of the future can never be anything purely eccentric and dissociated. The poetry of the present cannot be purely eccentric and dissociated. Eccentric and dissociated poetry is poetry that tries to exist or is intended to exist separately from the poem, that is to say in a style that is not identical with the poem. It never achieves anything more than a shallow mannerism, like something seen in a glass. Now, a time of disbelief is precisely a time in which the frequency of detached styles is greatest. I am not quite happy about the word detached. By detached, I mean the unsuccessful, the ineffective, the arbitrary, the literary, the non-umbilical, that which in its highest degree would still be words. For the style of the poem and the poem itself to be one there must be a mating and a marriage, not an arid love-song.

Yes: but the gods—how they come into it and make it a delicious subject, as if we were here together wasting our time on something that appears to be whimsical but turns out to be essential. They give to the subject just that degree of effulgence and excess, no more, no less, that the subject requires. Our first proposition, that the style of a poem and the poem itself are one was a definition of perfection in poetry. In the presence of the gods, or of their images, we are in the presence of perfection in created beings. The gods are a definition of perfection in ideal creatures. These remarks expound the second proposition that the style of the gods and the gods themselves are one. The exhilaration of their existence, their freedom from fate, their access to station, their liberty to command fix them in an atmosphere which thrills us as we share it with them. But these are merely attributes. What matters is their manner, their style, which tells us at once that they are as we wished them to be, that they have fulfilled us, that they are us but purified, magnified, in an expansion. It is their style that makes them gods, not merely privileged beings. It is their style most of all that fulfills themselves. If they lost all their privileges, their freedom from fate, their liberty to command, and yet still retained their style, they would still be gods, however destitute. That alone would destroy them, which deprived them of their style. When the time came for them to go, it was a time when their aesthetic had become invalid in the presence not of a greater aesthetic of the same kind, but of a different aesthetic, of which from the point of view of greatness, the difference was that of an intenser humanity. The style of the gods is derived from men. The style of the gods is derived from the style of men.

One has to pierce through the dithyrambic impressions that talk of the gods makes to the reality of what is being said. What is being said must be true and the truth of it must be seen. But the truth about the poet in a time of disbelief is not that he must turn evangelist. After all, he shares the disbelief of his time. He does not turn to Paris or Rome for relief from the monotony of reality. He turns to himself and he denies that reality was ever monotonous except in comparison. He asserts that the source of comparison having been eliminated, reality is returned, as if a shadow had passed and drawn after it and taken away whatever coating had concealed what lay beneath it. Yet the revelation of reality is not a part peculiar to a time of disbelief or, if it is, it is so in a sense singular to that time. Perhaps, the revelation of reality takes on a special meaning, without effort or consciousness on the part of the poet, at such a time. Why should a poem not change in sense when there is a fluctuation of the whole of appearance? Or why should it not change when we realize that the indifferent experience of life is the unique experience, the item of ecstasy which we have been isolating and reserving for another time and place, loftier and more secluded. There is inherent in the words *the revelation of reality* a suggestion that there is a reality of or within or beneath the surface of reality. There are many such realities through which poets constantly pass to and fro, without noticing the imaginary lines that divide one from the other. We were face to face with such a transition at the outset, for Baudelaire's line

A long time I passed beneath an entrance roof

opens like a voice heard in a theatre and a theatre is a reality within a reality. The most provocative of all realities is that reality of which we never lose sight but never see solely as it is. The revelation of that particular reality or of that particular category of realities is like a series of paintings of some natural object affected, as the appearance of any natural object is affected, by the passage of time, and the changes that ensue, not least in the painter. That the revelation of reality has a character or quality peculiar to this time or that or, what is intended to be the same thing, that it is affected by states of mind, is elementary. The line from Baudelaire will not have the same effect on everyone at all times, any more than it will continue to have the same effect on the same person constantly. I remember that when a friend of mine in Ireland quoted the line, a few years ago, in a letter, my feeling about it was that it was a good instance of the value of knowing people of different educations. The chances are that my friend in Dublin and I have done much the same reading. The chances are, also, that we have retained many different things. For instance, this man had chosen Giorgione as the painter that meant most to him. For my own part, Giorgione would not have occurred to me. I should like you to be sure that in speaking of the revelation of reality I am not attempting to forecast the poetry of the future. It would be logical to conclude that, since a time of disbelief is also a time of truth-loving and since I have emphasized that I recognize that what I am trying to say is nothing unless it is true and that the truth of it must be seen, I think that the main characteristic of the poetry of the future or the near future will be an absence of the poetic. I do not think that. I cannot see what value it would have if I did, except as a value to me personally. If there is a logic that controls poetry, which everything that I have been saying may illustrate, it is not the narrow logic that exists on the level of prophecy. That there is a larger logic I have no doubt. But certainly it has to be large enough to allow for a good many irrelevancies.

One of the irrelevancies is the romantic. It looks like something completely contemptible in the light of literary intellectualism and cynicism. The romantic, however, has a way of renewing itself. It can be said of the romantic, just as it can be said of the imagination, that it can never effectively touch the same thing twice in the same way. It is partly because the romantic will not be what has been romantic in the past that it is preposterous to think of confining poetry hereafter to the revelation of reality. The whole effort of the imagination is toward the production of the romantic. When, therefore, the romantic is in abeyance, when it is discredited, it remains true that there is always an unknown romantic and that the imagination will not be forever denied. There is something a little romantic about the idea that the style of a poem and the poem itself are one. It seems to be a much more broadly romantic thing to say that the style of the gods and the gods themselves are one. It is completely romantic to say that the style of men and men themselves are one. To collect and collate these ideas of disparate things may seem to pass beyond the romantic to the fantastic. I hope, however, that you will agree that if each one of these ideas is valid separately, or more or less valid, it is permissible to have brought them together as a collective source of suppositions. What is romantic in all of them is the idea of style which I have not defined in any sense uniformly common to all three. A poem is a restricted creation of the imagination. The gods are the creation of the imagination at its utmost. Men are a part of reality. The gradations of romance noticeable as the sense of style is used with reference to these three, one by one, are relevant to the difficulties of the imagination in a truth-loving time. These difficulties exist only as one foresees them. They may never exist at all. An age in which the imagination might be expected to become part of time's *rejectamenta* may behold it established and protected and enthroned on one of the few ever-surviving thrones; and, to our surprise, we may find posted in the portico of its eternal dwelling, on the chief portal, among the morning's ordinances, three regulations which if they were once rules of art will then have become rules of conduct. By that time the one that will matter most is likely to be the last, that the style of man is man himself, which is about what we have been saying.

It comes to this that we use the same faculties when we write poetry that we use when we create gods or when we fix the bearing of men in reality. That this is obvious does not make the statement less. On the contrary, it makes the statement more, because its obviousness is that of the truth; and in things that are central to us the last sanction is that of the truth. The three ideas are sources of perfection. They are of such a nature that they are instances of aesthetic ideas tantamount to moral ideas, a subject precious in itself but beyond our scope today. For today, they mean that however one time may differ from another, there are always available to us the faculties of the past, but always vitally new and strong, as the sources of perfection today and tomorrow. The unity of style and the poem itself is a unity of language and life that exposes both in a supreme sense. Its collation with the unity of style and the gods and the unity of style and men is intended to demonstrate this.

◇◇◇◇◇◇◇◇◇◇◇◇◇◇◇◇◇◇◇◇◇◇◇◇◇◇◇◇◇◇◇◇◇◇◇◇◇◇◇◇◇◇◇◇◇◇◇◇◇◇◇

## A COLLECT OF PHILOSOPHY

It is often the case that the concepts of philosophy are poetic. I thought, therefore, that you might like to consider the poetic nature of at least a few philosophic ideas. I have in mind ideas that are inherently poetic, as, for example, the concept of the infinity of the world. But when I wrote to Jean Wahl, who is both a poet and a philosopher, about ideas that are inherently poetic, he said immediately that no ideas are inherently poetic, that the poetic nature of any idea depends on the mind through which it passes. This is as true of the poetic aspect of nature as it is of the poetic aspect of ideas. The sun rises and sets every day and yet it brings to few men and to those men only infrequently a sense of the universe of space. However, the idea of the infinity of the world, which is the same thing as a sense of the universe of space, is an idea that we are willing to accept as inherently poetic even at moments when it means nothing at all, just as we are willing to assume that the rising and the setting of the sun are inherently poetic, even at moments when we are indifferent to them. The idea of the infinity of the world is a poetic idea because it gives the imagination sudden life. Bruno became the orator of the Copernican theory. He said,

By this knowledge we are loosened from the chains of a most narrow dungeon, and set at liberty to rove in a more august empire; we are removed from presumptuous boundaries and poverty to the innumerable riches of an infinite space, of so worthy a field, and of such beautiful worlds. . . . It is not reasonable to believe that any part of the world is without a soul, life, sensation and organic structure. From this infinite All, full of beauty and splendor, from the vast worlds which circle above us to the sparkling dust of stars beyond, the conclusion is drawn that there are an infinity of creatures, a vast multitude, which, each in its degree, mirrors forth the splendor, wisdom and excellence of the divine beauty. . . . There is but one celestial expanse, where the stars choir forth unbroken harmony.

If this is sixteenth century philosophy, it is, equally, sixteenth century poetry. One understands why Victor Hugo said, in his time, that the stars are no longer mentionable in poetry. The remark also illustrates Jean Wahl's point that that is poetic which the mind conceives to be so.

I

It will help to define what is intended by the poetic nature of concepts of philosophy to speak of a few of the things that are not intended. One of these things is a poetic way of thinking on the part of the philosopher. For the moment, I do not refer to a poetic way of writing as, for example, in the case of Plato and in modern times of Nietzsche, say, or Bergson. There is a poetic style or way of thinking. A poet's natural way of thinking is by way of figures, and while this includes figures of speech it also includes examples, illustrations and parallel cases generally. Take Leibniz, for instance. The following passage from his *Theodicy* is a compact of figurations:

> We know a very small part of eternity, which is immeasurable in its extent. . . . Nevertheless from so slight an experience we rashly judge regarding the immeasurable and eternal, like men who, having been born and brought up in prison, or perhaps in the subterranean salt mines of the Sarmatians, should think that there is no other light in the world than that of the feeble lamp which hardly suffices to direct their steps. If you look at a very beautiful picture, having covered up the whole of it except a very small part, what will it present to your sight . . . but a confused mass of colors, laid on without selection and without art? . . . The experience of the eyes in painting corresponds to that of the ears in music. Eminent composers very often mingle discords with harmonies so as . . . to prick the hearer, who becomes anxious as to what is going to happen, and is so much the more pleased when presently all is restored to order; just as . . . we delight in the show of danger that is connected with performances on the tight-rope, or sword-dancing; and we ourselves in jest half let go a little boy, as if about to throw him from us, like the ape which carried Christiern, king of Denmark, while still an infant in swaddling clothes, and then, as in jest, relieved the anxiety of everyone by bringing him safely back to his cradle.

We associate the name of Leibniz with his *Monadology*. He held that reality consists of a mass of monads, like bees clinging to a branch, although for him the branch was merely a different set of monads. Bertrand Russell said that Leibniz's monads were gods. Monad by monad, then, by way of the course of an immense unity, he achieved God. The concept of this monadic creation seems to be the disappointing production of a poet *manqué*. Leibniz

268

had a poet's manner of thinking but there was something a little too methodical about it. He had none of the enthusiasm of Bruno. There are those who regard a world of monads as poetic. Certainly the idea transforms reality. Moreover, in a system of monads, we come, in the end, to a man who is not only a man but sea and mountain, too, and to a God who is not only all these: man and sea and mountain but a God as well. Yet the idea seems to be completely lacking in anything securely lofty. Leibniz was a poet without flash. It is worth while stopping to think about him a moment because with all the equipage of a poet he never exposed any of a poet's brilliant excess in accomplishment. This may be because he was too intent on exposing something else and because he wanted his figures of speech to be the most understandable that would serve. It is worth while stopping to think of him because he stands for a class: the philosopher afraid of ornament. Men engaged in the elucidation of obscurity might well feel a horror of the metaphor. But the class I have in mind is the class to which metaphor is native and inescapable, which chooses to make its metaphors plain, and thinks from the true abundance of its thought. The disposition to metaphor cannot be kept concealed by the choice of metaphor; and one cannot help thinking that the presence of discipline is as much of an intrusion as the absence of it and, in the case of a man of genius, a deprivation and destruction. For a comparison between thinking like a philosopher and thinking like a poet, compare the quality of the image of the resemblance between the tension produced by a composer and the tension produced by a performer on the tight-rope with the quality of the image used by Jowett in his introduction to the *Phaedo*:

Is the soul related to the body as sight to the eye, or as the boatman to his boat?

Poets and philosophers often think alike, as we shall see. For the present, we must deny ourselves the definitions of poetry which are exceeded only by the definitions of philosophy. Leibniz, to sum it up, was a man who thought like a poet but did not write like one, although that seems strangely impossible; and, in consequence, his *Monadology* instead of standing as one of the world's revelations looks like a curious machine, several centuries old.

Another thing not intended is a poetic way of writing. If thinking in a poetic way is not the same thing as writing in a poetic way, so writing in a poetic way is not the same thing as having ideas that are inherently poetic conceptions. This is an accurate statement in the sense in which I mean it. Yet Plato wrote in a poetic way and certainly the doctrines of which he

269

was so constantly prolific are with great frequency concepts poetic per se. When I say that writing in a poetic way is not the same thing as having ideas that are inherently poetic concepts, I mean that the formidable poetry of Nietzsche, for example, ultimately leaves us with the formidable poetry of Nietzsche and little more. In the case of Bergson, we have a poetry of language, which made William James complain of its incessant euphony. But we also have the *élan vital*. In the case of Santayana, who was an exquisite and memorable poet in the days when he was, also, a young philosopher, the exquisite and memorable way in which he has always said things has given so much delight that we accept what he says as we accept our own civilization. His pages are part of the *douceur de vivre* and do not offer themselves for sensational summary.

Nor are we interested in philosophic poetry, as, for example, the poetry of Lucretius, some of the poetry of Milton and some of the poetry of Pope, and those pages of Wordsworth, which have done so much to strengthen the critics of poetry in their attacks on the poetry of thought. Theoretically, the poetry of thought should be the supreme poetry. Hegel called poetry the art of arts, specifically because in poetry the material of which the poem is made, that is to say, the language of the poem, is wholly subordinated to the idea. A poem in which the poet has chosen for his subject a philosophic theme should result in the poem of poems. That the wing of poetry should also be the rushing wing of meaning seems to be an extreme aesthetic good; and so in time and perhaps, in other politics, it may come to be. It is very easy to imagine a poetry of ideas in which the particulars of reality would be shadows among the poem's disclosures. If we are to dismiss from poetry expectations of that nature, we might equally well dismiss from philosophy all the profound expectations on which it is based. Of course, poems like the *De Rerum Natura* and the *Essay on Man* do not stir us particularly one way or the other, that is to say, either as poetry or as philosophy. The great poetry I have projected is a compensation of time to come. In our consideration of the poetic aspect of philosophy it is enough to dismiss the philosophic poem as irrelevant and yet, at the same time, to point out the perfection latent in it. After all, Socrates left descendants and one of them, in his youth, may choose to be concerned with the self, not in the sense common to youthful poets, but in the major sense common to the descendants of Socrates. Paul Weiss says in his *Nature and Man* that every object in the universe has some pertinence to the self. That is the sense of the self common to the descendants of Socrates.

When one says that the poetry of thought should be the supreme poetry and when one considers with what thought has been concerned throughout so many ages, the themes of supreme poetry are not hard to identify. Dr. Weiss, who was kind enough to write several letters to me last summer in relation to this paper, sent me a formulation of central doctrines to assist in the selecting of ideas which I have described as inherently poetic. I quote from one of these letters because to do so is like turning the pages of one of those books of the future about which I have been speculating. He said,

Plato: all things participate in the good; all beings love what they do not have, to wit, the good. Aristotle: all beings strive to realize their peculiar goods, already exemplified in some being somewhere in the natural world. St. Francis and St. Bonaventure: all beings have at least a trace of God in them. St. Thomas Aquinas: all existence is owed to God. Descartes: all bodies are machines. Leibniz: the world is at once the best and most rational of worlds; all the things we know in experience are combinations of spirits. Spinoza: all things happen by necessity; all things are in God. Kant: to be free is to be moral, and to be moral is to be free. Hegel: negation is a force; the absolute works out its own destiny; what comes to be is right.

Dr. Weiss did not limit himself to these formulations. He recognized that they were over-simplified. He said,

If by a poetic view we mean one which probes beneath those used in daily living, or one which cuts across the divisions which are normative to ordinary discourse, then all philosophy must be said to be poetic in conception and doctrine. It writes a cosmic poetry in prose, making use of such abstract terms as being, individuality, causality, etc. in order to talk about the presuppositions of all there is.

That all philosophy is poetic in conception and doctrine is no more true than that all poetry is philosophic in conception and doctrine. But if it was true, it would not mean that the object of all philosophic study is to achieve poetry. It would only mean what I have intended from the beginning and that is that it is often the case that the concepts of philosophy are poetic. Dr. Weiss's last remark is a statement of one of the reasons why that is true. Certainly a sense of the infinity of the world is a sense of something cosmic. It is cosmic poetry because it makes us realize in the same way in which an escape from all our limitations would make us realize that we are creatures, not of a part, which is our every day limitation, but of a whole for which, for the most part, we have as yet no language. This sudden change of a lesser life for a greater one is like a change of winter for spring or any other transmutation of poetry. Not all philosophy probes beneath daily living. Does the philosophy of science? Not all the abridgements of abstraction draw us away into metaphysical spheres. Was John Locke a mystic? It is true that philosophy is poetic in conception and doctrine to the extent that the ideas of philosophy may be described as poetic concepts. It is true all the way and not merely to an extent as Dr. Weiss puts it. To the extent stated, however, it demonstrates itself and nothing more is required. A realization of the infinity of the world is equally a perception of philosophy and a typical metamorphosis of poetry.

II

Essentially what I intend is that it shall be as if the philosophers had no knowledge of poetry and suddenly discovered it in their search for whatever it is that they are searching for and gave the name of poetry to that which they discovered. Whether one arrives at the idea of God as a philosopher or as a poet matters greatly. The philosopher if he sees God himself as a philosopher, and he usually does, adorns him with the regalia and immanences with which it would be natural for a poet to adorn him. There are levels of thought or vision where everything is poetic. But there are levels of philosophy and for that matter of poetry where nothing is poetic. Our object is to stay on the levels where everything is poetic and to give attention to what we find there, that is to say, to identify at least a few philosophic ideas that are inherently poetic and to comment on them, one by one and, then, in general. We have already noticed the idea of the infinity of the world and the somewhat furious poetry that it brought about in Bruno and we have spoken of Leibniz's world of monads or spirits. Before we stop to look at another eccentric philosophic apparatus on the grand scale in the *World as Will* of Schopenhauer, let us take a look or two at some of the poetic concepts that have resulted from the study of perception.

According to the traditional views of sensory perception, we do not see the world immediately but only as the result of a process of seeing and after the completion of that process, that is to say, we never see the world except the moment after. Thus, we are constantly observing the past. Here is an idea, not the result of poetic thinking and entirely without poetic intention, which instantly changes the face of the world. Its effect is that of an almost inappreciable change of which, nevertheless, we remain acutely conscious. The material world, for all the assurances of the eye, has become immaterial. It has become an image in the mind. The solid earth disappears and the whole atmosphere is subtilized not by the arrival of some venerable beam of light from an almost hypothetical star but by a breach of reality. What we see is not an external world but an image of it and hence an internal world. Berkeley rushed into this breach. He said,

> It is indeed an opinion strangely prevailing amongst men, that houses, mountains, rivers, and in a word all sensible objects, have an existence, natural or real,

272

distinct from their being perceived by the understanding. But with how great an assurance and acquiescence soever this principle may be entertained in the world, yet whoever shall find in his heart to call it in question may, if I mistake not, perceive it to involve a manifest contradiction. For what are the fore-mentioned objects but the things we perceive by sense? And what do we perceive besides our own ideas or sensations? And is it not plainly repugnant that any one of these, or any combination of them, should exist unperceived?

This was only one phase of Berkeley's philosophy. We are not interested, here, in following it beyond this stage. The point is that poetry is to a large extent an art of perception and that the problems of perception as they are developed in philosophy resemble similar problems in poetry. It may be said that to the extent that the analysis of perception in philosophy leads to ideas that are poetic the problems are identical. Whitehead has an important chapter related to this, "The Romantic Reaction," in his *Science and the Modern World*. He refers particularly to Wordsworth and Shelley. We have time only to mention this and, for the sake of disclosing another part of what he calls "the perceptual field," to quote one or two sentences, as follows:

My theory involves the entire abandonment of the notion that simple location is the primary way in which things are involved in space-time. In a certain sense, everything is everywhere at all times, for every location involves an aspect of itself in every other location. Thus every spatio-temporal standpoint mirrors the world.

These words are pretty obviously words from a level where everything is poetic, as if the statement that every location involves an aspect of itself in every other location produced in the imagination a universal iridescence, a dithering of presences and, say, a complex of differences.

I spoke a moment ago of the *World as Will*. Many of the ideas with which we are concerned have been very briefly summarized by Rogers in his *A Student's History of Philosophy*. I shall make use of his summary of Schopenhauer, as I have made use, elsewhere in this paper, of others of his summaries. He says,

While the world is illusion, mere appearance, there exists behind it a reality which appears—the thing-in-itself of Kant. . . . Is this thing really unknow-able, however, as Kant had claimed? . . . Schopenhauer . . . agrees that we cannot reach it by the pathway of the reason. . . . Our insight into its nature is rather the outcome of a direct intuition of genius. . . . Now the inner essence of man's nature is *will*. It is as will that the reality of his own body comes home to him immediately. The various parts of the body are the visible expression of desires; teeth, throat and bowels are objectified hunger; the brain is the will to know, the foot the will to go, the stomach the will to digest. It is only as a secondary outcome of this original activity that the thought life arises. We

273

think in order to do; the active impulse precedes, and is the necessary basis for, any conscious motion. And this insight, once attained, throws a flood of light on the outer world. The eternally striving, energizing power which is working everywhere in the universe—in the instinct of the animal, the life process of the plant, the blind force of inorganic matter—what is this but the will that underlies all existence? . . . Reality, then, is will. . . . We must leave out of our conception of the universal will that action for intelligent ends which characterizes human willing. . . . The will is thus far deeper seated than the intellect; it is the blind man carrying on his shoulders the lame man who can see.

These words depict, in the imagination, a text of the grotesque, both human and inhuman. It is the text of a poem although not a happy one. It is, in a way, the same poem as the poem of Leibniz although the terms are different. It is the cosmic poem of the ascent into heaven. I suppose that some kinds of faith require logical, even though fantastic, structures of this kind to support them on the way of that ascent. The number of ways of passing between the traditional two fixed points of man's life, that is to say, of passing from the self to God, is fixed only by the limitations of space, which is limitless. The eternal philosopher is the eternal pilgrim on that road. It is difficult to take him seriously when he relies on the evidence of the teeth, the throat and the bowels. Yet in the one poem that is unimpeachably divine, the poem of the ascent into heaven, it is possible to say that there can be no faults, since it is precisely the faults of life that this poem enables us to leave behind. If the idea of God is the ultimate poetic idea, then the idea of the ascent into heaven is only a little below it. Conceding that not all philosophy is concerned with this particular poem, nevertheless a great deal of it is, and always has been, and the philosophy of Schopenhauer is. The poets of that theme find things on the way and what they find on the way very often interests as much as what they find in the end. Thus, Samuel Alexander in *Space, Time and Deity* finds the order of compresence. He says,

What is of importance is the recognition that in any experience the mind enjoys itself and contemplates its object or its object is contemplated, and that these two existences, the act of mind and the object as they are in the experience, are distinct existences united by the relation of compresence. The experience is a piece of the world consisting of these two existences in their togetherness. The one existence, the enjoyed, enjoys itself, or experiences itself as an enjoyment; the other existence, the contemplated, is experienced by the enjoyed. The enjoyed and the contemplated are together.

Dr. Alexander expresses himself with the same straining for the utmost exactness in the words he uses as the straining of a poet for like exactness.

As a matter of fact, it is what philosophers find on the way that constitutes the body of philosophy for if the end is appointed in advance neither logic nor the lack of it can affect their passage. Jean Wahl wrote to me, saying

I am just now reading the *Méditations cartésiennes* by Husserl. Very dry. But he affirms that there is an enormous (*ungeheueres*) a priori in our minds, an inexhaustible infinity of a priori. He speaks of the approach to the unapproachable.

This enormous a priori is potentially as poetic a concept as the idea of the infinity of the world. Jean Wahl spoke, also, of other things in which you might be interested: of Pascal in a frightened mood saying "Le silence de ces espaces infinis m'effraie," adding appropriately that in Victor Hugo one might find echoes of that idea. He quoted again from Pascal: "La sphère dont le centre est partout et la circonférence est nulle part," as a concept belonging to our category. He spoke of the idea of the *ricorsi* of Vico; the idea of the *ewige Wiederkehr* of Nietzsche; the idea of freedom as developed in the French philosopher Lequier; the idea of "les vérités éternelles" of Malebranche. He particularly suggested the poems of Traherne. We have, however, excluded poems of philosophical intentions from our discussion. He had spoken in an earlier letter of Novalis influenced by the ideas of Fichte; Hölderlin influencing, in his opinion, the young Hegel; Shelley influenced by Plato; Blake; Mallarmé influenced by the Kabbala and Hegel. But these were all poets and I was approaching the subject the other way and with a different end in view. I was not interested in the philosophy of poets but in the poetry of philosophers. He made many other suggestions which I am happy to acknowledge for there is no one, what with his immense reading, to whom I could be more easily or more willingly indebted. I am not a philosopher.

Jean Paulhan sent some notes. He said,

It seems to me that the old psychological theory of perception considered as a true hallucination is the very type of the call to poetry. . . . The first word of the philosophy of the sciences, today, is that science has no value except its effectiveness and that nothing, absolutely nothing, constitutes an assurance that the external world resembles the idea that we form of it. Is that a poetic idea? Anti-poetic, rather, in that it is opposite to the confidence which the poet, by nature, reposes, and invites us to repose, in the world. Let us say that it needs poetry to rise above itself; hence that it is an invitation to much poetry. It is an indirect way of being poetic.

Later on, he expressed himself as thinking that the philosophy of the sciences would lend itself better to the kind of poetry that I am trying to specify. His attitude toward the problem was not that of a man looking at the past but that of a man looking at the present and asking himself whether the concepts of the philosophy of the sciences are poetic. He said,

It is admitted, since Planck, that determinism—the relation of cause to effect—exists, or so it seems, on the human scale, only by means of an aggregate of statistical compensations and as the physicists say, by virtue of macroscopic approximations. (There is much to dream about in these macroscopic approximations.) As to the true nature of corpuscular or quantic phenomena, well, try to imagine them. No one has yet succeeded. But the poets—it is possible.

And later, because his mind had been engaged by the subject, he sent a last word. He said,

It comes to this that philosophers (particularly the philosophers of science) make, not discoveries but hypotheses that may be called poetic. Thus Louis de Broglie admits that progress in physics is, at the moment, in suspense because we do not have the words or the images that are essential to us. But to create illuminations, images, words, that is the very reason for being of poets.

### III

Let us see, now, what deductions can be made from all this material.

First of all, since a similarity has been established between poets and philosophers and since it can no longer be necessary to argue that a measure of identity exists between them, what is the fundamental respect that separates them. The habit of forming concepts unites them. The use to which they put their ideas separates them. By the habit of forming concepts, I do not, of course, mean merely thinking, for all men have in common the habit of thinking. The habit of forming concepts is a habit of the mind by which it probes for an integration. Where we see the results of that habit in the works of philosophers we may think that it is a habit which they share with no one else. This is untrue. The habit of probing for an integration seems to be part of the general will to order. We must, therefore, go a step farther and look for the respect that separates the poet and the philosopher in the kind of integrations for which they search. The philosopher searches for an integration for its own sake, as, for example, Plato's idea that knowledge is recollection or that the soul is a harmony; the poet searches for an integration that shall be not so much sufficient in itself as sufficient for some quality that it possesses, such as its insight, its evocative power or its appearance in the eye of the imagination. The philosopher intends his integration to be fateful; the poet intends his to be effective.

And yet these integrations, although different from each other, have something in common, such as, say, a characteristic of the depth or distance

276

at which they have been found, a facture of the level or position of the mind or, if you like, of a level or position of the feelings, because in the excitement of bringing things about it is not always easy to say whether one is thinking or feeling or doing both at the same time. The probing of the philosopher is deliberate, as the history of the part that logic has played in philosophy demonstrates. Yet one finds it simple to assume that the philosopher more or less often experiences the same miraculous shortenings of mental processes that the poet experiences. The whole scheme of the world as will may very well have occurred to Schopenhauer in an instant. The time he spent afterward in the explication of that instant is another matter. The idea of the Hegelian state, one of the masterpieces of idealism, may very well have come into Hegel's mind effortlessly and as a whole, as distinct from its details, in the same way that the gist of a poem comes into the poet's mind and takes possession of it. It remains true, however, that the probing of the philosopher is deliberate. On the other hand, the probing of the poet is fortuitous. I am speaking of the time before he has found his subject, because, once he has found his subject, that is to say, once he has achieved the integration for which he has been probing, he becomes as deliberate, in his own way, as the philosopher. Up to the point at which he has found his subject, the state of vague receptivity in which he goes about resembles one part of something that is dependent on another part, which he is not quite able to specify. In any case, it is misleading to speak of the depth or distance at which their integrations are found, or of the level or position of the mind or feelings, if the fact is that they probe in different spheres and if, in their different spheres, they move about by means of different motions. It may be said that the philosopher probes the sphere or spheres of perception and that he moves about therein like someone intent on making sure of every foot of the way. If the poet moves about in the same sphere or spheres, and occasionally he may, he is light-footed. He is intent on what he sees and hears and the sense of the certainty of the presences about him is as nothing to the presences themselves. The philosopher's native sphere is only a metaphysical one. The poet's native sphere is the sphere of which du Bellay wrote: "my village . . . my own small house . . ."

> My Gaulish Loire more than the Latin Tiber,
> My tiny Lyré more than the Palatine hill,
> And more than sea-salt air, the sweet air of Anjou.

This seductive quotation takes one away from the sphere of perception a little too abruptly and too completely; for, after all, the philosopher, also, has a solid land that he loves. The poet's native sphere, to speak more accurately, is what he can make of the world.

The uses to which the philosopher and the poet put the world are different and the ends that they have in mind are different. This statement raises the question of the final cause of philosophy and the final cause of poetry. The answers to this question are as countless as the definitions of philosophy and poetry. The other day I read a phrase in Alain: "the history of doctrines." These words give us a single sense and an inadequate sense of what philosophy is. If I say that poetry constantly requires a new station, it is a way, and an inadequate way, of saying what poetry is. To define philosophy and to define poetry are parts of the repertory of the mind. They are classic exercises. This could not be true if the definitions were adequate. In view of this difficulty about definitions, any discussion of the final causes of philosophy and poetry must be limited, here, to pointing out the relation between the question of purposes and the miscellany of definitions. And yet for all the different kinds of philosophy it is possible to generalize and to say that the philosopher's world is intended to be a world, which yet remains to be discovered and which, at bottom, the philosophers probably hope will always remain to be discovered and that the poet's world is intended to be a world, which yet remains to be celebrated and which, at bottom, the poets probably hope will always remain to be celebrated. If the philosopher's world is this present world plus thought, then the poet's world is this present world plus imagination. If we think of the philosopher and the poet as raised to their highest exponents and made competent to realize everything that the figures of the philosopher and the poet, as projected in the mind of their creator, were capable of or, in other words, if we magnify them, what would they compose, by way of fulfilling not only themselves but also by way of fulfilling the aims of their creator? This brings us face to face once more with all the definitions. But whatever they composed, they could not compose the same thing and, perhaps, we should wonder what had ever led us to believe that they were close together.

Yet we should never be able to get away, even under this extreme magnifying, from the sense that they had in common the idea of creating confidence in the world:

la confiance que le poète fait naturellement—et nous invite à faire—au monde.

The confidence of the philosopher might be a certainty with respect to something to be left behind. The confidence of the poet might be a more immediate certainty. These are ancient routines. The means used by philosophers and poets alike change and disappear. Other means take their place. An immense amount of philosophy is no longer part of our thought and yet perpetuates itself. The soul and Leibniz's swarms of spirits and Schopenhauer's manifestations of will, which appear to us to be eccentric conceptions, are not junk. Thus the soul lives as the self. When we read the *Phaedo*, we stand in the presence of Socrates, in the chamber in which he is shortly to die and we listen to him as he expounds his ideas concerning immortality. We observe that his confidence in the immortality of what was really Socrates was no less a confidence in the world, in which he reclined and spoke, a hostile and a fatal world. When we look over the shoulder of Jean Paulhan, in Paris, while he writes of "la confiance . . . au monde" and stop to consider what a happy phrase that is, we wonder whether we shall have the courage to repeat it, until we understand that there is no alternative. So many words other than *confidence* might have been used—words of understanding, words of reconciliation, of enchantment, even of forgetfulness. But none of them would have penetrated to our needs more surely than the word *confidence*.

The most significant deduction possible relates to the question of supremacy as between philosophy and poetry. If we say that philosophy is supreme, this means that the reason is supreme over the imagination. But is it? Does not philosophy carry us to a point at which there is nothing left except the imagination? If we rely on the imagination (or, say, intuition), to carry us beyond that point, and if the imagination succeeds in carrying us beyond that point (as in respect to the idea of God, if we conceive of the idea of God as this world's capital idea), then the imagination is supreme, because its powers have shown themselves to be greater than the powers of the reason. Philosophers, however, are not limited to the reason and, as the concepts, to which I have referred, show, their ideas are often triumphs of the imagination. To call attention to ideas in which the reason and the imagination have been acting in concert is a way of saying that when they act in concert they are supreme and is not the same thing as to say that one is supreme over the other. I might have cited the idea of God when I was speaking of the infinity of the world, of the infinite spaces, which terrified Pascal, the most devout of believers and, in the same abandonment to the superlative, the most profound of thinkers; and it would have been possible, in that case, to conclude what I have to say by placing here at the end a figure which would leave the question of supremacy a question too difficult to attempt to solve. In his words about the sphere of which the center is everywhere and the circumference nowhere, which I quoted a moment ago, we have an instance of words in which traces of the reason and traces of the imagination are mingled together.

However, instead of placing at the end the figure of Pascal, let me place here the figure of Planck. I recognize that Pascal was a much greater human being. On the other hand, Planck, who died only four years ago at Göttingen, at the age of ninety, was a much truer symbol of ourselves; and in that true role is a more significant figure for us than the remote and almost fictitious figure of Pascal. I referred to him earlier and in relation to the quantum theory. There has recently been published in Europe a group of his posthumous texts, of which one is a thesis on *The Concept of Causality in Physics*. He was, of course, the patriarch of all modern physicists. André George published a note on these last writings of this great scholar in *Les Nouvelles Littéraires*, which I summarize to the extent that it is in point, particularly in respect to the thesis on causality. He says:

. . . The last pages of the thesis are quite curious. One feels there, as it were, a supreme hesitation; the believer henceforth is no longer able to conceal a certain trouble. The most convinced determinist, Planck declares, in so many words, is not able to satisfy himself entirely with such an interpretation. For, in the end, a universal principle like the rigorous causal bond between two successive events ought to be independent of man. It is a principle of cosmic importance, it ought to be an absolute. Now, Planck not only recognizes that it is part of human aptitude to foresee events but to foresee them by means of science, "the provisional and changing creation of the power of the imagination." How then liberate the concept from such an anthropomorphic hypothesis? Only an intelligence external to man, "not constituting a part of nature," would be able to liberate it. This supra-natural intelligence would act through the deterministic power . . . Planck thereupon concludes that the law of causality is neither true nor false. It is a working hypothesis.

George says, finally, that this conclusion is far away from the rigid concept, firmly determinist, which seemed up to now to constitute Planck's belief. He calls it a nuance but a nuance of importance, worth being signalized.

I think we may fairly say that it is a nuance of the imagination, one of those unwilled and innumerable nuances of the imagination that we find so often in the works of philosophers and so constantly in the works of poets. It is unexpected to have to recognize even in Planck the presence of the poet. It is as if in a study of modern man we predicated the greatness of poetry as the final measure of his stature, as if his willingness to believe beyond belief was what had made him modern and was always certain to keep him so.

# A NOTE ON "LES PLUS BELLES PAGES"

Apparently the poem means that the conjunction of milkman and moonlight is the equivalent of the conjunction of logician and saint. What it really means is that the interrelation between things is what makes them fecund. Interaction is the source of potency. Sex is an illustration. But the principle is not confined to the illustration. The milkman and the moonlight are an illustration. The two people, the three horses etc. are illustrations. The principle finds its best illustration in the interaction of our faculties or of our thoughts and emotions. Aquinas is a chance example: a figure of great modern interest, whose special force seems to come from the interaction between his prodigious logic and his prodigious love of God. The idea that his theology, as such, is involved, is dismissed in the last line. That the example is not of scholarly choice is indicated by the title. But the title also means that les plus belles pages are those in which things do not stand alone but are operative as the result of interaction, interrelation. This is an idea of some consequence, not a casual improvisation. The interrelation between reality and the imagination is the basis of the character of literature. The interrelation between reality and the emotions is the basis of the vitality of literature, between reality and thought the basis of its power.

# RAOUL DUFY

Raoul Dufy's sudden death in March, 1953, was like a rip in the rainbow. His work for the lithographs in the present portfolio had been completed. The collection was far advanced toward its appearance. It was based on his largest and most significant fresco. It had engaged him seriously for a long period of time. He regarded it as a typical and sympathetic undertaking and he looked forward to its publication as a kind of radiant realization. But this realization of the spirit of the artist was destined to be a realization on the part of others after his death. The work reveals Dufy, on a scale beyond comparison with anything else he has done, exploiting, as artist, the world we know and the world of what we know, which are always the same. It is an exploitation of fact by a man of elevation. It is a surface of prose changeable with the luster of poetry and thought.

The lithographs enable us to see how Dufy, for all the documentation that was inevitable, for all the ten supernumeraries from the *Comédie-Française* who posed for him, for all the costuming, for all the full year of study and observation, prevails, in the end, purely as artist; and how all the ideas, documentation, study and observation, of which the original fresco was composed, are subdued, finally, by Dufy's sense; and seeing this clearly, seeing how the artist is enabled to carry lightly the burden imposed on him by a great work, until, when it is finished, we have, not a memorial of work but the happiness of the artist who has achieved what he wanted to achieve as artist (and in this case the peculiar *allégresse* associated with Dufy's name), we experience a confidence that in the many futures of knowledge, the artist will always come through as one of the masters of his particular time.

Dufy was asked to do a mural painting for the electricity pavilion at the International Exposition at Paris in 1937. For this purpose he produced a work about thirty feet high and a little less than two hundred feet wide, in which he traced the history of light and power from pastoral time to the present time. He included figures as large as life of the principal characters who, in the course of history, and this means universal history, contributed by their discoveries or inventions to the coming on of electricity, its uses and the engineering incidental thereto. To overcome the notion of electricity as an abstraction, he symbolized it as *La Fée Electricité*, a fay rather plump and wholesome from the American point of view respecting fays and, perhaps, an improvement on that point of view. Now, what is Dufy's attitude toward all this material? It is the same attitude to which he has accustomed us in his work generally. His personalizing of the scenes that have interested him has always been slight. He has never forged blatant Dufyisms out of what he saw. There was never any melodrama and, although there was poetry, it was pretty much the radiance of exact prose, a gaiety of strokes like a gaiety of words. In consequence, this epic of *La Fée Electricité*, composed, episodically, day by day, over a long period of time, has all the interest and meaning of a simple prose narrative. Yet it is a scroll of poetry in its truth and the implications of its truth. Dufy does not engage in "the dire delight, negative and cantankerous, of men who are lacking in sense." He remains steadfast in his own intelligence delineating and allowing history to crowd its figures upon him. An artist has no being who has no identity. Here in this large work one finds the identity that we recognize as Dufy, engaged in all the delectations that make up his identity, extended and prolonged. He is not speculating about the future of the world, the potentialities of changes inherent in knowledge nor the integrity of the artist. These are glosses. He is not discursive. He knows that everything depends on concentration. He concentrates effortlessly on what is within his focus, so that it is natural for the highest point of his painting to be a collection of electrical machinery in a power plant in Paris, say, instead of some sparkling fantasy acted by his planetary heroine.

The lithographs are original works. To reproduce the original fresco it had to be done over again. When he painted the work for the first time Dufy had to enlarge everything. After the work had been schematized and reduced, Dufy repainted it for this portfolio, in its new scale, making a few changes, as, for example, eliminating figures which in the process of reduction had become too small. The lithographs are the only form in which the work is available, short of the construction of a special building to contain the fresco itself.

Near the figure of Goethe there is a quotation from one of Goethe's letters, as follows:

I shall turn myself toward the artisans—chemistry—The hour of the beautiful has gone by; today, misery and implacable necessity lay claim to our time.

That approach to the modern goes far back, as the lithographs show; but regardless of the degree of remoteness the words of Goethe, or similar words, have always been in the air above the approach. Today more than ever those words are heard on the approach to what is presently modern, since the finality of what is modern is never fully and ultimately attainable. At the moment, the approach is precise, taking nothing for granted. Dufy's La Fée Electricité is most definitely a union of drudge and dazzling angel.

The intelligence is part of the comedy of life. It was not only that Dufy tried to dress each of the many figures that appear in his fresco in clothes that were appropriate and which they might have worn; nor that he had a scholar from the Sorbonne tutor him a little in respect to electricity; nor that he visited various central electric stations throughout France; it was not only that he tried to grasp the truth. He tried, also, to express his own intelligence respecting these things, that is: to produce a painting that interests us by its reality and which, in these lithographs, gives us an experience as with a multitude of actualities, an experience intense and yet without extravagance. The lithographs leave us feeling that the dissipations of life inevitably arrange themselves in a final scene, a scene that fills us with optimism and satisfaction as the characters leave the stage with all the lights burning. Is not that, after all, the chief effect of this pageant? Is it not the principal thing that the individuality of Dufy should be the coordinating force and high issue of all these details? And is not this high issue one of those choices of the intelligence of an artist who, by making this choice, goes forward with the train of his characters, of whom he is really one, committed to the same purpose? These great blues of Dufy are a kind of assertion of strength. They create a human self-confidence, as if one had known from the beginning the eventual denouement of knowledge, so long postponed and so incredible.

✿◈✿◈✿◈✿◈✿◈✿◈✿◈✿◈✿◈✿◈✿◈✿◈✿◈✿◈✿◈✿◈✿◈✿◈✿◈✿◈✿◈✿◈✿◈✿◈✿◈✿◈✿◈✿◈✿◈✿◈✿◈✿◈✿◈✿◈✿◈✿◈✿◈◈✿◈

## THE WHOLE MAN: PERSPECTIVES, HORIZONS

The subject of "The Whole Man" would have excited the attention of Professor Whitehead. One of his constant concerns was with the effect of types of individuals or groups on society and, in the long run, this was a concern with civilization. For example, he said, "College faculties are going to want watching. . . . I don't need to tell you that there is a good deal of sniffing on this, the Harvard College and graduate schools side of the Charles River, sniffing at the new Harvard School of Business Administration on the opposite bank. . . . If the American universities were up to their job they would be taking business in hand and teaching it ethics and professional standards."

These remarks illustrate the existence of a relation between an imaginative thinker like Professor Whitehead and business. To consider the effect of his presence as a member of the board of directors of a corporation of national scope or, for that matter, as a member of the executive committee of one of the larger unions, makes a dazzling parenthesis. I am trying to make a point by citing Professor Whitehead as an example of an all-round man, because I do not think the definition of an all-round man necessarily includes a man of any actual technical business experience. He need not be a banker who collects books or a manufacturer who reads philosophy. It is a question of breadth of character and, say, diversity of faculties. In order to establish in your minds Professor Whitehead's right to the title, let me quote him again: "The mischief of elevating the type that has aptitude for economic advancement is that it denies the superior forms of aptitude which exist in quite humble people. Who shall say that to live kindly and graciously and meet one's problems bravely from day to day is not a great art, or that those who can do it are not great artists. Aesthetics are understood in too restricted a sense."

This sketches for you a man who did as much as any man can do to qualify as an all-round man. He began life as a mathematician and ended it as a philosopher. He is a wholly contemporaneous figure although no longer alive. My quotations are from his *Dialogues* as recorded by Lucien Price.

Last week I received a letter, greetings on my seventy-fifth birthday, from a young scholar, a Korean. When he was at New Haven, he used to come up to Hartford and the two of us would go out to Elizabeth Park, in Hartford, and sit on a bench by the pond and talk about poetry. He did not wait for the ducks to bring him ideas but always had in mind questions that disclosed his familiarity with the experience of poetry. He spoke in the most natural English. He is now studying in Switzerland at Fribourg, from where his letter came. It was written in what appeared to be the most natural French. Apparently they prize all-round young men in Korea, too. In his letter, he said, "Seventy-five years is not a great deal, when one thinks that the poets and philosophers of the Far East, nourishing themselves only on the mist, have been able to prolong life up to one hundred and even one hundred and fifty years. Historians tell us that they have then been able to enter into fairyland, which is beyond our comprehension today."

That is my idea of a specialist. If these venerable men, by reducing themselves to skin and bones and by meditation prolonged year after year, could perceive final harmony in what all the world would concede to be final form, they would be supreme in life's most magnificent adventure. But they would still be specialists. They would, of course, be specialists in precisely that respect which led us to regard Professor Whitehead as a specimen of the all-round man.

There is an inevitable rapport between all men who seek the truth and who hope, thereby, to be made free and to remain free. I, for one, do not regard the all-round man as the apt opposite of the vertical man. It is illusory so to regard him. There is not the same contradistinction that would exist, say, between the horizontal and the vertical or between the latitudinal and the longitudinal. What really exists is the difference between the theorist and the technician, the difference between Hamlet and Horatio, the difference between the man who can talk about pictures and the man who can afford to buy them. None of these differences involve direct and total opposites. The best technician, the purest mechanic, is necessarily something of a theorist. Hamlet was far more pushing than Horatio ever thought of being, when it came to the point. More often than the satirists admit, the man who can afford to buy pictures is entirely competent to take their measure and at the same time to take the measure both of the artist and of the dealer.

Admitting, however, that human nature contains no built-in iron curtains, the relation of the theorist to society is one thing and the relation of the technician is another. They do not make their impacts by what they have in common but by that in which they differ. The community does not reflect their likenesses but their unlikenesses. If we personalize a university, it corresponds to the all-round man. It is a complex of theorists and of some exceedingly vertical characters. As a whole, however, it is articulate only through its theorists. The world is the world through its theorists. Their function is to conceive of the whole and, from the center of their immense perspectives, to tell us about it. If we say that the basic consideration underlying this evening's discussion is that there are grades of importance in the multitude of man's concerns and that things of first importance must have precedence over things of secondary or lesser importance, it becomes clear that the man who applies himself to considerations of first importance must have precedence over the man who applies himself to things of secondary or lesser importance. This does not require demonstration. Let me try, nevertheless. Modern art often seems to be an attempt to bridge the gap between fact and miracle. To succeed in doing this, if it can be done at all, seems to be exclusively the task of the specialist, that is to say, the painter. If we want to build a bridge, we are bound to employ a bridge builder. It would not help us to invoke even the ghost of Professor Whitehead, which is, no doubt, an exceedingly able-bodied ghost. Sooner or later, however, some all-round man is going to think about this particular bit of bridge building. He will say that there is a kind of corollary to the relation between the theorist and the technician (or if you prefer between the humanist and the scientist) and the relation between art, on the one hand, and painting, on the other. It seems likely that modern art will be affected more by what he has to say by way of approval, if he should approve, or by way of disapproval, if he should disapprove, than by what the painters themselves will have to say.

I suppose it is true that nothing keeps painting alive from one time to another except its form. What is true of painting is no less true of poetry and music. Form alone and of itself is an ever-youthful, ever-vital beauty. The vigor of art perpetuates itself through generations of form. But if the vigor of art is itself formless, and since it is merely a principle it must be, its form comes from those in whom the principle is active, so that generations of form come from generations of men. The all-round man is certain to scrutinize form as he scrutinizes men, that is to say, in relation to all past form. It is inevitable that, from his scrutiny of past form, some ideal should have been created, whether it is derived from something actual in the past or something desired to become actual in the future. Modern art is inescapably framed within these large horizons, which, certainly, are not the horizons of a school, whether of time or place. I repeat that what is true of painting is no less true of poetry and music. The principle of poetry is not confined to its form however definitely it may be contained therein. The principle of music would be an addition to humanity if it were not humanity itself, in other than human form, and while this hyberbole is certain to be repulsive to a good many people, still it may stand. This is the life of the arts which the all-round man thinks of in relation to life itself.

You may be saying that I am going beyond the intentions of this evening's general subject, that I am changing the man with more interests than one into a figure slightly fabulous and also that I am changing the specialist, who is, after all, a creature of necessity, into an illiberal bigot; and that the figures with whom we are really concerned are the educated, intelligent, widely experienced man on the one hand, and the educated, intelligent, less widely experienced man on the other. The trouble is that a man's scope may be independent of his education, intelligence, and experience. Furthermore, one may at least express uncertainty about this scope always having a relation to his effect on society. Notwithstanding this, I prefer my slightly fabulous creature of thought and my technician. As to the latter, it may be said that the ever-increasing mass of people could not live together in the world without the technician and that the elevating of the level of life for people in general is, in all except its concept, a technical problem. The all-round man was in his heyday, in this country, a hundred and fifty or even two hundred years ago. Looking back at them, many of our original political philosophers seem to have been just such all-round men: Franklin, Washington, Jefferson, Madison. There were no technicians, or few. A city the size of New York today could not exist without technicians. We live here today by the aid of types living a century and more apart. What a many-sided man Dr. Benjamin Rush of Philadelphia seems to us to have been. In what a leisurely, spacious city he lived. Did Dr. Rush have much choice about it? Could Philadelphia have been anything but what it was? Could Franklin, Washington, Jefferson, Madison have lived different lives? If we account for our technicians by saying that they are part of the struggle for survival, can we account for our all-round men in any other way? Are the all-round men any less the result of pressure than the technicians? What pressure? What other pressure could it be than the pressure of society itself, the developing forces, the demands and permissions of people adapting themselves to the circumstances in which they find themselves, devising the formulae of civilized existence? The human struggle, however, is immensely more than the mere struggle to survive than these questions suggest.

It is possible to conceive of a neo-Platonic republic in which technicians would be political and moral neuters. In such a republic, one class would be the class of all-round men: the general thinkers, the over-all thinkers, men capable of different sights, the sturdy fathers of that very republic and the authors of its political and moral declarations. Since most of us are technicians on at least one side or, say, to some extent, those in whom we reposed the profoundest confidence would actually be few, perhaps a group composed of men with minds like the rapacious and benign mind of Professor Whitehead. To be ruled by thought, in reality to govern ourselves by the truth or to be able to feel that we were being governed by the truth, would be a great satisfaction, as things go. The great modern faith, the key to an understanding of our times, is faith in the truth and particularly in the idea that the truth is attainable, and that a free civilization based on the truth, in general and in detail, is no less attainable.

◇◇◇◇◇◇◇◇◇◇◇◇◇◇◇◇◇◇◇◇◇◇◇◇◇◇◇◇◇◇◇◇◇◇◇◇◇◇◇◇◇◇◇◇◇◇◇◇◇◇◇◇◇◇◇◇◇

## ON RECEIVING THE NATIONAL BOOK
## AWARD FOR POETRY (1955)

When a poet comes out of his cavern or wherever it is that he secretes himself, even if it is a law office or a place of business, and suddenly finds himself confronted by a great crowd of people, the last thing in the world that enters his mind is to thank those who are responsible for his being there. And this is particularly true if the crowd has come not so much on his account as on account, say, of a novelist or some other figure, who is, as a rule, better known to it than any poet. And yet the crowd will have come, to some extent on his account, because the poet exercises a power over life, by expressing life, just as the novelist does; and I am by no means sure that the poet does not exercise this power at more levels than the novelist, with more colors, with as much perception and certainly with more music, not merely verbal music, but the rhythms and tones of human feeling.

I think then that the first thing that a poet should do as he comes out of his cavern is to put on the strength of his particular calling as a poet, to address himself to what Rilke called the mighty burden of poetry and to have the courage to say that, in his sense of things, the significance of poetry is second to none. We can never have great poetry unless we believe that poetry serves great ends. We must recognize this from the beginning so that it will affect everything that we do. Our belief in the greatness of poetry is a vital part of its greatness, an implicit part of the belief of others in its greatness. Now, at seventy-five, as I look back on the little that I have done and as I turn the pages of my own poems gathered together in a single volume, I have no choice except to paraphrase the old verse that says that it is not what I am, but what I aspired to be that comforts me. It is not what I have written but what I should like to have written that constitutes my true poems, the uncollected poems which I have not had the strength to realize.

Humble as my actual contribution to poetry may be and however modest my experience of poetry has been, I have learned through that contribution and by the aid of that experience of the greatness that lay beyond, the power over the mind that lies in the mind itself, the incalculable expanse of the imagination as it reflects itself in us and about us. This is the precious scope which every poet seeks to achieve as best he can.

Awards and honors have nothing to do with this. The role of awards and honors in the life of a poet is simply to bring him back to reality, to remind him, in the midst of all his hopes for poetry, that he lives in the world of Darwin and not in the world of Plato. He does not accept them as a true satisfaction because there is no true satisfaction for the poet but poetry itself. He accepts them as tokens of the community that exists between poetry on the one hand and men and women on the other. He accepts them not for their immediate meaning but as symbols and it is their secondary value that makes him the richer for having received them.

And having said this much, I feel better able to express my obligation to this body and to the judges for the privilege of being here today and for the honor they have done me and to say that I am grateful to them and thank them. And I am grateful to my publisher, Alfred Knopf, and his staff, and thank them for the notably handsome job they made of the *Collected Poems*.

289

# A FOOTNOTE TO SAUL BELLOW'S
## "PAINS AND GAINS"

Some years ago a cable car in San Francisco let go and by the time it arrived at the foot of California Street the passengers were all over the place. A man who had not seen what had happened came out of a side street and went to the nearest victim and asked him what it was all about. The man who was lying in the street said to him, "Well, there has been an accident and we are waiting for the adjuster for the street car company to turn up." "Do you mind," said the newcomer, "if I lie down with you."

# TWO PREFACES

### I

### *Gloire du long désir, Idées*

Denis Saurat refers to *Eupalinos* as Valéry's "prose masterpiece," not meaning more, however, than that it was one of a number of masterpieces by Valéry in prose, not to speak of his masterpieces in verse. He cites a brief passage or two and then says, "You have to go back to Bossuet to find such writing in prose." It is easy to believe this of *Eupalinos* if you give yourself up to some of the more rhetorical episodes. There is, for example, the passage in which Socrates speaks of the chance that had placed in his hands an object which became, for him, the source of reflections on the difference between constructing and knowing. Phaedrus asked him to help him to see the object, and thereupon Socrates said:

Well then, Phaedrus, this is how it was. I was walking on the very edge of the sea. I was following an endless shore. . . . This is not a dream I am telling you. I was going I know not whither, overflowing with life, half-intoxicated by my youth. The air, deliciously rude and pure, pressing against my face and limbs, confronted me—an impalpable hero that I must vanquish in order to advance. And this resistance, ever overcome, made of me, too, at every step an imaginary hero, victorious over the wind, and rich in energies that were ever reborn, ever equal to the power of the invisible adversary. . . . That is just what youth is.

290

I trod firmly the winding beach, beaten and hardened by the waves. All things around me were simple and pure: the sky, the sand, the water.

Merely to share the balance and the imagery of these words is to share the particular exhilaration of the experience itself. Then, too, toward the close of the work, in the speech in which Socrates states the conclusions to which the speakers have been brought, he substitutes for oral exhilaration the exhilaration that comes from the progression of the mind. Only enough of this true apostrophe can be cited to identify it. Socrates says to Phaedrus:

> O coeternal with me in death, faultless friend, and diamond of sincerity, hear then:
> It served no purpose, I fear, to seek this God, whom I have tried all my life to discover, by pursuing him through the realm of thought alone; by demanding of him that most variable and most ignoble sense of the just and the unjust, and by urging him to surrender to the solicitings of the most refined dialectic. The God that one so finds is but a word born of words, and returns to the word. For the reply we make to ourselves is assuredly never anything other than the question itself; and every question put by the mind to the mind is only, and can only be, a piece of simplicity. But on the contrary, it is in acts, and in the combination of acts, that we ought to find the most immediate feeling of the presence of the divine, and the best use for that part of our strength that is unnecessary for living, and seems to be reserved for the pursuits of an indefinable object that infinitely transcends us.

Valéry himself has commented on the work. In a letter to Paul Souday written in 1923, he said:

> I was asked to write a text for the album *Architectures*, which is a collection of engravings and plans. Since this text was to be magnificently printed in folio format and fitted in exactly with the decoration and pagination of the work, I was requested to limit its size quite precisely to 115,800 *letters* . . . 115,800 characters! It is true, the characters were to be sumptuous.
> I accepted. My dialogue was at first too long. I shortened it; and then a little too short—I lengthened it. I came to find these exigencies very interesting, though it is possible that the text itself may have suffered a little in consequence.
> After all, the sculptors never complained who were obliged to house their Olympian personages inside the obtuse triangle of pediments! . . .

There is, also, a letter to Dontenville, *inspecteur d'Académie*, written in 1934. The letter to Paul Souday was written a few months after the composition of *Eupalinos*. The letter to Dontenville was written after the lapse of ten years. Valéry, referring again to the requirement of 115,800 characters, said:

> This rigor, at first astounding and repellent, albeit required of a man accustomed enough to the rigor of poems in fixed form, made this man wonder at first—but then find that the peculiar condition proposed to him might be easily

enough satisfied by employing the very elastic form of the *dialogue*. (An insignificant rejoinder, introduced or cut out, allows us a few fumblings to conform with fixed requirements of measurement.) The adjustment was, in effect, easily made in the proofs.

The vast proof sheets I received gave me the strange impression that I had in my hands a work of the sixteenth century and was 400 years dead.

The name of Eupalinos was taken by me from the article "Architecture" in the *Encyclopédie Berthelot*, when I was looking for the name of an architect. I since learned, from a study by the learned Hellenist Bidez (of Ghent), that Eupalinos, an engineer more than an architect, dug canals and built scarcely any temples; I gave him my ideas, as I did Socrates and Phaedrus. Moreover, I have never been in Greece; and as for Greek, I have unfortunately remained the most indifferent of scholars, getting lost in the original text of Plato and finding him, in the translations, terribly long and often boring. . . .

Since Valéry describes Eupalinos as of Megara, and since it was at Megara that the school of Euclid flourished, Valéry's ascription of the name of Eupalinos to the *Encyclopédie Berthelot* dispels the idea of any relation between Eupalinos and Euclid. Finally, to return to the letter to Paul Souday, Valéry said of "these dialogues":

They are works made to order, in which I have not managed or known how to establish a true thought in its most favorable light. I should have tried to show that pure thought and the search for truth in itself can only ever aspire to the discovery or the construction of some *form*.

What, then, are the ideas that Valéry has chosen to be discussed by the shades of Socrates and his friend Phaedrus, as they meet, in our time, in their "dim habitation" on the bank of Ilissus? They are alone and remain alone. Eupalinos does not appear and takes no part in the discussion, unless, as he is spoken of, an image of him passes, like the shade of a shade. The talk is prolonged, and during its course, one or the other speaker propounds ideas. If we attempt to group a number of the ideas propounded, we have something like the following:

There are no details in execution.

Nothing beautiful is separable from life, and life is that which dies.

We must now know what is truly beautiful, what is ugly; what befits man; what can fill him with wonder without confounding him, possess him without stupefying him. . . . It is that which puts him, without effort, above his own nature.

By dint of constructing, . . . I truly believe that I have constructed myself. . . . To construct oneself, to know oneself—are these two distinct acts or not?

292

What is important for me above all else is to obtain from *that which is going to be,* that it should with all the vigor of its newness satisfy the reasonable requirements of *that which has been.*

O body of mine . . . keep watch over my work. . . . Grant me to find in thy alliance the feeling of what is true; temper, strengthen, and confirm my thoughts.

No geometry without the word.

Nothing can beguile, nothing attract us, . . . nothing by us is chosen from among the multitude of things, and causes a stir in our souls, that was not in some sort pre-existent in our being or secretly awaited by our nature.

An artist is worth a thousand centuries.

Man . . . fabricates by abstraction.

Man can act only because he can ignore.

That which makes and that which is made are indivisible.

The greatest liberty is born of the greatest rigor.

Man's deepest glances are those that go out to the void. They converge beyond the All.

If, then, the universe is the effect of some act; that act itself, the effect of a Being, and of a need, a thought, a knowledge, and a power which belong to that Being, it is then only by an act that you can rejoin the grand design, and undertake the imitation of that which has made all things. And that is to put oneself in the most natural way in the very place of the God.
Now, of all acts the most complete is that of constructing.

But the constructor whom I am now bringing to the fore . . . takes as the starting point of his act, the very point where the god had left off. . . . Here I am, says the Constructor, I am the act.

Must I be silent, Phaedrus?—So you will never know what temples, what theaters, I should have conceived in the pure Socratic style! . . . And exercising an ever stricter control over my mind, at the highest point I should have realized the operation of transforming a quarry and a forest into an edifice, into splendid equilibriums! . . .
Then out of raw materials I was going to put together my structures entirely ordained for the life and joy of the rosy race of men. . . . But you shall learn no more. You can conceive only the old Socrates, and your stubborn shade. . . .

This is the substance of the dialogue between Socrates and Phaedrus, or, at least, these sayings, taken from their talk, indicate what they have been talking about. And what in fact have they been talking about? And why is

Valéry justified when, in his closing words, Socrates says: ". . . all that we have been saying is as much a natural sport of the silence of these nether regions as the fantasy of some rhetorician of the other world who has used us as puppets!" Have we been listening to the talk of men or of puppets? These questions are parts of the fundamental question, What should the shades of men talk about, or in any case what may they be expected, categorically, to talk about, in the Elysian fields? Socrates answers this question in the following manner:

Think you not that we ought now to employ this boundless leisure which death leaves us, in judging and rejudging ourselves unwearyingly, revising, correcting, attempting other answers to the events that took place, seeking, in fine, to defend ourselves by illusions against nonexistence, as the living do against their existence?

This Socratic question (and answer) seems empty. The Elysian fields would be the merest penal habitude, if existence in them was not as absolute as it is supposed to be eternal and if our disillusioned shades were dependent, there, on some fresh illusion to be engendered by them for themselves in that transparent realm. It cannot be said freely that Valéry himself fails to exhibit Socrates and Phaedrus engaged in any such discussion, for as the talk begins to reach its end, there emerges from it an Anti-Socrates, to whom an Anti-Phaedrus is listening, as if their conversation had been, after all, a process of judging and rejudging what they had done in the past, with the object of arriving at a state of mind equivalent to an illusion. The dialogue does not create this impression. It does not seem to us, as we read it, that we are concerned with the fortunes of the selves of Socrates and Phaedrus, notwithstanding that that would be a great concern.

We might well expect an existence after death to consist of the revelation of the truth about life, whether the revelation was instantaneous, complete, and dazzling, or whether it was a continuity of discoveries made at will. Hence when a conversation between Socrates and Phaedrus after death occurs, we somehow expect it to consist of resolutions of our severest philosophical or religious difficulties, or of some of them. The present dialogue, however, is a discussion of aesthetics. It may even be said to be the apotheosis of aesthetics, which is not at all what we have had in mind as that which phantoms talk about. It makes the scene seem more like a place in provincial France than either an archaeological or poetic afterworld. In view of Valéry's reference to "the very admirable Stephanos," it is clear that the scene is the afterworld of today, since Mallarmé died in 1898. The trouble is that our sense of what ought to be discussed in the afterworld is derived from specimens that have fallen into disuse. Analysis of the point would be irrelevant. It seems enough to suppose that to the extent that the dead exist in the mind of the living, they discuss whatever the living discuss, although it cannot be said that they do it in quite the same way, since when Phaedrus told Socrates how Socrates, if he had been an architect, would have surpassed "our most famous builders," Eupalinos included, Socrates replied: "Phaedrus, I beg of you! . . . This subtle matter of which we are now made does not permit of our laughing. I feel I ought to laugh, but I cannot. . . . So refrain!"

This elevation of aesthetics is typical of Valéry's thought. It is itself an act of construction. It is not an imbalance attributable to his nature as a poet. It is a consequence of reasonable conviction on his part. His partiality for architecture was instinctive and declared itself in his youthful *Introduction to the Method of Leonardo da Vinci*. It was not an artificiality contrived to please the company of architects who had commanded *Eupalinos*. It seems most natural that a thinker who had traced so much of man's art to man's body should extend man's art itself to the place of God and in that way should relate man's body to God, in the manner in which this is done in *Eupalinos*. Socrates said: "I cannot think that there exists more than one Sovereign Good."

Phaedrus then spoke of what Eupalinos had said concerning forms and appearances. He repeated the words of Eupalinos:

Listen, Phaedrus . . . that little temple, which I built for Hermes, a few steps from here, if you could know what it means to me!—There where the passer-by sees but an elegant chapel—'t is but a trifle: four columns, a very simple style—there I have enshrined the memory of a bright day in my life. O sweet metamorphosis! This delicate temple, none knows it, is the mathematical image of a girl of Corinth, whom I happily loved. It reproduces faithfully the proportions that were peculiarly hers. It lives for me! It gives me back what I have given it. . . .

Eupalinos had then spoken of buildings that are mute, of others that speak, and of others that sing, for which he gave the reasons.

Socrates interrupted Phaedrus with a reference to his prison, which he called "a drab and indifferent place in itself." But he added, "In truth, dear Phaedrus, I never had a prison other than my body."

Eupalinos had gone on to speak to Phaedrus of the effect on the spirit of the sites of ports: ". . . the presence of the pure horizon, the waxing and the waning of a sail, the emotion that comes of being severed from the earth, the beginning of perils, the sparkling threshold of lands unknown." He did not profess to be able to connect up an analysis with an ecstasy. He said:

I feel my need of beauty, proportionate to my unknown resources, engendering of itself alone forms that give it satisfaction. I desire with my whole being. . . . The powers assemble. The powers of the soul, as you know, come strangely up out of the night. . . . By force of illusion they advance to the very borders of the real. I summon them, I adjure them by my silence. . . .

He continued:

O Phaedrus, when I design a dwelling (whether it be for the gods, or for a man), and when I lovingly seek its form, . . . I confess, how strange soever it may appear to you, *that it seems to me my body is playing its part in the game.*

Eupalinos ended with the prayer to his body, which Socrates called "an unexampled prayer," when Phaedrus repeated it. It is Socrates himself—in the apostrophe to Phaedrus, beginning "O coeternal with me in death," in the closing pages of the dialogue—who says that man by his acts puts himself in the place of God, not meaning that he becomes God but that he puts himself in the very place of God: *la place même du Dieu.*

It follows that for Eupalinos and for men like him what they do is their approach to the divine and that the true understanding of their craft and the total need that they feel to try to arrive at a true understanding of it and also at an exact practice of it are immeasurably the most important things in the world, through which the world itself comes to the place of the divine. The present work has to be read with all this in mind. Any rigorous intellectual discipline in respect to something significant is a discipline in respect to everything significant. Valéry's own discipline appears in every page of the dialogue. The need to understand uncommon things and to manifest that understanding in common things shows itself constantly. The modeling of the cluster of roses is an instance. The comparison of the object found on the shore of the sea, a natural object, with an object made by man is another. The parable of the Phoenician and how he went about making a ship is a third. It is the parable of the artist. The image of the Phoenician's boat recalled to Socrates ". . . the black, loose-flapping sails of the vessel with its load of priests, which as it labored back from Delos, dragging on its oars. . . ."

At this, Phaedrus exclaimed, "How little you seem to relish living your beautiful life over again!"

Socrates then asked, "Is there anything vainer than the shadow of a sage?"

And Phaedrus said, "A sage himself." The image of the man of action makes the shade of the man of thought regret his life. It is, in a way, the triumphant image of the constructor as it faces the image of the man of thought. Perhaps on his own grounds, it was Valéry, for all his life of study, full of the sea, watching the departure of the Phoenician's supreme boat on its maiden voyage: "Her scarlet cheeks took all the kisses that leapt up to meet her on her course; the well-stretched triangles of her full, hard sails held down her quarter to the wave. . . ."

Is it not possible that one of the most perceptive texts of modern times, although neither immense nor varied, and containing little of life and the nature of man, is yet a masterpiece? Within the limits of the work, Valéry expresses ideas relevant to the thought of his time as it came to consider, with an unprecedented interest, the problems of art. In the dialogue, Socrates speaks of these expatiations as if with a nuance of their triviality. As he continued to probe, his interest heightened to such an extent that he lost his own traditional character; and in this, he became part of the new time in which his shade comes close to us. The nuance of triviality had vanished by the time he reached the noble speech beginning "O coeternal with me in death," when he was ready to say:

> The Demiurge was pursuing his own designs, which do not concern his creatures. The converse of this must come to pass. He was not concerned about the troubles that were bound to spring from that very separation which he diverted or perhaps bored himself with making. He has given you the means of living, and even of enjoying many things, but not generally those which you particularly want.
> But I come after him. I am he who conceives what you desire a trifle more exactly than you do yourselves. . . . I shall make mistakes sometimes, and we shall have some ruins; but one can always very profitably look upon a work that has failed as a step which brings us nearer to the most beautiful.

In the end, Socrates had become the constructor, and if he had, then Valéry had. The thinker had become the creator. Jean Wahl might have diminished this to a defense mechanism. Perhaps it was an appearance of what Alain called the inimitable visage of the artist. To be a little more exact in quoting Alain, one should say that the creator had asserted its parentage of the thinker, for Alain had spoken of thought as the daughter of poetry in a passage peculiarly applicable to Valéry. He had said that of all the indicators of thought the most sensitive were poets, first because they take risks a little further than logic permits; also because the rule they adopt always carries them a little beyond what they hoped for. Mallarmé and Valéry announce a new climate of thought. They want clear enigmas, those that are developable, that is to say, mathematical. Alain says:

And if it is true, as I believe, that Thought, daughter of Poetry, resembles her mother, we shall see everywhere a clarity of details, a clarity won by conquest, in

297

the place of our vague aspirations; and the young will make us see another manner of believing—which will be a refusal to believe.

*Eupalinos* is a work of this "clarity of details." This is its precise description. In it Valéry made language itself a constructor, until Socrates asked:

What is there more mysterious than clarity? . . . What more capricious than the way in which light and shade are distributed over hours and over men? . . . Orpheuslike we build, by means of the word, temples of wisdom and science that may suffice for all reasonable creatures. This great art requires of us an admirably exact language.

It has been said that Rilke, who translated so much of Valéry, including *Eupalinos*, felt an intense interest, as a poet, in the language of the work. The page on music—". . . a mobile edifice, incessantly renewed and reconstructed within itself, and entirely dedicated to the transformations of a soul"; the page on the sea shore—"This frontier between Neptune and Earth"; the page on in the beginning—"In the beginning . . . there was what is: the mountains and the forests . . ."—are pages of true poetry. It was natural for such pages to give Rilke pleasure. But what impressed him was what he called the composure and finality of Valéry's language. Rilke read *Eupalinos* when it came out in the *Nouvelle Revue Française,* and his translation of it was the last work he did before he died.

It seems sometimes, in the fluidity of the dialogue, as if the discussion was casual and fortuitous or, say, Socratic. But a discussion over which the mind of Socrates presides derives much of its vitality from this characteristic, so that when the talk is over, we have a sense of extended and noble unity, a sense of large and long-considered form.

II

*Chose légère, ailée, sacrée*

In 1930, Louis Séchan published a work on *La Danse grecque antique,* which contained a chapter on Valéry's *Dance and the Soul.* M. Séchan was Professor of Greek Language and Literature at the University of Montpellier. He sent a copy of this book to Valéry, who acknowledged it in a letter, which it seems worth while to copy at length, as follows:

I thank you greatly for your attention in sending me your fine work on Greek dancing. I learn from it many things I ignored—and even ignored about myself. Your kind chapter on my little dialogue generously attributes to me much more

298

erudition than I ever possessed. Neither Callimachus nor Lucian, Xenophon nor the Parthenia was known to me; and would not in any case have been of much use to me. Documents in general impede rather than help me. They result in difficulties for me, and consequently in peculiar solutions, in all those compositions in which history must play some part.

In reality, I confined myself to dipping into Emmanuel at the Library, and I left open on my table the book of Marey which I have had for the last thirty years. Those outline drawings of jumping and walking, some memories of ballets were my essential resources. The flutist does come from the Throne. The head compact like a pine cone from a living dancer.

The constant thought of the Dialogue is physiological—from the digestive troubles of the prelude-beginning to the final swoon. Man is slave to the sympathetic and pneumogastric nerves. Sumptuary sensations, the gestures of luxury, and spectacular thoughts exist only by the good favor of these tyrants of our vegetative life. Dance is the type of the runaway.

As for the form of the whole, I have tried to make of the Dialogue itself a sort of ballet of which the Image and the Idea are Coryphaeus in turn. The abstract and the sensible take the lead alternately and unite in the final vertigo.

To sum up: I in no degree strove for historic or technical rigor (and for very good reason). I freely introduced what I needed to maintain my Ballet and vary its figures. This extended to *the ideas themselves*. Here they are *means*. It is true that this idea (that ideas are means) is familiar to me, and perhaps *substantial*. It leads on, moreover, to wicked thoughts about philosophy (cf. "Leonardo and the Philosophers," which I published last year).

I should never have planned to write on the dance, to which I had never given serious thought. Moreover, I considered—and I still do—that Mallarmé had exhausted the subject in so far as it belongs to literature. This conviction made me first refuse the invitation of the *Revue Musicale*. Other reasons made me resolve to accept it. What Mallarmé had prodigiously written then became a peculiar condition of my work. I must neither ignore him nor espouse his thought too closely. I adopted the line of introducing, amid the divers interpretations which the three characters give of the dance, the one whose formulation and incomparable demonstration through style are to be found in the *Divagations*.

I have explained myself at considerable length. But I feel I owe this to one who has been such an attentive and even fervent critic of my Dialogue. You have perfectly presented its spirit, which, in truth, is neither *this* nor *that*—neither with Plato, nor according to Nietzsche, but an act of transformation.

The nature of M. Séchan's book can be gathered from Valéry's comment on it. M. Séchan thought that Valéry's attitude toward *Dance and the Soul* as something fortuitous was typical of Valéry. He discussed Mallarmé's remarks in *Divagations* on the dance as corporeal writing or hieroglyphic, and he dwelt on the resemblance between the dance and the meditations of the spirit in moments of tension. He referred to the analysis of *Dance and the Soul* by Paul Souday in the latter's work on Valéry and, in particular, to the contrasting conceptions of the dance by the persons taking part in the present dialogue, thus: the conception of Eryximachus (the Eryximachus of Plato's *Symposium*) that the dance is purely sensory; the conception of Phaedrus (the Phaedrus of *Eupalinos*) that the dance is psychologically evocative; and the conception of Socrates, which reconciles the other two, that the dance is an interpretation of a secret and physical order. And finally M. Séchan speaks of the fact that both Schopenhauer and Nietzsche were influential forces at the time when Valéry was maturing. But he regards *Dance and the Soul* as Apollonian rather than Dionysian, because as Apollonian it corresponds better with the Greek genius. It is, in fact, possible, if only because Valéry published *Eupalinos* and *Dance and the Soul* together and because they seem to be inseparable companions, that Valéry had a sense that *Eupalinos* was Apollonian and that *Dance and the Soul* was Dionysian. On the other hand, it is certain that Valéry's own genius was Apollonian and that the Dionysian did not comport with it, and, with that, the subject may be dismissed.

*Dance and the Soul* is a lesser work than *Eupalinos*, since it does not contain the proliferation of ideas which characterizes *Eupalinos*. Socrates is always and everywhere proliferation. In this dialogue, however, he confines himself to the proliferation of a single idea. He asks repeatedly the question, "O my friends, what in truth is dance?" and again, "But what then is dance, and what can steps say?" and again, "O my friends, I am only asking you what is dance. . . ."

While these questions are being asked, a dance is going on, a ballet is being danced. The scene is a banqueting place with a banquet in course. There are servants serving food and no end of wine. The persons are Socrates, Phaedrus, and Eryximachus, great numbers of multicolored groups of smiling figures, whirling and dissolving in enchanted sequences, Athikte, the *première danseuse*, who is commencing, the *musiciennes*, one of whom, coral-rose, is blowing an enormous shell, another, a tall flute-player, who denotes the measure with her toe. Socrates is conscious of ideas that come to him as he watches Athikte and observes the majesty of her movements. Eryximachus exclaims: "Dear Socrates, she teaches us that which we do, showing clearly to our souls that which our bodies accomplish obscurely."

Phaedrus adds: "In which respect this dancer would, according to you, have something Socratic, teaching us, in the matter of walking, to know ourselves a little better."

These remarks illustrate the constant allusions to the dancers which keep the reader of the dialogue in the presence of the dancers. He hears the voices of the speakers and watches the movements of the dancers at one and the same time, without the least confusion, as he would do in reality; and as his interest in what is being said grows greater as the discussion approaches its resolutions, and as his absorption in the spectacle becomes deeper with his increased understanding of it and because of the momentum toward the ultimate climax, he realizes, for the first time, the excitement of a meaning as it is revealed at once in thought and in act.

The work is regenerative. M. Séchan quoted the words of Plato on the poet: *chose légère, ailée, sacrée*. These words apply equally to Valéry's text. Here again we have what we had in *Eupalinos*, the body as source and the act in relation to the body. Socrates says to Eryximachus:

Do you not see then, Eryximachus, that among all intoxications the noblest, the one most inimical to that great tedium, is the intoxication due to acts? Our acts, and more particularly those of our acts which set our bodies in motion, may bring us into a strange and admirable state. . . .

Still speaking to Eryximachus, he made a gesture in the direction of

. . . that ardent Athikte, who divides and gathers herself together again, who rises and falls, so promptly opening out and closing in, and who appears to belong to constellations other than ours—seems to live, completely at ease, in an element comparable to fire—in a most subtle essence of music and movement, wherein she breathes boundless energy, while she participates with all her being in the pure and immediate violence of extreme felicity.

As he continues, he says what sums up his argument and sums up the whole work:

If we compare our grave and weighty condition with the state of that sparkling salamander, does it not seem to you that our ordinary acts, begotten by our successive needs, and our gestures and incidental movements are like coarse materials, like an impure stuff of duration—whilst that exaltation and that vibration of life, that supremacy of tension, that transport into the highest agility one is capable of, have the virtues and the potencies of flame; and that the shames, the worries, the sillinesses, and the monotonous foods of existence are consumed within it, making what is divine in a mortal woman shine before our eyes?

There is a series of speeches by Socrates in the closing pages of the dialogue which are full of the noble rhetoric of the truth. But they are still rhetoric; and it is the presence of this rhetoric of the truth that makes the work regenerative. It is rhetoric to say: "In a sonorous world, resonant and rebounding, this intense festival of the body in the presence of our souls offers light and joy. . . . All is more solemn, all more light, all more lively, all stronger; all is possible in another way; all can begin again indefinitely. . . ." So, too, it is rhetoric to say: "I hear the clash of all the glittering arms of life! . . . The cymbals crush in our ears any utterance of secret thoughts.

They resound like kisses from lips of bronze. . . ." It is, however, this rhetoric, the eloquent expression of that which is precisely true, that gives what it expresses an irresistible compulsion as when Socrates says: "A body, by its simple force, and its act, is powerful enough to alter the nature of things more profoundly than ever the mind in its speculations and dreams was able to do!"

While Socrates is pronouncing his subtle and solemn words, our eyes remain fastened on Athikte, while she tries to make us see that which Socrates is seeking to tell us. She moves through jewels, makes gestures like scintillations, filches impossible attitudes from nature, so that Eryximachus says, "Instant engenders form, and form makes the instant visible." She continues to dance until she falls. When she has fallen and lies, white, on the ground, she says something to herself, the simplest possible thing. Phaedrus asks what it is and Eryximachus replies, "She said: 'How well I feel!' "—a remark immense with everything that Socrates himself had been saying a moment or two before. She has spoken in a rhetoric which achieves the pathetic essential almost without speech. It is obvious that this degree of agitation has been reached in what is, after all, an exegetical work, through the form of the work. Valéry's slim and cadenced French adds its own vitality to the original. It seems enough to present the work in this brief manner. André Levinson said in relation to *Dance and the Soul*: "To explain a thing is to deform it; to think is to substitute what is arbitrary for the unknowable truth." What *Dance and the Soul* requires is not so much explanation as—what Valéry called M. Séchan—attentive and fervent critics or, say, readers, willing to experience the transformation which knowing a little about themselves brings about as by miracle or, say, by art.

Man has many ways to attain the divine, and the way of Eupalinos and the way of Athikte and the various ways of Paul Valéry are only a few of them.

❀◇❀◇❀◇❀◇❀◇❀◇❀◇❀◇❀◇❀◇❀◇❀◇❀◇❀◇❀◇❀◇❀◇❀◇❀◇❀◇❀◇❀◇❀◇❀◇❀◇❀◇❀◇❀◇❀◇❀◇❀◇❀◇❀◇❀◇❀◇❀◇❀◇

# CONNECTICUT COMPOSED

The thrift and frugality of the Connecticut Yankee were necessary to life in the Colony and still are. They were imposed on him by the character of the natural world in which he had come to live, which has not changed.

It required thrift and frugality to live in Connecticut and still does. And now after three centuries or more of this tradition, the people of the state are proud of it. They are proud of the kind of strength of character which they have derived from this necessity, proud of the intelligent ingenuity with which they faced their many hardships and with which they rose to the high general level of intelligence and dignified style of living that is now so characteristic of them. The other day, early in April, when the weather was still bleak and everything still had the look of winter, I went from Hartford to Boston, on the railroad by way of Willimantic. Everything seemed gray, bleached and derelict and the word *derelict* kept repeating itself as part of the activity of the train. But this was a precious ride through the character of the state. The soil everywhere seemed thin and difficult and every cutting and open pit disclosed gravel and rocks, in which only the young pine trees seemed to do well. There were chicken farms, some of them abandoned, and there were cow-barns. The great barns of other states do not exist. There were orchards of apples and peaches. Yet in this sparse landscape with its old houses of gray and white there were other houses, smaller, fresher, more fastidious.

And spring was coming on. It was as if the people whose houses I was seeing shared the strength that was beginning to assert itself. The man who loves New England and particularly the spare region of Connecticut loves it precisely because of the spare colors, the thin lights, the delicacy and slightness of the beauty of the place. The dry grass on the thin surfaces would soon change to a lime-like green and later to an emerald brilliant in a sunlight never too full. When the spring was at its height we should have a water-color not an oil and we should all feel that we had had a hand in the painting of it, if only in choosing to live there where it existed. Now, when all the primitive difficulties of getting started have been overcome, we live in the tradition which is the true mythology of the region and we breathe in with every breath the joy of having ourselves been created by what has been endured and mastered in the past. We think of the state not only as a matrix, but as a very mother, above all in the spring, when the reward of discipline is visible and tangible, or seems to be. We seem to be conscious then, more than at any other time, of the extent to which those who helped to prepare each present season are part of it, and of the extent to which the nature of the land is part of them and of ourselves.

There are only some two million people living in the state, which is the third smallest state in the country. Of these a quarter of a million are foreign-born. Of those who were born in the state, many are the children of parents who were themselves foreign-born, or of parents whose parents,

generation back of generation, were foreign-born. All of us together constitute the existing community. Those who descend from earlier generations
know that the forces that moulded them are today moulding those who
descend from later generations. The children look alike. There are no
foreigners in Connecticut. Once you are here you are or you are on your
way to become a Yankee. I was not myself born in the state. It is not that
I am a native but that I feel like one. It interests me to think of our sea-
coast—the coast-line of Connecticut, much of it merely the coast of Long
Island Sound. I like to think of all the small ports and harbors on that
coast, the little fishing towns; also the towns up and down the Connecticut
River, the anchorages of the whalers. Those who did not do too well at
making livings in Connecticut made their livings in China or the Marquesas
or Jamaica and used the banks of the Connecticut River as the sites of
their dwellings and of the gazebos in the gardens of their dwellings, in
which they sat and planned and fostered the temples and universities and
the many practical enterprises to which their imaginations were addicted.

But that was when they had come home. There is nothing that gives the
feel of Connecticut like coming home to it. I am not thinking of the
thousands of commuters who come home to it every night from New York;
nor even, since it is not a question of distance, of those returning after
remoter and longer absences. It is easy to see the picture in the mind of
those who are far away as if the state was a single metropolis, in the way
they say that England is a park. Truly Connecticut is much like a single
metropolis, highly industrial, with factories and mills and shops and schools
and homes spread out everywhere, with a few major concentrations in
Bridgeport, New Haven, Hartford, New London. One could say in a few
words simply that Connecticut is an industrial and business center. That
would leave out the saltwater of Noank and Stonington, the hills in which
the various Cornwalls are situated, the sense of being on high land, of
being on a large plateau, at Pomfret, the rare rich fields over East, the
heights and depths of our Western and part of our Northern borders, the
special countries of the Housatonic and the Thames. Yet to return to these
places would not be quite what I had in mind when I spoke of the coming
home that gives one the feel of Connecticut. What I had in mind was
something deeper that nothing can ever change or remove. It is a question
of coming home to the American self in the sort of place in which it was
formed. Going back to Connecticut is a return to an origin. And as it happens, it is an origin which many men all over the world, both those who
have been part of us and those who have not, share in common: an origin
of hardihood, good faith and good will.

# QUESTIONNAIRE

# RESPONSES

# RESPONSES TO *NEW VERSE* QUESTIONNAIRE

## AN ENQUIRY

1. *Do you intend your poetry to be useful to yourself or others?*
2. *Do you think there can now be a use for narrative poetry?*
3. *Do you wait for a spontaneous impulse before writing a poem; if so, is this impulse verbal or visual?*
4. *Have you been influenced by Freud and how do you regard him?*
5. *Do you take your stand with any political or politico-economic party or creed?*
6. *As a poet what distinguishes you, do you think, from an ordinary man?*

1. Not consciously. Perhaps I don't like the word *useful*.
2. There can now be a use for poetry of any sort. It depends on the poet.
3. Most often. While the immediate impulse is verbal, there is, no doubt, a group of impulses.
4. No. I have not read Freud except the *Interpretation*.
5. I am afraid that I don't.
6. Inability to see much point to the life of an ordinary man. The chances are an ordinary man himself sees very little point to it.

# RESPONSES TO *TWENTIETH CENTURY VERSE* QUESTIONNAIRE

## ENQUIRY

1. *Do you think a representative "American poetry" exists now, distinct from English poetry, that an "American tradition" is in process of cre-*

*ation? To put the question another way, do you think the American Renaissance of 1912 and the following years had permanent value?*

2. *Do you regard yourself as part of the "American tradition," as an American poet, regional or national; or as a poet simply, dissociated from nationality?*

3. *Do you think the poetry written by Americans during the last ten years shows any line of development (progression)?*

QUESTION 1—

The relationship between Americans is at least approximately racial, and does not pretend to be anything else. We have the country in common, even if we do not always have each other. This does not make for tradition. In the case of any poem professing to be an American poem, most Englishmen would be competent to determine for themselves, by now, whether it was genuinely American. In short, there exists a clear sense of what is American. Conceding that we are racially a bit tentative, does not the sense of what we are answer your question? The less said about permanent values now-a-days, the better.

QUESTION 2—

I should not say that I was flagrantly American, but I hope that I am American.

QUESTION 3—

The older poets have to be considered as individuals; the younger poets, whom it is easier to see as a group, lack a leader. After all, the fury of poetry always comes from the presence of a madman or two and, at the moment, all the madmen are politicians.

❖❖❖❖❖❖❖❖❖❖❖❖❖❖❖❖❖❖❖❖❖❖❖❖❖❖❖❖❖❖❖❖❖❖❖❖❖❖❖❖❖❖❖❖❖

# RESPONSES TO *PARTISAN REVIEW* QUESTIONNAIRE (1939)

## THE SITUATION IN AMERICAN WRITING: SEVEN QUESTIONS

1. *Are you conscious, in your own writing, of the existence of a "usable past"? Is this mostly American? What figures would you designate as*

*elements in it? Would you say, for example, that Henry James's work is more relevant to the present and future of American writing than Walt Whitman's?*

2. *Do you think of yourself as writing for a definite audience? If so, how would you describe this audience? Would you say that the audience for serious American writing has grown or contracted in the last ten years?*

3. *Do you place much value on the criticism your work has received? Would you agree that the corruption of the literary supplements by advertising—in the case of the newspapers—and political pressures—in the case of the liberal weeklies—has made serious literary criticism an isolated cult?*

4. *Have you found it possible to make a living by writing the sort of thing you want to, and without the aid of such crutches as teaching and editorial work? Do you think there is any place in our present economic system for literature as a profession?*

5. *Do you find, in retrospect, that your writing reveals any allegiance to any group, class, organization, region, religion, or system of thought, or do you conceive of it as mainly the expression of yourself as an individual?*

6. *How would you describe the political tendency of American writing as a whole since 1930? How do you feel about it yourself? Are you sympathetic to the current tendency towards what may be called "literary nationalism"—a renewed emphasis, largely uncritical, on the specifically "American" elements in our culture?*

7. *Have you considered the question of your attitude towards the possible entry of the United States into the next world war? What do you think the responsibilities of writers in general are when and if war comes?*

1. The material of the imagination is reality and reality can be nothing else except the usable past. In my own case this is wholly an American past. However, it does not follow that this or that particular figure of the past is relevant to the future. It is just as easy to be diffident about James as it is to be diffident about Whitman. I suppose you have chosen these two figures as symbols; neither of them means anything to me. The projections of the past are as incalculable as the stock market; otherwise it would be nothing but a bore.

2. I do not visualize any audience. To me poetry is one of the sanctions of life and I write it because it helps me to accept and validate my ex-

perience. Writing poetry is one thing; publishing it is another. Often I wish that I did not publish it, because the act of publishing it invokes a seriousness different from the seriousness of writing it. I think that the audience for serious American writing must have grown in the last ten years.

3. Much of the criticism one receives is a good deal keener than people who have not been subjected to the same thing can know. Besides, critics are perhaps the most important part of one's audience. I doubt if business and political pressures influence the criticism of poetry to any considerable extent. The Marxist point of view is exclusive, and I suppose that extremists encounter a good deal of opposition, but that there is anything corrupt about the opposition is something else.

4. I have not tried to make a living by writing. However, the fact that writers commonly take advantage of "such crutches as teaching and editorial work" is nothing that entitles writers to indulge themselves in spasms of self-pity. Most people avail themselves of crutches of one sort or another: lawyers promote business enterprises; doctors marry rich women and buy and sell securities. I think that there is a place in the present economic system for literature as a profession.

5. Unquestionably and notwithstanding the fact that I indulge in a good deal of abstraction, I do not regard my poems as mainly an expression of myself, nor as modern in the sense in which that unpleasant commonplace is so frequently used. Still, some time ago, when I sent one of my books to an honest man in England, he wrote to me saying that he found it personal and modern, and that these qualities were not his dish of tea.

6. I don't believe in factitious Americanism. An American has to be an American because there is nothing else for him to be and also, I hope, because it would not matter if there was. Even so, I believe in forgetting about it except as a quality, a savor.

7. I don't think that the United States should enter into the next world war, if there is to be another, unless it does so with the idea of dominating the world that comes out of it, or unless it is required to enter it in self-defense. The question respecting the responsibility of writers in war is a very theoretical question respecting an extremely practical state of affairs. A war is a military state of affairs, not a literary one. Conceding that the propagandists don't agree, does it matter that they don't agree? The role of the writer in war remains the fundamental role of the writer intensified and concentrated.

# RESPONSE TO *YALE LITERARY MAGAZINE* QUESTION

*What do you believe to be the major problem or problems facing the young writer in America today?*

Today, in America, all roles yield to that of the politician.

The role of the poet may be fixed by contrasting it to that of the politician. The poet absorbs the general life: the public life. The politician is absorbed by it. The poet is individual. The politician is general. It is the personal in the poet that is the origin of his poetry. If this is true respecting the relation of the poet to the public life and respecting the origin of his poetry, it follows that the first phase of his problem is himself.

This does not mean that he is a private figure. On the other hand, it does mean that he must not allow himself to be absorbed as the politician is absorbed. He must remain individual. As individual he must remain free. The politician expects everyone to be absorbed as he himself is absorbed. This expectation is part of the sabotage of the individual. The second phase of the poet's problem, then, is to maintain his freedom, the only condition in which he can hope to produce significant poetry.

If people are to become dependent on poetry for any of the fundamental satisfactions, poetry must have an increasing intellectual scope and power. This is a time for the highest poetry. We never understood the world less than we do now nor, as we understand it, liked it less. We never wanted to understand it more nor needed to like it more. These are the intense compulsions that challenge the poet as the appreciatory creator of values and beliefs. That, finally, states the problem.

I have not touched on form which, although significant, is not vital today, as substance is. When one is an inherent part of the other, form, too, is vital.

◇◇◇◇◇◇◇◇◇◇◇◇◇◇◇◇◇◇◇◇◇◇◇◇◇◇◇◇◇◇◇◇◇◇◇◇◇◇◇◇◇◇◇◇◇◇◇◇◇◇◇◇◇◇◇◇◇◇

# RESPONSES TO *PARTISAN REVIEW*
# QUESTIONNAIRE (1948)

## THE STATE OF AMERICAN WRITING, 1948:
## SEVEN QUESTIONS

1. *What, in your opinion, are the new literary tendencies or figures, if any, that have emerged in the forties? How does the literary atmosphere of this decade compare with that of the thirties? In what way, too, does the present period differ from the first postwar period? Can the differences between the two postwar periods be defined in relation to the European situation?*

2. *Do you think that American middlebrow culture has grown more powerful in this decade? In what relation does this middlebrow tendency stand to serious writing—does it threaten or bolster it?*

3. *What is the meaning of the literary revivals (James, Forster, Fitzgerald, etc.) that have taken place of late? Is this a publishing phenomenon or is it an organic literary interest in the sense that the rediscovered writers of the past are in some way truly expressive of current literary needs?*

4. *It is the general opinion that, unlike the twenties, this is not a period of experiment in language and form. If that is true, what significance can be attached to this fact? Does present writing base itself on the earlier experimentation, in the sense that it has creatively assimilated it, or can it be said that the earlier experimentation came to a dead end?*

5. *In the twenties most writers were free-lancers, whereas now many make their living by teaching in universities. Has this change affected the tone and mood of literature in our time? Can it with justice be said that American writing has grown more academic since the twenties?*

6. *In recent decades serious literary criticism has shown a special bent for the analysis and interpretation of poetry. What is the significance of this concentration at a time when poetry itself has had an ever-diminishing audience? Would literature benefit from a critical concern, equally intense, with other genres of writing? In our time, when the fate of culture as a whole is called into question, does the basic meaning of the literary effort stand in need of reexamination?*

7. *What is the effect on American writing of the growing tension between Soviet Communism and the democratic countries? How are cultural*

*interests affected by this struggle and do you think a writer should involve himself in it (as writer? as person?) to the point of commitment?*

These answers are limited to parts of questions 4, 6 and 7 and to poetry.

EXPERIMENT IN LANGUAGE. Poetry is nothing if it is not experiment in language. A recent remark by de Rougemont,

> Le vrai superstitieux se moque des superstitions comme le vrai poète des sujets et des mots poétiques,

explains this. The poet records his experience as poet in subjects and words which are part of that experience. He knows that nothing but the truth of that experience means anything to him or to anyone else. Experiment in respect to subjects and words is the effort on his part to record the truth of that experience.

In this statement the experience is central and experiment is the struggle with the experience and here experiment, also, is central. But often there is little, even no, experience and here experiment is merely experiment. The opinion that, unlike the twenties, this is not a period of experiment seems to be right in respect to experience in both senses. In respect to central experiment, the experience of the poet as poet may be too much or too little for him to record as yet: too much and too immediate or too little and not near enough; and so it may never be recorded at all. In respect to experiment that is merely experiment, this seems, in the circumstances, to be a pastime proper for Nero's children's children.

If these things are fluctuations of literary modes, what is the cause of the fluctuations? It may be simply our experience of life. To sum this up, central experiment is one of the constants of the spirit which is inherent in a true record of experience. But experiment for the sake of experiment has no such significance. Our present experience of life is too violent to be congenial to experiment in either sense. There is also the consideration that the present time succeeds a time of experiment. Theoretically a period of attempts at a world revolution should destroy or endanger all stationary poetic subjects and words and be favorable in the highest degree to the recording of fresh experience. But the vivification of reality has not yet occurred in spite of the excitement. Only the excitement has occurred.

EXPERIMENT IN FORM. So, too, experiment in form is one of the constants of the spirit. Much of what has been said about subjects and words applies to form. There is, however, a usage with respect to form as if form in poetry was a derivative of plastic shape. The tendency to visualize form is illustrated by the way a reference to form becomes a reference to the appearance of the poem on the page as in the case of a poem in the shape of a pear, say, or a poem without any shape at all. Such trivialities show that the record of a man's experience in the modern world is not a derivative of plastic shape. Modern poetry is not a privilege of heteroclites. Poetic form in its proper sense is a question of what appears within the poem itself. It seems worth while to isolate this because it is always form in its inimical senses that destroys poetry. By inimical senses one means the trivialities. By appearance within the poem itself one means the things created and existing there. The trivialities matter little today and most people concede that poetic form is not a question of literary mode.

ABOUT POETRY. It is not necessary to answer the last question relating to the fate of culture in order to consider the present position of poetry. That question implies that an understanding of the basic meaning of literary effort involves the fate of culture. Certainly a critical concern with poetry involves an understanding of the basic meaning of literary effort. Perhaps the present interest in the analysis and interpretation of poetry is in itself an attempt to get at the basic meaning of literary effort.

It seems that poetic order is potentially as significant as philosophic order. Accordingly, it is natural to project the idea of a theory of poetry that would be pretty much the same thing as a theory of the world based on a coordination of the poetic aspects of the world. Such an idea completely changes the significance of poetry. It does what poetry itself does, that is to say, it leads to a fresh conception of the world. The sense of this latent significance exists. Many sensitive readers of poetry, without being mystics or romantics or metaphysicians, feel that there probably is available in reality something accessible through a theory of poetry which would make a profound difference in our sense of the world. The interest in the analysis and interpretation of poetry is the same thing as an interest in poetry itself. For that reason it is not possible to speak of an enlarged audience for the analysis and interpretation of poetry and at the same time of a diminishing audience for poetry itself. The analysis and interpretation of poetry are perceptions of poetry.

You may not regard these answers as responsive to questions that contemplate literary tendencies, literary atmosphere, literary interest, literary criticism, and so on. One's interest is, however, an interest in life and in reality. From this point of view it is easy to say that the basic meaning of literary effort, and, therefore, of poetry, is with reference to life and reality and not with reference to politics. The basic meaning of the effort of any man to record his experience as poet is to produce poetry, not politics. The poet must stand or fall by poetry. In the conflict between the poet and the politician the chief honor the poet can hope for is that of remaining himself. Life and reality, on the one hand, and politics, on the other, notwithstanding the activity of politics, are not interchangeable terms. They are not the same thing, whatever the Russians may pretend.

❀❂❖❂❖❂❖❂❖❂❖❂❖❂❖❂❖❂❖❂❖❂❖❂❖❂❖❂❖❂❖❂❖❂❖❂❖❂❖❂❖❂❖❂❖❂❖❂❖

# RESPONSES TO MODERN AMERICAN POETRY QUESTIONNAIRE

## AMERICAN AND ENGLISH POETRY: A QUESTIONNAIRE

1.  *Is it nonsense to talk of a typical American poem? If not, what, in your opinion, are the qualities which tend to distinguish a poem as "American"?*
2.  *Do you consider that the language of American poetry (vocabulary, use of vocabulary, metric, cadences, syntax, punctuation) differs notably from that of English poetry? Is this difference (if any) fortuitous, or does it correspond to some underlying difference of sensibility?*
3.  *Has American poetry been affected by those trends in English poetry in the thirties typified by the work of Auden, Spender, Day Lewis and MacNeice?*
4.  *Has American poetry been affected by the romanticism now prevalent in English poetry, and represented in varying ways by the work of Dylan Thomas, George Barker, The New Apocalypse, Personalism, and the later poetry of Miss Edith Sitwell?*

1.  At bottom this question is whether there is such a thing as an American. If there is, the poems that he writes are American poems. And a typical American poem is merely a matter of choice as between one of his poems and another. It must be as easy to distinguish an American poem from a Maori poem as it is to distinguish an American from a Maori. While it is not always so easy to distinguish an American poem from an English poem, after all would *Snow-Bound* sound quite like an English poem to you? Would you be likely to mistake *Leaves of Grass* for something English? *Snow-Bound* is a typical American poem. **The**

315

poems in *Leaves of Grass* are typical American poems. Even if a difference was not to be found in anything else, it could be found in what we write about. We live in two different physical worlds and it is not nonsense to think that that matters.

2. No. At the same time, I think that there is an underlying difference of sensibility. We use the same language in pretty much the same way that you do, in print. While there are variations in vocabulary and no doubt variations in other respects, the difference, in print, is not notable.

3. My answer to this is included in my answer to 4.

4. Undoubtedly American poetry has been enriched by all of the poets mentioned in questions 3 and 4. I think that Americans find English poetry extremely to their liking. We give ourselves up to it, not at all because it is English, but because in the minute differences between it and our own poetry we find something that has a poetic value in itself.

# NOTES

### CHIAROSCURO

This poem and the three that follow ("Colors," "Testamentum," "Dolls") are reproduced as they appear in holograph manuscripts at the Huntington Library. "Chiaroscuro" also appears, untitled, in a notebook in which Elsie Stevens copied passages from her husband's letters before destroying some of them. An excerpt following the poem indicates that Stevens sent it to her in 1908, saying it would be in the booklet of manuscript poems he planned to give her on her birthday in June 1909. He apparently changed his mind, for it is not in "The Little June Book."

### COLORS

This poem is based on a passage in Stevens' letter to Elsie of 18 March 1909 and an entry in his journal of 14 May 1909; see Holly Stevens, *Souvenirs and Prophecies: The Young Wallace Stevens* (New York: Alfred A. Knopf, 1977), pp. 214, 222. With "Colors" and "Testamentum" is a cover sheet bearing the title "Intermezzi." Never published, the "Intermezzi" sequence may have included other poems dating from this period.

### INFERNALE

Carl Van Vechten recalled hearing Stevens read a version of this poem, along with "Dolls" and "Cy Est Pourtraicte, Madame Ste Ursule, et les Unze Mille Vierges," at a party in late 1914; see "Rogue Elephant in Porcelain," *Yale University Library Gazette*, 38 (October 1963), 49. As reproduced here, the text follows a typescript at the Huntington Library. Stevens sent a revised version entitled "The Guide of Alcestis" to Ronald Lane Latimer in 1935; see *Letters of Wallace Stevens*, ed. Holly Stevens (New York: Alfred A. Knopf, 1972), pp. 285–86.

### CARNET DE VOYAGE

Sections III–VII originally appeared in "The Little June Book," which Stevens presented to Elsie on her birthday in 1909.

### HOME AGAIN

This poem was included in the "Book of Verses" Stevens presented to Elsie on her birthday in 1908.

## PHASES

This is the version of the poem reconstructed by A. Walton Litz in *Introspective Voyager: The Poetic Development of Wallace Stevens* (New York: Oxford University Press, 1972), pp. 305–9. Sections I–V follow a holograph manuscript at the Huntington Library (which identifies "There was heaven . . ." as Section I) and the sequence of four poems published in *Poetry* magazine in November 1914; the latter were Sections II–V in the typescript Stevens sent to *Poetry*. The rest of the sequence, beginning with the fragmentary Section VI, follows the incomplete typescript in the Harriet Monroe Library of Modern Poetry, University of Chicago Library. After *Poetry* published Sections II–V, Stevens experimented with the order of the remaining sections, renumbering them and adding the title "Belgian Farm, October, 1914" to Section VII.

## "ALL THINGS IMAGINED ARE OF EARTH COMPACT . . ."

Robert Buttel describes this poem, so unlike Stevens' other work of this period, as a variation on the familiar lines about the lunatic, the lover, and the poet in *Midsummer Night's Dream*; see *Wallace Stevens: The Making of* Harmonium (Princeton: Princeton University Press, 1967), pp. 224–25. All but one of the poems tentatively dated 1913–1915 are reproduced from manuscripts at the Huntington Library. "I have lived so long with the rhetoricians . . ." is reprinted from Buttel, p. 183.

## HEADACHE

Numerous erasures and cancellations appear on the holograph draft of the poem. Still legible following the line "There are letters in the hair" are the lines "The alphabet is a collection / Of satirical design." Following the line "Bite, twitch their ears . . ." one can still read the fragmentary line "They leer. full of the devil."

## TO MADAME ALDA, SINGING A SONG, IN A WHITE GOWN

Stevens may have planned to use this poem as part of a sequence, for the number VI appears above the title in the typescript. At the bottom of the page is the address 441 West 21st Street, New York, where he lived between September 1909 and May 1916. Since this address also appears on the typescript of "Domination of Black," first published in March 1916, these may have been written about the same time and could have belonged to a projected sequence of poems; see the first paragraph of Stevens' "Note on a Personal Choice of Poems," p. 242.

## BLANCHE McCARTHY

The texts of this poem and the incomplete "For an Old Woman in a Wig" follow holograph manuscripts at the Huntington Library.

## EIGHT SIGNIFICANT LANDSCAPES

Stevens deleted Stanzas V and VII (here shown as they appear in the holograph manuscript at the Huntington Library) and renumbered the sequence to produce "Six Significant Landscapes," first published in the March 1916 issue of *Others* and reprinted in the *Collected Poems* (New York: Alfred A. Knopf, 1954).

## PRIMORDIA

Sections 7 and 9 of this sequence appear in the *Collected Poems* under the titles "In the Carolinas" and "Indian River." "To the Roaring Wind" retains its title in the same volume.

## LETTRES D'UN SOLDAT (1914–1915)

This is substantially the sequence of poems reproduced in A. Walton Litz, *Introspective Voyager*, pp. 310–15, with minor variations based on Stevens' typescript in the Harriet Monroe Library of Modern Poetry. As Litz observes, the sequence may originally have contained seventeen poems, since Section XIII ("Death was a reaper . . .") is numbered XVII in a holograph manuscript at the Huntington Library. The Huntington manuscript also contains another version of Section XVI; following the 17 *mars* epigraph it reads (with canceled passages in brackets),

> The cranes return. The soldier hears their cry.
> No: not as if the jades of willow-tree
> Or river-fern came coloring the sky.
> But still the cranes return.
>
> The soldier hears their cry. He knows the fire
> That touches them—knows that he must not know
> Nor burden his endurance with desire.
> [But still the cranes return . . .]
>
> Endurance that grows heavy from despair,
> Drowsed with the oblivion of oblivions—
> The chant of spring becomes an obsolete air—
> [But still] The cranes return . . .
>
> [Grows heavy from despair, too much alone
> To feel the spring infusing its relief
> In sleepiness, to resist that weight of sky.
> But still the cranes return.]

Sections II–VI and VIII–XI were published in the May 1918 issue of *Poetry*. Sections VI, VII, IX, and XI (the last under the title "The Death of a Soldier") are reprinted without their epigraphs in the *Collected Poems*.

## STANZAS FOR "LE MONOCLE DE MON ONCLE"

The title "The Naked Eye of The Aunt" appears on the cover sheet to these stanzas in the holograph manuscript at the Huntington Library. The first stanza is unnumbered.

## AN EARLY VERSION OF "ANECDOTE OF THE PRINCE OF PEACOCKS"

This poem is reproduced as it appears in a holograph manuscript at the Huntington Library, where it bears the same title as the poem beginning "In the moonlight / I met Berserk . . ." in the *Collected Poems*.

## PETER PARASOL

The epigraph of this poem also served as its title when Stevens submitted it to *Poetry* as part of the "Pecksniffiana" group. It may have been Harriet Monroe who supplied the current title, borrowing the pseudonym Stevens had signed to "Phases." Reprinted here is the version that appeared in the October 1919 issue of *Poetry*. The holograph manuscript in the Harriet Monroe Library of Modern Poetry differs from the printed version in its punctuation and the wording of lines 4–5, which read, "Ears, eyes, souls, skins, hair? // Ah, good God! . . . ."

## PIANO PRACTICE AT THE ACADEMY OF THE HOLY ANGELS

This poem was already in proof when Stevens asked that it be withdrawn from the "Pecksniffiana" group. Harriet Monroe wrote the words "Jewel never published" on the uncorrected proof, now in the Harriet Monroe Library of Modern Poetry. This presumably qualified "Piano Practice" for the "Jewel file" in which she kept the unpublished sections of Stevens' "Phases" and other poems she admired but was unable to print, such as T. S. Eliot's "The Death of Saint Narcissus."

## ANECDOTE OF THE ABNORMAL

The texts of this poem and "Romance for a Demoiselle Lying in the Grass," also tentatively dated 1919–1920, follow holograph manuscripts at the Huntington Library.

## FROM THE JOURNAL OF CRISPIN

For an account of how the Beinecke Rare Book and Manuscript Library at Yale acquired the typescript and a partial carbon copy of this poem, long thought to be lost, see Louis L. Martz, " 'From the Journal of Crispin': An Early Version of 'The Comedian as the Letter C,' " in *Wallace Stevens: A Celebration*, ed. Frank Doggett and Robert Buttel (Princeton: Princeton University Press, 1980), pp. 3–29. Reproduced here is the text of the original typescript with misspellings corrected and the variant *sea-glass* (rather than *sea-grass*) adopted from the carbon copy in Section I, line 31.

## THIS VAST INELEGANCE

Matthew Josephson wrote to Stevens on 22 February 1922, telling him he could not use this poem in the *Headsman*. On the original typescript now at the Huntington Library, Stevens canceled lines 2 and 4, probably after the poem was rejected.

## SATURDAY NIGHT AT THE CHIROPODIST'S

This poem exists in two forms at the Huntington Library—a typescript containing obvious errors and the holograph manuscript reproduced here.

## METROPOLITAN MELANCHOLY

In a letter to Harriet Monroe of 20 June 1928, Stevens mentions having written this poem the previous day (*Letters of Wallace Stevens*, p. 252). The text follows the holograph manuscript in the Harriet Monroe Library of Modern Poetry.

## GOOD MAN, BAD WOMAN

A. Walton Litz and Samuel French Morse both speculate that this poem and "The Woman Who Blamed Life on a Spaniard" consist of stanzas salvaged from a longer version of "Red Loves Kit." See Litz's *Introspective Voyager*, pp. 169–70; and Morse's *Wallace Stevens: Poetry as Life* (New York: Pegasus, 1970), pp. 142–43.

## THE WOMAN WHO BLAMED LIFE ON A SPANIARD

In an earlier version of Stanza III that Stevens sent to Harriet Monroe in December 1930, line 10 reads, "Well-witted; a destroying voice that sings . . . ." In the same holograph draft, which is in the Harriet Monroe Library of Modern Poetry, line 12 reads, "A skillful apprehension and proud eye . . . ."

## POLO PONIES PRACTICING

Stevens' typescript at the Huntington Library differs from the version published in the Autumn 1934 issue of *Westminster Magazine* in several places. Lines 3–4 read, "Is stale today. // Here at least is a world . . . ." Lines 8–9 read, "In hedges of dew, / In morning sun." The final line in the typescript reads, "On the words of the mind."

## LYTTON STRACHEY, ALSO, ENTERS INTO HEAVEN

In line 18 of the typescript at the Huntington Library, *theatre* is spelled as shown here. It was changed to *theater* when the poem was published in the Spring 1935 issue of *Rocking Horse*.

## TABLE TALK

The texts of this poem and "A Room on a Garden," also tentatively dated 1935, follow typescripts at the Huntington Library.

## OWL'S CLOVER

This is the original, longer version of the poem published by the Alcestis Press in 1936; a shorter version of the poem appeared in *The Man with the Blue Guitar and Other Poems* (New York: Alfred A. Knopf, 1937). Obvious errors in the Alcestis text have been corrected.

## STANZAS FOR "THE MAN WITH THE BLUE GUITAR"

These stanzas are reproduced from the holograph manuscript of the poem in the Poetry/Rare Books Collection, University Libraries, State University of New York at Buffalo, and are numbered accordingly. The manuscript contains thirty-seven stanzas, some of them extensively worked over. Two stanzas—those that became XXI and XXVI in *The Man with the Blue Guitar and Other Poems*—are dated 25 January and 13 February 1937, respectively. Stevens apparently dropped Stanzas III, IX, and X before preparing a typescript of the poem. He originally included Stanzas VII, XI, and XXI in the typescript, then decided not to publish them; these, which are all that remains of the typescript, are at the Huntington Library. The published version includes two stanzas, VII and XXXII, that do not appear in the holograph manuscript but were presumably in the typescript. The following notes pertain to individual stanzas:

III: In the holograph manuscript, this follows what became Stanza II in the published text. Stevens salvaged it for "Five Grotesque Pieces" (1942), where it appears slightly revised under the title "Communications of Meaning."

VII: Follows what became Stanza V in the published text. In the Huntington typescript, it is numbered VI and *negress* in line 10 has become *negro.*

IX: Follows what became Stanza VI in the published text.

XI: This stanza is numbered VIII in the Huntington typescript, which also revises lines 3–4 to read, "The shapings of the instrument / Distort . . . ."

XXI: Follows what became Stanza XVI in the published text. It also appears, unnumbered, in the Huntington typescript. In the lower right-hand corner of the holograph page, Stevens glossed the stanza as follows: "The blue guitar is the individuality of the poet. This matures best in solitude. The imagination developes best there 'where no people are.' Such a place is a place of blond weather. But things as they are—reality—are as they are without personal transformation. So for that matter are people. On that level they equal each other."

## STANZAS FOR "EXAMINATION OF THE HERO IN A TIME OF WAR"

Stanza II bears the number III in a holograph manuscript at the Houghton Library, Harvard University. No manuscript source has been located for Stanzas I and III, which are reproduced from the first edition of *Opus Posthumous.*

## FROM "FIVE GROTESQUE PIECES"

Sections I and V are the only new poems in this group, published in the March 1942 issue of *Trend*. Section II, "Hieroglyphica," was reprinted from the Autumn 1934 issue of *Direction* (see p. 69), minus lines 4–6 ("Even if . . . Hey-di-ho"). Section IV, "What They Call Cherry Pie," had appeared under the title "What They Call Red Cherry Pie" in the October 1934 issue of *Alcestis* (see p. 68). Section III, "Communications of Meaning," was salvaged from the holograph manuscript of "The Man with the Blue Guitar," where it appears as Section III (see p. 101). Stevens changed two words in the manuscript version of Section III when he published it in *Trend*: *balmy* in the first line became *palmy*, and *rose-leaves* in the last line became *petals*.

## THIS AS INCLUDING THAT

The opening couplet of this poem, reproduced from the typescript at the Huntington Library, suggests that it was written about the same time as Section IV ("Dry Birds Are Fluttering in Blue Leaves") of "The Pure Good of Theory," published in the Spring 1945 issue of *Voices*.

## RECITATION AFTER DINNER

This poem is reprinted as it appears in the typescript at the Huntington Library. A slightly different version appears in *The Saint Nicholas Society of the City of New York* (New York: Saint Nicholas Society, 1945), where its title is "Tradition." J. M. Edelstein compares the two versions in *Wallace Stevens: A Descriptive Bibliography* (Pittsburgh: University of Pittsburgh Press, 1973), p. 170.

## FIRST WARMTH

Stevens inscribed this poem on the false-title page of the copy of *Transport to Summer* belonging to his editor, Herbert Weinstock, in March 1947. Preceding the poem and incorporating the printed false-title are the words "The Only Copy of TRANSPORT TO SUMMER together with *First Warmth*, 1947." Following the poem are Stevens' signature and the words "For Herbert Weinstock."

## AS YOU LEAVE THE ROOM

This appears to be a later version of "First Warmth," which it incorporates with several changes.

## AS AT A THEATRE

This and the following five poems appeared in the Summer 1950 issue of *Wake*. The text reproduced here is that of the typescript at the Huntington Library; the *Wake* editor systematically replaced Stevens' spaced periods with single terminal periods.

## A DISCOVERY OF THOUGHT

Line 17 is based on the typescript at the Huntington Library rather than the version published in the Summer 1950 issue of *Imagi*, where a comma follows *secret*.

## THE COURSE OF A PARTICULAR

In the first printing of the 1957 edition of *Opus Posthumous*, the second-last line reads, "Than they are in the final finding of the air, in the thing . . . ." *Air* was subsequently replaced with *ear*, in keeping with the typescript now at the Huntington Library and the version published in the Spring 1951 issue of the *Hudson Review*.

## FAREWELL WITHOUT A GUITAR

In one typescript of the poem at the Huntington Library, the word *grass* appears in place of *green* in line 2, *snow* in place of *sun* in line 14.

## THE SAIL OF ULYSSES

Stevens read this poem at the Phi Beta Kappa exercises held at Columbia University on 31 May 1954. In the carbon typescript of the poem at the Huntington Library, the sections are glossed as follows:
>    lines 1–6: The place of the poem. Its theme.
>    Stanza I: To know is to be.
>       II: To know is the force to be.
>       III: The true creator.
>       IV: The center of the self.
>       V: Except for illogical receptions.
>       VI: Presence of an external master of knowledge.
>       VII: Truth as fate.
>       VIII: Shape of the sibyl of truth.

## CONVERSATION WITH THREE WOMEN OF NEW ENGLAND

Lines 9 and 29 follow the typescript at the Huntington Library. In the Autumn 1954 issue of *Accent*, line 9 reads, "In the central of earth or sky or thought, . . . ." Line 29 substitutes *difference* for *differences*.

## ON THE WAY TO THE BUS

The typescript of this poem is at the Huntington Library.

## THE REGION NOVEMBER

Although this poem was not published until some months after Stevens' death, he had sent it to Themistocles Hoetis, editor of *Zero*, on 15 November 1954.

## "A MYTHOLOGY REFLECTS ITS REGION . . ."

No title appears on the typescript of this poem at the Huntington Library.

## OF MERE BEING

This poem apparently survives in only one form, a typescript at the Huntington Library. There the final word of line 3 is *decor* rather than, as the first edition of *Opus Posthumous* has it, *distance*.

## MOMENT OF LIGHT

Stevens' translation of Jean Le Roy's "Instant de clarté" follows the holograph manuscript at the Van Pelt Library, University of Pennsylvania, in all but title. Stevens translated Le Roy's title rather literally as "Moment of Clearness." Though another hand canceled the title on the manuscript and wrote "Moment of Insight" above it, the poem is called "Moment of Light" in the October 1918 issue of *Modern School*. The *Modern School* version omits one line ("in front . . . ruddyings") and reverses the order of two others ("on which . . . scale of lives").

## THREE PARAPHRASES FROM LEON-PAUL FARGUE

According to Samuel French Morse, Stevens read his prefatory remarks and the three paraphrases at the YMHA Poetry Center in New York in 1951 (Introduction to first edition of *Opus Posthumous*, p. xxv). This text follows the typescript at the Huntington Library.

## *THREE TRAVELERS WATCH A SUNRISE*

There are four distinct versions of this play: an unrevised typescript in two copies, one in the Harriet Monroe Library of Modern Poetry and the other in the Beinecke Rare Book and Manuscript Library; a typescript with Harriet Monroe's revisions, in the Harriet Monroe Library; the proofs with Stevens' corrections, also in the Harriet Monroe Library; and the text published in the July 1916 issue of *Poetry*. This is essentially the *Poetry* version, with minor changes based on the proofs and revised typescript. For comparisons of the revised and unrevised versions, see George S. Lensing, *Wallace Stevens: A Poet's Growth* (Baton Rouge: Louisiana State University Press, 1986), pp. 248–52; and Louis L. Martz, "Manuscripts of Wallace Stevens," *Yale University Library Gazette*, 54 (October 1979), 54–59.

## *CARLOS AMONG THE CANDLES*

This is the text of the play published in the December 1917 issue of *Poetry*. Except for one sentence, the typescript at the Houghton Library differs chiefly in the stage directions. The sentence beginning "It is like the diverging angles" (p. 166) reads as follows in the typescript: "It is like nine triangles in water, composing themselves brilliantly in the polished surface."

## BOWL, CAT AND BROOMSTICK

As reproduced here, the play follows the carbon typescript at the Huntington Library (which is missing page 3) and a copy of the missing page, discovered after the Huntington acquired the rest of the typescript. Obvious errors have been corrected.

## A CEREMONY

Stevens may have written this piece, shown here as it appears in the typescript at the Huntington Library, for the entertainment of the Saint Nicholas Society, which he joined in 1944.

## FROM *SUR PLUSIEURS BEAUX SUJECTS*

These entries are taken from the first of two manuscript notebooks Stevens used as a commonplace book between 1932 and about 1953. The first selection can be dated about 1932, the last about 1937. He probably took the title of the commonplace book from a sixteenth-century French manuscript he read about in the *Bulletin of the Museum of Fine Arts* (Boston), 31 (August 1933), 56. For the complete text, see Sur Plusieurs Beaux Sujects: *Wallace Stevens' Commonplace Book*, ed. Milton J. Bates (Stanford: Stanford University Press / Huntington Library, 1989).

## ADAGIA

This is the complete text of the manuscript notebooks entitled *Adagia I* and *Adagia II*, discussed in A. Walton Litz, "Particles of Order: The Unpublished *Adagia*," in *Wallace Stevens: A Celebration*, pp. 57–75. The following notes apply to particular adages:

PAGE 186
*Usage is everything* . . . The quotation from Braque is a later addition, bracketed to the right of the adage.

PAGE 189
*Consider* . . . The word *Consider* is not separated from the previous entry by a skipped line, which suggests it may have been inserted after Stevens wrote propositions I and II.

PAGE 190
*Values other than* . . . This may be a continuation of the previous entry, since it appears at the top of the following page.

PAGE 196
*The World Reduced* . . . This entry appears to be a title rather than an aphorism. Stevens kept another notebook, *From Pieces of Paper*, specifically for titles; it is reproduced in Lensing, *Wallace Stevens: A Poet's Growth*, pp. 166–88.

PAGE 197
*Poetry must resist* . . . The word *almost* has been inserted above the line.

PAGE 197
*Life is a composite of* . . . Above "is a composite of" Stevens has written "se compose de."
PAGE 198
*The world is myself* . . . This adage is written in the left margin of the last page of *Adagia I*.
PAGE 199
*Poetry is the gaiety* . . . The word *gaiety* is written above *joy* (parentheses added).
PAGE 202
*Poetry is a renovation* . . . The second sentence is a later addition, to the right of the first.
PAGE 202
*The theory of poetry* . . . The second sentence is a later addition, to the right of the first.

## FROM "MATERIA POETICA"

In 1940 Stevens selected thirty-two aphorisms from the *Adagia* notebooks, revised some of them, and added seven new ones. These he submitted to *View* magazine, numbering them I–XXXIX on a typescript now at the Huntington Library. *View* published I–XXII in its September 1940 issue, which also contained an interview with Stevens. It did not publish the remaining seventeen aphorisms (omitting the numbers) until October 1942. Adage III in the typescript and *View* ("The poet confers his identity on the reader. He cannot do this if he intrudes personally") differs significantly from the notebook adage reproduced on p. 185. Stevens' revisions were otherwise minor, hence this selection reprints only the seven aphorisms that were not taken from the *Adagia* notebooks.

## FROM MISCELLANEOUS NOTEBOOKS

The first of these notebooks, all of which are at the Huntington Library, can be dated approximately from its second entry, which reads "Poetic Exercises of 1948." The second contains only the entry reprinted here. The third is the second of two notebooks in which Stevens excerpted lengthy passages from William McCausland Stewart's translation of Paul Valéry's *Eupalinos* for use in his preface "Gloire du long désir, Idées" (1955); the aphorism appears, canceled, at the top of the first page. The first two notebooks are reproduced in A. Walton Litz, "Particles of Order: The Unpublished *Adagia*," pp. 76–77.

## CATTLE *KINGS* OF FLORIDA

This essay may have originated in Stevens' friendship with Judge Arthur Powell of Atlanta and his involvement with the Hartford Live Stock Insurance Company (he had been on the board of directors from 1916 to 1920). As printed in the Sunday magazine supplement to the *Atlanta Journal*, the essay's subhead reads,

"Florida's Pioneer Cattlemen Frequently Carried Fortunes in Their Saddle Bags, and the Coffee Can or Cooking Pot on a Cabin Shelf Often Held a King's Ransom in Gold. An Unlettered Cowboy Financed the First Free School in Polk County and Provided the Land for Orlando's Famous Parks."

## ON "THE EMPEROR OF ICE-CREAM"

Stevens' statement appears, untitled, opposite his poem in *Fifty Poets: An American Auto-Anthology* (1933).

## WILLIAMS

This piece serves as the Preface to William Carlos Williams' *Collected Poems 1921–1931* (1934).

## A NOTE ON MARTHA CHAMPION

Stevens' note follows four poems by Champion in Ann Winslow's *Trial Balances* (1935), an anthology of poems by thirty-two young poets, each paired with an established poet or critic. Champion, who was born in 1911, is identified in a biographical note as a doctoral candidate in anthropology at Columbia University.

## A POET THAT MATTERS

Stevens' review of Marianne Moore's *Selected Poems* (1935) appeared in the December 1935 issue of *Life and Letters Today*.

## THE IRRATIONAL ELEMENT IN POETRY

As reproduced here, the text of this lecture delivered at Harvard on 8 December 1936 generally follows the typescript at the Huntington Library. In several places, however, it adopts the wording of the version (probably a corrected typescript, not located) used in the first edition of *Opus Posthumous*. The most significant variation occurs in Section VIII, where the Huntington typescript reads, "In that sense life is mysterious. I hope . . ." (cf. p. 231).

## JACKET STATEMENT FROM *THE MAN WITH THE BLUE GUITAR AND OTHER POEMS*

The second printing of the jacket (shown here) substituted *conjunctions* for *conjunctioning*, apparently at Stevens' request; see *Letters of Wallace Stevens*, p. 325.

## SURETY AND FIDELITY CLAIMS

This essay is reprinted, without the subheads used to break up the text, from the *Eastern Underwriter*, 25 March 1938, p. 45.

328

## A NOTE ON POETRY

Stevens' note introduced eleven of his poems in *The Oxford Anthology of American Literature* (1938).

## NOTES ON JEAN LABASQUE

No manuscript or printed source has been located for these notes, here reprinted from the first edition. Stevens owned at least one painting by Labasque, the portrait of Paris bookseller Anatole Vidal he mentions in his poem "The Latest Freed Man" (1938).

## POETRY AND WAR

This statement appears, untitled, at the end of Stevens' *Parts of a World* (1942), where it follows "Examination of the Hero in a Time of War."

## NOTE ON A PERSONAL CHOICE OF POEMS

Entitled simply "Note," this statement accompanied a list of eighteen poems Stevens sent to Whit Burnett on 10 August 1942, for inclusion in Burnett's anthology *This Is My Best* (1942). Stevens' list, which is at the Princeton University Library together with his statement, included "Earthy Anecdote"; "In the Carolinas"; "Domination of Black"; "The Snow Man"; "The Load of Sugar-Cane"; "The Emperor of Ice-Cream"; "Sunday Morning"; "Anecdote of the Jar"; "To the One of Fictive Music"; "Dance of the Macabre Mice"; "The Pleasures of Merely Circulating"; "The Man with the Blue Guitar," Sections V, XV, XVII, XVIII, and XXVIII; "Country Words"; and "Asides on the Oboe." Due to circumstances described by Glen MacLeod in "A New Version of Wallace Stevens," *Princeton University Library Chronicle*, 41 (Autumn 1979), 22–29, Burnett was able to use only "Domination of Black" and the portion of Stevens' statement beginning "The themes of life" and concluding "something less than a man of reason."

## A NOTE ON SAMUEL FRENCH MORSE

This piece serves as the Introduction to Morse's *Time of Year* (1944).

## JOHN CROWE RANSOM: TENNESSEAN

Stevens' typescript at the Huntington Library reflects his uncertainty regarding the home states of Ransom and Allen Tate. At the suggestion of Tate, who assembled the Summer 1948 issue of the *Sewanee Review* honoring Ransom, Stevens revised two sentences in the first paragraph of the typescript: "They say that there are even more Ransoms than Tates in Tennessee" and "To be a Ransom in Tennessee (even if you get your start in Kentucky) is something more precious than it is easy to say."

## POETRY AND MEANING

After the *Explicator* published two essays on "The Emperor of Ice-Cream" in its April 1948 issue, a reader wrote to ask Stevens if their interpretations were correct. This is Stevens' reply, which appears untitled in the November issue.

## MARCEL GROMAIRE

Stevens wrote this note for a catalogue of Gromaire's paintings on exhibit at the Louis Carré Gallery in New York, 5–31 December 1949.

## ON RECEIVING THE GOLD MEDAL FROM THE POETRY SOCIETY OF AMERICA

Following this speech, which Stevens delivered at Sherry's in New York on 24 January 1951, he read his poems "A Rabbit as King of the Ghosts" and "The Candle a Saint." The typescript is at the Huntington Library.

## ON RECEIVING THE NATIONAL BOOK AWARD FOR POETRY (1951)

Stevens received the National Book Award for *The Auroras of Autumn* (1950). He delivered his acceptance speech, here reproduced as it appears in the typescript at the Huntington Library, on 6 March 1951.

## ON RECEIVING AN HONORARY DEGREE FROM BARD COLLEGE

Bard conferred the Honorary Doctor of Letters Degree on Stevens on 16 March 1951. This text follows the typescript at the Huntington Library rather than the slightly different version published in the *Quarterly Review of Literature* after his death.

## TWO OR THREE IDEAS

This paper was delivered as a lecture at Mount Holyoke College on 28 April 1951, then published as a chapbook by the sponsor of the lecture, the New England College English Association. This is the published version, which differs chiefly in its punctuation from the holograph manuscript and original typescript at the Houghton Library. A carbon typescript is at the Huntington Library.

## A COLLECT OF PHILOSOPHY

This is the text of the typescript at the Huntington Library, which seems to be the final version of the lecture Stevens delivered at the University of Chicago on 16 November 1951 and again at the City College of New York, Harlem campus, on 26 November. From holograph and typed manuscripts in the Beinecke Rare Book and Manuscript Library, Peter Brazeau has reconstructed three different conclusions to the lecture; see " 'A Collect of Philosophy': The Difficulty of Finding What Would Suffice," in *Wallace Stevens: A Celebration*, pp. 46–56.

## A NOTE ON "LES PLUS BELLES PAGES"

According to Samuel French Morse, Stevens wrote this commentary on his poem "Les Plus Belles Pages" (1941) in 1952, for the Poetry Collection of the Lamont Library at Harvard (Introduction to first edition of *Opus Posthumous*, p. xxxvii). In the holograph manuscript, currently at the Houghton Library, the word *God* is not capitalized in the sentence beginning "Aquinas is . . . ."

## RAOUL DUFY

Despite Stevens' reference to "the present portfolio," this piece did not accompany Dufy's *La Fée Electricité* (1953). It was issued as a separate, unillustrated pamphlet.

## THE WHOLE MAN: PERSPECTIVES, HORIZONS

Stevens presented this paper at the Metropolitan Museum of Art in New York on 21 October 1954, before delegates attending the Forty-fifth Anniversary Convention of the American Federation of Arts. The young Korean scholar to whom he refers is Peter H. Lee.

## ON RECEIVING THE NATIONAL BOOK AWARD FOR POETRY (1955)

Stevens received the National Book Award on 25 January 1955 for his *Collected Poems* (1954). The text of his speech is reproduced from the original typescript at the Beinecke Rare Book and Manuscript Library; the Huntington Library has a carbon copy.

## A FOOTNOTE TO SAUL BELLOW'S "PAINS AND GAINS"

Stevens conceived this anecdote in response to Bellow's similar story, published in the previous issue of *Semi-Colon*, of a woman who trips on a sidewalk but refuses to be helped to her feet until she can establish grounds for a lawsuit. Stevens originally set his story at the foot of Montgomery Street, then realized it was California Street he had in mind.

## TWO PREFACES

Stevens' prefaces to Paul Valéry's *Eupalinos* and *L'Ame et la danse* appear thus in *Dialogues*, the last of four volumes of Valéry in the Bollingen Series (New York: Pantheon, 1956). Stevens' typescript at the Huntington Library contains several short passages dropped from the published version; otherwise, it differs chiefly in its use of French for the quotations from Valéry.

## CONNECTICUT COMPOSED

This is the uncut version of the script (currently at the Huntington Library) that Stevens wrote for the Voice of America's "This Is America" series, completing it several weeks after the two prefaces to Valéry. A shorter version entitled "This Is Connecticut" was broadcast in July 1955 and distributed to newspapers.

## RESPONSES TO *NEW VERSE* QUESTIONNAIRE

In this and all subsequent questionnaire responses, the questions are reprinted in italic type, Stevens' responses in roman.

## RESPONSES TO *PARTISAN REVIEW* QUESTIONNAIRE (1948)

The typescript of Stevens' responses is at the Huntington Library, together with his letter of 26 April 1948 to Delmore Schwartz, then an editor of *Partisan Review*. In the typescript the last sentence of the "Experiment in Language" section reads, "Only the excitement has occurred and is occurring."

# Index of Titles

334

## A NOTE ABOUT THE AUTHOR

Wallace Stevens was born in Reading, Pennsylvania, on October 2, 1879, and died in Hartford, Connecticut, on August 2, 1955. After attending Harvard University and working for a time as a newspaper reporter in New York, he secured a law degree from the New York Law School and was admitted to the bar in 1904. In 1909 he married Elsie Kachel of Reading. From 1916 to his death he was associated with the Hartford Accident & Indemnity Company, of which he became vice-president in 1934.

Although he began writing poems and stories while still in school, and published a number of pieces in the *Harvard Advocate*, it was not until 1915 that "Sunday Morning," his first major poem, appeared in Harriet Monroe's magazine, *Poetry*. *Harmonium*, his first volume of poems, was published by Alfred A. Knopf in 1923; it was followed by *Ideas of Order* (1936), *The Man with the Blue Guitar* (1937), *Parts of a World* (1942), *Transport to Summer* (1947), *The Auroras of Autumn* (1950), *The Necessary Angel* (a volume of essays, 1951), *The Collected Poems of Wallace Stevens* (1954), *The Letters of Wallace Stevens* (1966), *The Palm at the End of the Mind* (1971), and *Souvenirs and Prophecies: The Young Wallace Stevens* (the last three edited by his daughter, Holly Stevens).

Wallace Stevens was awarded the Bollingen Prize in Poetry in 1950. He won the National Book Award in Poetry twice —in 1951 and 1955—and the Pulitzer Prize in Poetry in 1955.

# A NOTE ON THE TYPE

*This book is set in Linotype* ELECTRA, *a face designed by* W. A. DWIGGINS (1880–1956), *who was responsible for so much that is good in contemporary book design. Although much of his early work was in advertising and he was the author of the standard volume* Layout in Advertising, *Mr. Dwiggins later devoted his prolific talents to book typography and type design, and worked with great distinction in both fields. In addition to his designs for Electra, he created the Metro, Caledonia, and Eldorado series of type faces, as well as a number of experimental cuttings that were never issued commercially.*

*Electra cannot be classified as either modern or old-style. It is not based on any historical model, nor does it echo a particular period or style. It avoids the extreme contrast between thick and thin elements which marks most modern faces, and attempts to give a feeling of fluidity, power, and speed.*

Composition by Heritage Printers, Inc.,
Charlotte, North Carolina.
Printed and bound by The Murray Printing Company,
Westford, Massachusetts.
Typography adapted from original designs
by W. A. Dwiggins.